Christianities in the Trans-Atlantic World, 1500-1800

Series Editors

Crawford Gribben
Queen's University Belfast School of
History and Anthropology
School of History and Anthropology
Belfast,
United Kingdom

Scott Spurlock
University of Glasgow Department of
Theology and Religious Studies
Department of Theology and Religious Studies
Glasgow,
United Kingdom

Building upon the recent recovery of interest in religion in the early modern trans-Atlantic world, this series offers fresh, lively and inter-disciplinary perspectives on the broad view of its subject. Books in the series will work strategically and systematically to address major but under-studied or overly simplified themes in the religious and cultural history of the early modern trans-Atlantic.

More information about this series at
http://www.springer.com/series/14892

Philip Lockley
Editor

Protestant Communalism in the Trans-Atlantic World, 1650–1850

palgrave
macmillan

Editor
Philip Lockley
University of Oxford
Oxford, United Kingdom

Christianities in the Trans-Atlantic World, 1500-1800
ISBN 978-1-137-48486-4 (hardcover)   ISBN 978-1-137-48487-1   (eBook)
ISBN 978-1-349-69487-7 (softcover)
DOI 10.1057/978-1-137-48487-1

Library of Congress Control Number: 2016938645

Printed on acid-free paper

This Palgrave Macmillan imprint is published by Springer Nature
The registered company is Macmillan Publishers Ltd. London

Contents

NOTES ON CONTRIBUTORS

Jeff Bach is Associate Professor in the Department of Religious Studies, Elizabethtown College, Pennsylvania, and Director of the Young Center for Anabaptist and Pietist Studies. He holds a PhD in Religion from Duke University (1997) and is the author of *Voices of the Turtledoves: The Sacred World of Ephrata* (2003) and co-editor and translator with Michael Birkel of *Genius of the Transcendent: Mystical Writings of Jakob Boehme* (2010).

Hermann Ehmer holds a doctorate in Theology from the University of Tübingen (1972). Trained as an archivist he worked for the archives service of the state of Baden-Württemberg, 1972–1988, then as Head of Archives for the Protestant Church of Württemberg (Landeskirchliches Archiv) in Stuttgart, 1988–2008. From 1996 to 2012 he lectured on Württemberg church history at the Faculty of Protestant Theology at the University of Tübingen, and was made honorary professor in 2007. He has published extensively on the regional history of southwest Germany and German church history.

Christian Goodwillie is Director of Special Collections, Hamilton College, New York—a major repository of Shaker and other communal society source material. He has published numerous articles on Shaker history, is co-author of a history of Hancock Shaker Village and is editor of a three-volume edition of *Writings of Shaker Apostates and Anti-Shakers, 1782–1850* (2013).

Matthew J. Grow is Director of Publications at the Church History Department of the Church of Jesus Christ of Latter-day Saints. He holds a PhD in American History from the University of Notre Dame (2006) and was previously an assistant professor of history and director of the Center for Communal Studies at the University of Southern Indiana. He is author of the award-winning *"Liberty to the Downtrodden": Thomas L. Kane, Romantic Reformer* (2009) and (with Terryl Givens) *Parley P. Pratt: The Apostle Paul of Mormonism* (2011).

Peter Hoehnle is President of the Communal Studies Association and editor of the journal *Communal Societies*. He hold a PhD from Iowa State University (2003) and has published extensively on Inspirationist history and other communal topics, including the monograph *The Amana People: The History of a Religious Community* (2003). He further serves as administrator of the Amana Church Society.

Bradley Kime is a Jefferson Fellow and doctoral student in religious studies at the University of Virginia. His work has been published in the *Journal of Mormon History*, *Religion in the Age of Enlightenment* and *Wesley and Methodist Studies*.

Philip Lockley is British Academy Postdoctoral Fellow in the Faculty of Theology and Religion, University of Oxford. He holds a doctorate in history from the University of Oxford (2010). He is the author of *Visionary Religion and Radicalism in Early Industrial England: From Southcott to Socialism* (2013), a study of the relationship between millennial religion and the earliest English socialisms.

LIST OF FIGURES

MAPS

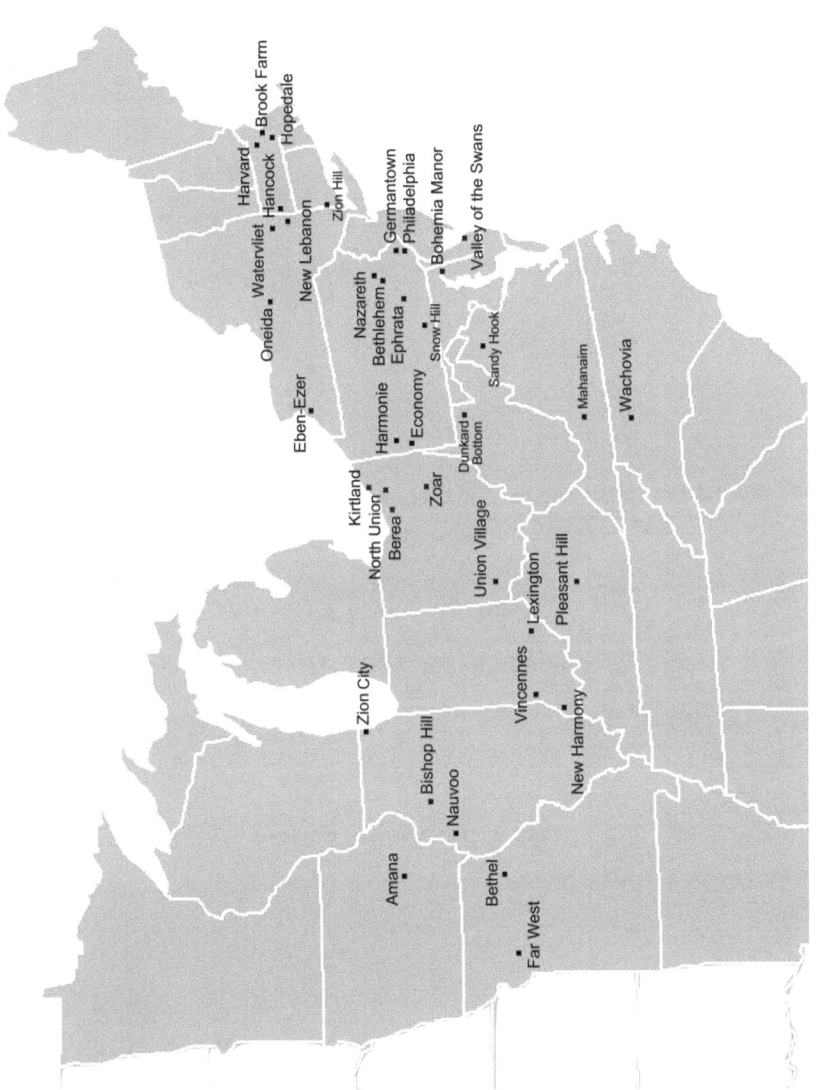

Map 1   Locations in North America

Map 2 Locations in England

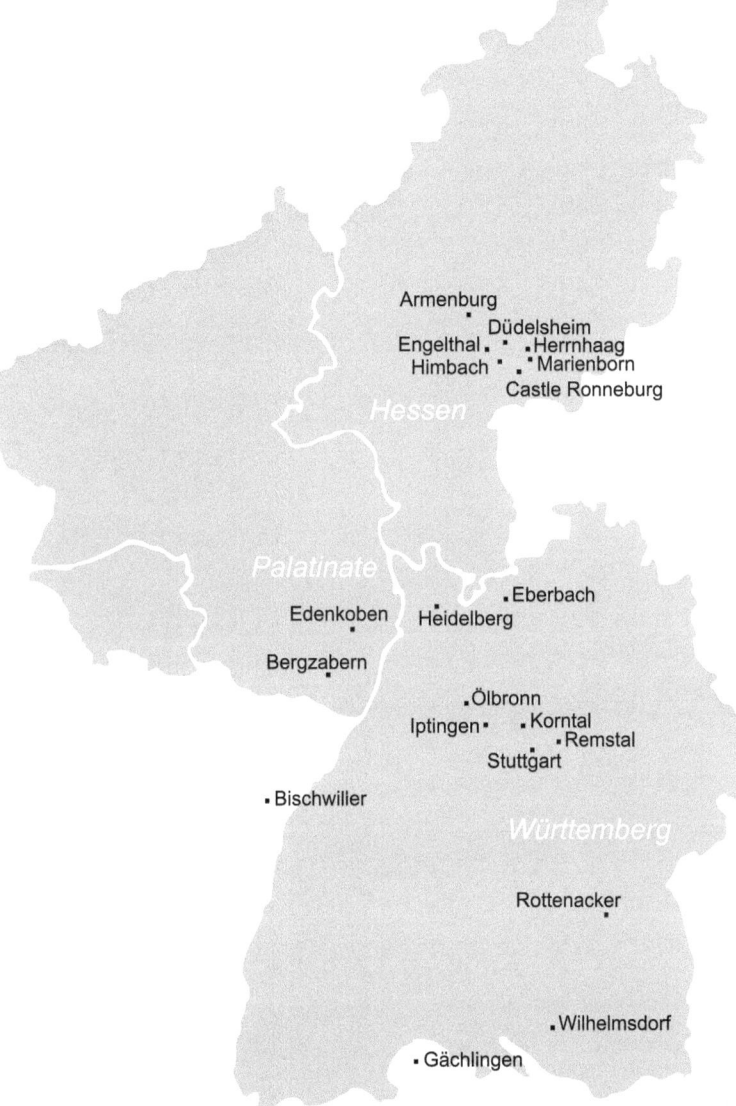

Map 3 Locations in southwest Germany

CHAPTER 1

Introduction

Philip Lockley

This book recovers the trans-Atlantic histories, networks, ideas and influences of Protestant Christian traditions of communal property across two centuries of early modernity. Between 1650 and 1850 a distinctive if disparate North Atlantic Protestant culture emerged, grew and continued among a variety of religious communities set apart from mainstream Protestant Christianities in both Europe and North America by their attitude to property and collective social practice. Across this period, small Protestant groups, often with a trans-Atlantic reach, came to embrace communalism, or the holding of property in common in single or interlinked settlements, as a mark of their ideal Christian practice.

Several groups displayed no communal propensity in Europe, yet came to adopt shared property soon after arriving in North America, such as the Shakers and the German-speaking Ephrata community in Pennsylvania in the eighteenth century. Others evolved elements of a communal outlook in Europe, adapting and expanding this further after migration to the new environment of the United States. These included the Community of True Inspiration and the Harmony Society—both traditions of radical German Pietism. Still other traditions developed in nineteenth-century American soil, or only practised communalism in America, yet maintained a trans-Atlantic component to their history, mission or recruitment, among them

P. Lockley
University of Oxford, Oxford, UK

© The Editor(s) (if applicable) and The Author(s) 2016
P. Lockley (ed.), *Protestant Communalism in the Trans-Atlantic World, 1650–1850*, DOI 10.1057/978-1-137-48487-1_1

1

the Church of Jesus Christ of Latter-day Saints—the Mormons. While some communal traditions were short-lived, others endured for generations. All such communities co-existed with the tensions and opportunities presented by host cultures of individualism and private property—cultures themselves rooted in a predominant Protestant social ethic, in central Europe, in Britain or in North America.

A primary aim of this volume is to correct a still prevailing interpretation of many of these Protestant communal groups which sees such societies belonging to an explicitly *American* communal tradition, or a recognized tradition of 'American utopia'. Countless essay collections, dictionaries and annotated guides have drawn more or less direct lines of comparison and precedent from these migrating and mission communities in the seventeenth, eighteenth and nineteenth centuries to the communes and radical alternatives of the 1960s counterculture.[1] Taken as a whole, this utopian tradition may be seen to appeal to some as a comforting testimony to 'another America'. The perennial presence of such groups arguably reveals shared work and common ownership to be as 'American' a pursuit as the proverbial happiness conferred by individual interest, private property and other assumed legacies of American Protestantism.

While this book does not set out to dismantle this interpretation, it nevertheless confronts this reading by recovering and emphasizing the formative and persistent trans-Atlantic dynamic to the wider communal tradition as a whole, and to specific groups and traditions in their individual and collective histories and influences. This dynamic is illustrated in new understandings of the European roots, relationships and reputations of some communities, and the consciously 'Atlantic' rather than 'American' worldviews and influences assumed by others.

The comparative study of such communal religious traditions has a distinguished history. Yet this is in turn dominated by their American context—from Charles Nordhoff's *Communistic Societies of the United States* (1875) to Arthur Bestor's *Backwoods Utopias* (1950), and on to Donald

---

[1] Among the best existing volumes belonging to this tendency are Donald E. Pitzer (ed.), *America's Communal Utopias* (Chapel Hill: University of North Carolina Press, 1997); and Robert P. Sutton, *Communal Utopias and the American Experience: Religious Communities, 1732–2000* (Westport, CT: Praeger, 2003). Two reference works include Robert S. Fogarty, *Dictionary of American Communal and Utopian History* (Westport, CT: Greenwood Press, 1980) and Foster Stockwell, *Encyclopaedia of American Communes, 1663–1963* (Jefferson, NC: McFarland, 1998).

Pitzer's edited collection on *America's Communal Utopias* (1997).[2] These works have been almost exclusively concerned with the 'Americanness' of such communal phenomena. Robert Sutton's two-volume collection *Communal Utopias and the American Experience* (2003–2004), which discusses Ephrata, Shakers, Harmonists, Inspirationists and others, acknowledges a persistent concern in its title: the extent to which such communalisms reflected an 'American experience' above all.[3]

Today, historians of the early modern and modern period are deeply engaged by the dynamics of Atlantic exchange and the nature and extent of intercontinental relationships across this ocean.[4] Broader movements within Pietism and its recognized English-language relatives—revivalism and evangelicalism—are historical subjects which have benefitted greatly from the transnational perspective.[5] Yet, the full spectrum of communal traditions related in diverse ways to this Protestant renewal remains understudied from a trans-Atlantic perspective.

---

[2] Charles Nordhoff, *The Communistic Societies of the United States: from personal visit and observation: including detailed accounts of the Economists, Zoarites, Shakers, the Amana, Oneida, Bethel, Aurora, Icarian and other existing societies; their religious creeds, social practices, numbers, industries, and present condition* (London: J. Murray, 1875); Arthur Bestor, *Backwoods Utopias: The Sectarian and Owenite Phases of Communitarian Socialism in America, 1663–1829* (Philadelphia: University of Pennsylvania Press, 1950); Pitzer (ed.), *America's Communal Utopias.*

[3] Sutton, *Communal Utopias*; see also Robert P. Sutton, *Communal Utopias and the American Experience: Secular Communities, 1824–2000* (Westport, CT: Praeger, 2004).

[4] David Armitage, 'Three Concepts of Atlantic History', in David Armitage and Michael J. Braddick (eds), *The British Atlantic World, 1500–1800* (Basingstoke and New York: Palgrave Macmillan, 2002), pp. 11–27; Nicholas Canny and Philip Morgan (eds), *The Oxford Handbook of the Atlantic World, 1450–1850* (Oxford: Oxford University Press, 2011); Karen Ordahl Kupperman, *The Atlantic in World History* (New York: Oxford University Press, 2012); Lars Maischak, *German Merchants in the Nineteenth-Century Atlantic* (Cambridge: Cambridge University Press, 2013).

[5] This trans-Atlantic literature is vast, and may be dated either from Richard Carwadine, *Trans-Atlantic Revivalism: Popular Evangelicalism in Britain and America* (Westport, CT: Greenwood Press, 1978) or Susan O'Brien 'A Trans-Atlantic Community of Saints', *American Historical Review*, 91 (1986), 811–32. More recent notable contributions include: W.R. Ward, *Early Evangelicalism: A Global Intellectual History, 1670–1789* (Cambridge: Cambridge University Press, 2006); Jonathan Strom, Hartmut Lehmann and James Van Horn Melton (eds), *Pietism in Germany and North America 1680–1820* (Burlington, VT: Ashgate, 2009); Jonathan Strom, *Pietism and Community in Europe and North America: 1650–1850* (Leiden: Brill, 2010); Crawford Gribben, *Evangelical Millennialism in the Trans-Atlantic World, 1500–2000* (Basingstoke: Palgrave Macmillan, 2011).

In recent years, innovative research has begun to pay closer attention to the European origins and American connections of some individual communal traditions, but certainly not all. For instance, Clarke Garrett's *Origins of the Shakers* sought to locate the 'Shaking Quakers' who migrated from the northwest of England to New York State in 1774 within a diffuse culture of 'spirit possession and popular religion' identified on either side of the Atlantic.[6] One of several radical Pietist groups to leave southwest Germany during and after the Napoleonic Wars, the Separatists of Zoar, Ohio, have had their roots in early nineteenth-century Württemberg uncovered by Eberhard Fritz, in two articles originally published in German and translated for English readers in 2002 in the journal *Communal Societies*.[7] The earlier cloistered community of Ephrata, Pennsylvania, founded by German Baptist immigrants, has likewise had elements of its 'sacred world' dissected for European precedents in *Voices of the Turtledoves* by Jeff Bach—who brings more recent research to bear in his contribution to this volume.[8]

Moravians—the revived *Unitas Fratrum* movement—are perhaps the most prominent Protestant tradition to have an identifiable history of communal property ownership, though this was limited to a specific period in the eighteenth century. Moravian history has fared especially well in the scholarly turn towards the transnational of the last decade or more. A growing body of scholarship now strongly emphasizes the trans-Atlantic dimension to Moravian group identity and collective practice.[9]

---

[6] Clarke Garrett, *Origins of the Shakers: From the Old World to the New World* (Baltimore and London: Johns Hopkins University Press, 1998). This study was first published as *Spirit Possession and Popular Religion* in 1987.

[7] Eberhard Fritz, 'Roots of Zoar, Ohio, in Early 19th Century Württemberg', *Communal Societies*, 22 (2002), 27–44, and *Communal Societies*, 23 (2003), 29–44. This article was first published as Eberhard Fritz, 'Separatisten in Rottenacker. Eine ortliche Gruppe als Zentrum eines "Netwerks" im fruhen 19. Jahrhundert', *Blatter für Wurttembergische Kirchengeschichte*, 98 (1998), 66–158.

[8] Jeff Bach, *Voices of the Turtledove: The Sacred World of Ephrata* (University Park: Pennsylvania State University Press, 2003).

[9] Craig Atwood, *Community of the Cross* (University Park: Pennsylvania State University Press, 2004); Michele Gillespie and Robert Beachy (eds), *Pious Pursuits: German Moravians in the Atlantic World* (New York and Oxford: Berghahn, 2007); Aaron Spencer Fogleman, *Jesus Is Female: Moravians and Radical Religion in Early America* (Philadelphia: University of Pennsylvania Press, 2007); Gisela Mettele, *Weltbürgertum oder Gottesreich: Die Herrnhuter Brüdergemeine als Globale Gemeinschaft, 1727–1857* (Göttingen: Vandenhoeck & Ruprecht, 2009); Katherine Carté Engel, *Religion and Profit: Moravians in Early America* (Philadelphia: University of Pennsylvania Press, 2009); Leland Ferguson, *God's Fields: Landscape, Religion,*

Yet, while the Moravian concept of community has gained much attention within such studies, their time-limited practice of shared property has rarely been related to a context of wider Pietist, and indeed Protestant, tendencies towards communalism in either the period or similar geographical settings.

The essays in this book do not set out to be exhaustive in their dissection of all instances of Protestant communalism across their period. Instead, they seek to offer a range of broad or focused accounts and perspectives which will go some distance towards defining the culture of communalism it recognizes, and locating this Protestant culture across an Atlantic geography encompassing northwest Europe, the British Isles, the eastern seaboard of North America and the continent beyond.

In the second chapter, I attempt to 'map' Protestant communalism across 200 years and two sides of an ocean. This provides an overview of each of the groups and traditions discussed in greater detail elsewhere in the volume, and locates other communal movements, including Moravians and Anglican monasticism, emerging earlier and later from similar or drastically different beliefs. Across this survey chapter, the adoption of communal practices is shown to have been grounded repeatedly in theological ideas before or soon after its practical implementation. Eschatology in its broadest forms was the branch of theology most frequently involved in providing this theological conduit to communalism, though communal property was not dependent on an eschatological outlook: some attempts to revive monastic communities in Protestantism are found to have owed more to an intended return to Catholic traditions of asceticism and order.

In Chap. 3, Jeff Bach presents the first of five extensive case studies of distinct Protestant communal traditions forged in trans-Atlantic histories. Bach narrates the rise, flourishing and decline of the eighteenth-century Ephrata community in Lancaster County, Pennsylvania—a settlement with celibate orders and married families originating in the 1730s. Bach

and Race in Moravian Wachovia (Gainesville: University Press of Florida, 2011); Katherine Carté Engel, 'Moravians in the Eighteenth-Century Atlantic World', *Journal of Moravian History*, 12:1 (2012), 1–19; Amy C. Schutt, *A Harmony of Spirits: Translation and the Language of Community in Early Pennsylvania* (Chapel Hill, NC: University of North Carolina Press, 2012); Markéta Křížová, 'The Moravian Church and the Society of Jesus: American Mission and American Utopia in the Age of Confessionalisation', *Journal of Moravian History*, 13:2 (2013), 197–226; Aaron Spencer Fogleman, *Two Troubled Souls: An Eighteenth-Century Couple's Spiritual Journey in the Atlantic World* (Chapel Hill, NC: University of North Carolina Press, 2013).

argues that an accurate interpretation of Ephrata must take account of how diverse religious and cultural influences from Europe combined in the American context. Ephrata maintained lasting communications with contacts in Switzerland and Germany, while further drawing on pockets of radical Christian views among the Pennsylvania population. Much of the past interpretation of Ephrata has focused on the unique location of America as a place for religious freedom. Through tracing outward communications and networks of relationships that spanned the Atlantic, the chapter shows both the patterns of Ephrata's recruitment and its theological foundations to have remained intimately linked to Europe.

In Chapter 4, Christian Goodwillie offers a fresh and strikingly detailed group biography of the original trans-Atlantic English Shakers who founded one of the most recognizable traditions of Protestant communalism. The life of the Shaker leader, Mother Ann Lee has been narrated many times, not least in later Shaker writings reflecting a generation or more of oral tradition and collective memory. Of the eight other English Shakers who accompanied Ann Lee on her 1774 crossing to America, and the further handful of believers who joined them in America the following year, less has been written. This is despite Shaker sources taking care to record memories of some of their other founders, including Ann Lee's brother, William Lee, and the first Shaker leader after Mother Ann's death in 1784, James Whittaker. Goodwillie painstakingly compiles the evidence of the lives of these and each of the other English Shakers, from both Shaker and non-Shaker sources. He reveals how several played significant roles in shaping the emerging body of Shaker principles and communal settlements in New York and New England in the 1780s and 1790s.

In a third case-study chapter, Hermann Ehmer narrates a new European and American history of the Harmony Society, the radical German Pietist association led by George Rapp, which relocated from Württemberg in southwest Germany to western Pennsylvania in 1804. The Harmonists' three successive settlements in nineteenth-century America—Harmony, Pennsylvania, New Harmony, Indiana, and Economy, Pennsylvania— are among the best-known historic sites of communal experiment in the United States today. In his revisionist study, Ehmer notably brings to bear a wealth of German-language scholarship on the history of Pietism and Württemberg's social and political history, setting the emerging theology and practice of Rapp's society within this specific German context. Ehmer argues that the emigration of the Harmony Society to the United States may only be understood in light of the group's millennial beliefs. Their communalism in the United States was a further expression both of Pietist theology and inherited forms of communal behaviour transported from the German village to the American frontier.

In Chapter 6, Peter Hoehnle writes on the Community of True Inspiration—yet another radical German Protestant group with its origins in the eighteenth century. Hoehnle uncovers a notable 'axis of communalism' along which this persisting Pietist tradition moved between the early and mid-nineteenth century, and from central Germany to central Iowa, via upstate New York. This movement towards communal property, Hoehnle shows, was not simply a response to the demands of the American landscape, or even a following of precedent set by other Pietist traditions in the United States. Rather, many surviving and newly converted Inspirationists had already gathered together on a series of estates leased from tolerant landowners in the Hessen region. Several of these estates had once been Roman Catholic monasteries or convents; one was 'Herrnhaag', a Moravian communal settlement since left in a state of disrepair. On these German estates in the 1820s and 1830s, the Inspirationists took significant steps towards communalism, sharing many assets, living in communal buildings and working in common industries. The Inspirationist experience of Protestant communalism is thus shown to have been forged in circumstances and practices on both sides of the Atlantic, expressing an evolving bond of community embodied in their trans-Atlantic crossing.

Chapter 7 concludes the series of case studies with a perhaps unexpected tradition: Matthew J. Grow and Bradley Kime re-examine the origins, points of influence and repercussions of communal experiments among the Mormons in the nineteenth century. As Grow and Kime show, communalism in the Church of Jesus Christ of Latter-day Saints was inextricably bound up with millennialism—a theological concern animating several of the groups already encountered in the volume. From Joseph Smith's early prophecies directing his followers to realize God's intended unified and equal society, to the developing vision of 'Zion'—a righteous place which the Latter-day Saints sought to build in Ohio, Missouri, Illinois and then Utah—early Mormonism challenged mainstream ideas of individualism and private property in America. Mormon prophetic and millennial beliefs in particular were utilized in missionary contact with prominent traditions of Protestant communalism, and converts won from both these traditions went on to influence organizational aspects of nascent Mormon communalism. In addition, some of the earliest and most successful trans-Atlantic Mormon missions were to the northwest of England—a region closely associated with cooperative trading. Grow and Kime trace how cooperative principles were not only brought over to Utah by such converts, but the Mormon press took a consistent interest in the development of cooperation in the trans-Atlantic world. This interest and influence directly contributed to the brief 'United Order' initiative across Utah in the 1870s—a distinctive communal experiment in Mormon economic and social history. In a comparative and reflective conclusion, the chapter points forward to how mid-century Mormon communal experience was in turn a critical influence on the later trans-Atlantic communalism of John Alexander Dowie and a continuing inspiration for Latter-day Saints' own understanding of their social aims and divine direction in the twentieth century.

The final chapter in the collection represents a shift in perspective as I explore the renown and reputation of Protestant communalism among outsiders in the early nineteenth-century Atlantic world, in particular among the earliest secular socialists in Britain and North America. One of the first socialist theorists, Robert Owen, has long been linked to the Harmony Society, as he crossed the Atlantic to purchase their Indiana community in the mid-1820s. However, the interactions between early socialism and Protestant communalism stretched further, and over a longer period than this single property deal. Accounts of Shaker, Harmonist and other communal settlements were promoted enthusiastically by socialist journals and readers in Europe over several decades. Sympathizers regularly set out to visit communities for themselves, and in some cases chose not to leave but to join. Tracing the rise and fall of this socialist interest in Protestant communal groups helps to highlight the trans-Atlantic scope of not just their internal history but their external influence before 1850, so presenting a fuller picture of the notice, consequence and effects of Protestant communalism in the trans-Atlantic world.

CHAPTER 2

Mapping Protestant Communalism, 1650–1850

Philip Lockley

The European Reformation left a complex legacy for Protestant approaches to Christian community. Close to a thousand years of monastic tradition upholding the principle of common property came to an end wherever Catholic convents and monasteries were dissolved across northern Europe. Many of the ascetic disciplines, most notably celibacy, as well as the mystical theologies developed by men and women living the cloistered life, were also rejected by Lutheran and Reformed churches. Magisterial Protestant reformers invariably endorsed the family unit and promoted the order and obligations of private-property ownership as the location for godly living. Among radical Anabaptist groups in Switzerland and regions of the modern-day Czech Republic an alternative impulse towards shared communal property was manifested between the 1520s and 1550s, and in the case of the 'Hutterite' Brethren preserved for extended periods later.[1]

[1] G.H. Williams, *The Radical Reformation* (London: Weidenfeld & Nicholson, 1962), pp. 124–46, 429–34, 680; James Stayer, *The German Peasants' War and Anabaptist Community of Goods* (Montreal: McGill-Queen's University Press, 1991). The Hutterite Brethren was the one branch of Anabaptism to have reinstituted the practice of community of goods in the later sixteenth century, and preserved it since. Most Hutterites migrated east to the Ukraine in the 1770s, and west across the Atlantic to the Dakotas in the 1870s.

P. Lockley
University of Oxford, Oxford, UK

© The Editor(s) (if applicable) and The Author(s) 2016   9
P. Lockley (ed.), *Protestant Communalism in the Trans-Atlantic World, 1650–1850*, DOI 10.1057/978-1-137-48487-1_2

Such communal practices alarmed political and ecclesiastical authorities almost as much as the Anabaptist denial of infant baptism (a rejection of an essential measure of Christian citizenship), intensifying their intolerance. In due course, the traumatic memory of Münster—the besieged city in northern Germany where a community of goods was instituted in 1534— confirmed official attitudes still further. And yet for Protestants drawn to read their Bibles, and more particularly to look to the first church in Jerusalem depicted in Acts 2 and 4, the precedent of the earliest Christian community where 'all that believed were together, and had all things in common' remained potent.[2]

Before the middle of the seventeenth century, experiments in shared property, beyond a few persisting Hutterite bodies in Eastern Europe, were rare, brief and often obscured by subsequent reputation within the Protestant world. The enigmatic late sixteenth-century network of the Family of Love, who tended to gather in discreet communities in England and parts of Northwest Europe, were commonly thought to deny ownership—or that 'no man … clameth any thing to be his Owne'.[3] More openly, if conveniently forgotten in later repute, the Calvinist 'Pilgrim' émigrés who disembarked the *Mayflower* in Massachusetts in 1620 adopted community of property for their first 3 years, before ceasing the practice.[4]

From around 1650 until well into the nineteenth century, a diverse range of Protestant traditions of communal property subsequently emerged in the trans-Atlantic world. This chapter maps the history of this Protestant communalism, identifying the geographical contexts, migration patterns and theologies behind such groups and practices in early modernity. Traditions explored in later chapters are introduced in overview, and set within a longer narrative of the development, decline and revival of communal interest and experiment on both sides of the Atlantic. The mapping exercise reveals the sharing of property in common to have been inspired by old and new forms of Christian belief. The chapter concludes with an attempt to categorize this variety of communal theologies across the period, so charting frameworks of ideas as well as the communities that believed them.

[2] Acts 2:44.

[3] Hendrick Niclaes, quoted in Alastair Hamilton, *The Family of Love* (Cambridge: James Clarke, 1981), p. 10. See also C.W. Marsh, *The Family of Love in English Society, 1550–1630* (Cambridge: Cambridge University Press, 1994).

[4] John Demos, *A Little Commonwealth Family: Family Life in Plymouth Colony* (New York: Oxford University Press, 1970).

EARLY EXPERIMENTS, C.1650–1700

The civil wars that disrupted the British Isles in the 1640s and after produced unfettered religious experimentation as well as political turmoil. In this period, new denominations like Baptists and Quakers made their first appearance, as also did small collective bodies like Gerrard Winstanley's group of 'Diggers'—labourers and landless farmers who gathered on a Surrey hillside in 1649 and pronounced the earth to be 'a common treasury'.[5] By 1650, Winstanley's community had been forced off their original plot of land on St George's Hill, but moved to nearby Cobham Heath, building several houses and replanting the land. Related colonies sprang up in Northamptonshire, Buckinghamshire, Kent and elsewhere in southern England, apparently influenced by Digger literature insisting that land was created by God for all to share, and never to be held in private hands.[6] Winstanley notably believed a new age was just beginning, in which the Spirit of Christ would be newly present within people, leading them to act with greater justice and overcome all poverty and inequality. Digger communities were a sign of this new age which would overcome the Fall—a millennium, or thousand years of harmony prophesied in Revelation 20. Yet, no Digger community survived very long, being dispersed within a year in the face of local landowner opposition.

An appetite for experiment nevertheless remained during the Cromwellian protectorate. In 1658, a Dutch Socinian, Pieter Cornelius Plockhoy, is known to have crossed from Amsterdam to England and attracted supporters in Bristol, London and parts of Ireland for his plan 'bringing together a fit, suitable, and well qualified people unto one … little-common-wealth'.[7] The Restoration of the English monarchy in 1660 put paid to Plockhoy's plans being realized in England, but he returned to the Netherlands, and interested the authorities there in funding a group of Mennonite settlers—descendants of former communal Anabaptists—to establish a 'little-common-wealth' in the mid-Atlantic Dutch colonies.

[5] Timothy Kenyon, *Utopian Communism and Political Thought in Early Modern England* (London: Pinter, 1989).

[6] Andrew Bradstock, *Radical Religion in Cromwell's England* (London: I.B. Tauris, 2011), pp. 56–7.

[7] Pieter Plockhoy, *The Way to Peace and Settlement of These Nations: Fully Discovered* (London: 1659); and, idem, *A Way Propounded to Make the Poor in These and Other Nations Happy, by bringing together a fit, suitable, and well qualified people unto one household-government, or little-common-wealth* (London: 1659).

About 40 settlers then sailed for modern-day Delaware in May 1663, landing in July at a site named Zwaanendael, or the Valley of the Swans (near contemporary Lewes). Few if any records survive of the settlement or its theology, though it seems to have lasted barely longer than the Digger colonies in England, razed to the ground by the Royal Navy in an offensive against the Dutch in 1664.[8]

After the Restoration, elements within the re-established Church of England more sympathetic to Catholic traditions tried quietly to overcome Anglicanism's missing monasticism. Greg Peters has traced several small-scale attempts to introduce recognizably monastic forms of religious life between the 1660s and early eighteenth century, occasionally linked to the administering of charity.[9] Among these were small groups of wealthy women, typically widows, who pooled their private means and sought the oversight of sympathetic male clergy. William Sancroft, later Archbishop of Canterbury, while Dean of St Paul's in London ministered to and directed a group of 'about 12 Protestant ladies of gentle birth and considerable means who had an idea of founding a convent in London'.[10] George Wheler, another Anglican clergyman, published *The Protestant Monastery: or, Christian Oeconomicks. Containing directions for the religious conduct of a family* in 1698, which further advocated convents for single women, believing 'monasteries ... duly ordered, would undoubtedly be both a reputation to the Church, and Advantageous to the Nation'.[11]

In Calvinist regions of Europe, especially Geneva and the Dutch Republic, the radical figure of Jean de Labadie stirred a rather different tendency to recapture elements of communal life and discipline previously

---

[8] Donald F. Durnbaugh, 'Communitarian Societies in Colonial America', in *America's Communal Utopias*, ed. D. Pitzer (Chapel Hill: University of North Carolina Press, 1997), pp. 15–17; Leland Harder and Marvin Harder, *Plockhoy from Zurik-zee: The Study of a Dutch Reformer in Puritan England and Colonial America* (Newton, KS: [Mennonite] Board of Education and Publication, 1952). See also, P.C. Plockhoy, 'An Invitation to the Society of Little Commonwealth', in *Every Need Supplied: Mutual Aid and Christian Community in the Free Churches, 1525–1675*, ed. Donald F. Durnbaugh (Philadelphia: Temple University Press, 1974), pp. 143–55.

[9] Greg Peters, *Reforming the Monastery: Protestant Theologies of the Religious Life* (Eugene, OR: Cascade, 2014), pp. 53–90.

[10] Walter Joseph Travers quoted in Peters, *Reforming the Monastery*, p. 56; Peter Anson, *The Call of the Cloister: Religious Communities and Kindred Bodies in the Anglican Communion* (London: SPCK, 1964), pp. 14–18.

[11] George Wheler, *The Protestant Monastery: or, Christian Oeconomicks. Containing directions for the religious conduct of a family* (London, 1698).

absent from Reformed Protestantism.[12] Labadie preached a powerful message combining features of French Catholic Jansenism with both Calvinism and older traditions of central European mysticism. Advocating Christian withdrawal from all worldly distractions and pleasures, Labadie emphasized the guidance of 'the inner light'—which burned brighter and more clearly within the elect through prayer, fasting, the mortification of the flesh and disciplined periods of silence. Labadie's separatist fervour eventually proved too much for the official Reformed Church in the Netherlands, and in 1668 he was suspended. Several dozen followers gathered around Labadie in the southern Dutch city of Veere, and afterwards Amsterdam, soon adopting the community of goods. Unwelcome in Amsterdam, Labadie's community spent the following years in a succession of sympathetic jurisdictions in the Holy Roman Empire and the Northern Netherlands, establishing another community of goods in Wieuward in West Friesland.

Labadie died in 1674, yet his surviving followers were expansionist in outlook, dispatching agents to scout out suitable sites for colonies on both the North and South American continents. A community founded in Dutch-controlled Surinam lasted from 1680 to 1688. An alternative group of Labadists secured land in Maryland, close to Chesapeake Bay, and brought around 100 settlers from the Netherlands to found a community called Bohemia Manor in 1683. Poverty, obedience, chastity and the separation of the sexes for much of the day were strictly observed at Bohemia Manor. Meals appear to have been deliberately meagre, with all additional produce from the land being sold to serve the common fund. As some among the immigrant membership withdrew and settled elsewhere, the community attracted a few replacements among the local population.[13] Bohemia Manor nonetheless disbanded during the 1720s.

Developments in the 1680s laid the groundwork for one American colony to become the pre-eminent location for Protestant communal experiments for over a century: Pennsylvania. William Penn secured a royal charter for his new colony in 1682, and immediately launched a series of recruitment drives through central Europe, inviting any seeking religious

---

[12] Trevor J. Saxby, *The Quest for the New Jerusalem: Jean de Labadie and the Labadists, 1610–1744* (Dordrecht: Nijhoff, 1987).

[13] Everett Gordon Alderfer, *The Ephrata Commune: An Early American Counterculture* (University of Pittsburgh Press, 1985), p. 32.

freedom.[14] Penn's promotional pamphlets distributed through southwest Germany eventually attracted remnants of Anabaptist and Mennonite peasant groups, now several generations passed the practice of communal property, and who now mostly made the crossing to Philadelphia as indentured servants, then earned their freedom before heading west and north in extended family units.[15]

Smaller and more recently established Protestant traditions were also attracted to Pennsylvania as early as the 1690s, including the 'Society of the Woman in the Wilderness'—a group of forty German-speaking scholars of theology, astronomy, mathematics and the mystical writings of the sixteenth-century shoemaker, Jakob Böhme. This group originally gathered around Johann Jakob Zimmerman, a Heidelberg professor and pastor in Württemberg with a penchant for predicting the arrival of the Millennium—the thousand-year period in Revelation. Zimmerman first calculated this age would be in 1685, then recalibrated this to 1694, and advised his followers to flee with him to 'the wilderness', in the manner of the woman depicted in a vision in Revelation 12. Zimmerman died on the eve of departure from Rotterdam; but the group left regardless, and named Johannes Kelpius their new leader.

The Kelpius party first stopped in England, and followed up links with the principal English following of Böhme, the Philadelphian Society. Several Philadelphians in London, including their leading prophetic figure, Jane Lead, were known to have pooled their property communally since the 1670s. The Philadelphians believed there 'must be no Self-Appropriation; the very Root of Self must be removed: for the Blessings of the Kingdom are not to be enjoyed in Propriety, but in Community'.[16] Kelpius's group soon continued their trans-Atlantic journey, and eventually settled in

---

[14] Steve Longenecker, *Piety and Tolerance: Pennsylvania German Religion, 1700–1850* (Metuchen, NJ: Scarecrow Press, 1994); Aaron S. Fogleman, *Hopeful Journeys: German Immigration, Settlement, and Political Culture in Colonial America, 1717–1775* (Philadelphia: University of Pennsylvania Press, 1996).

[15] Kenneth Rexroth, *Communalism: From Its Origins to the Twentieth Century* (New York: Seabury, 1974), p. 173. The most recognizable group of Anabaptist emigrants today, the Amish, migrated in waves from Switzerland and the Alcase region in the mid-eighteenth and nineteenth centuries. Donald Kraybill et al., *The Amish* (Baltimore: Johns Hopkins University Press, 2013).

[16] Jane Lead, *Signs of the Times* (London, 1699) quoted in Paula Mcdowell, *The Women of Grub Street: Press, Politics, and Gender in the London Literary Marketplace 1678–1730* (Oxford: Oxford University Press, 1998), p. 199. On the Philadelphian Society, see Ariel Hessayon (ed.), *Jane Lead and Her Transnational Legacy* (Basingstoke: Palgrave Macmillan, 2016).

Germantown, Pennsylvania, in 1694. Despite Zimmerman's predicted Millennium not arriving, within two years the group had founded their own small celibate communities of shared property: 'the Contented of the God-Loving Soul or Chapter of Perfection' and 'Irenia or the True Church of Brotherly Love'. Members of each community practised a hermit-like existence rather than an entirely communal life, though a large building was reportedly constructed for meetings.[17] The scholars seem to have spent much of their time consulting manuscripts and watching the night sky through telescopes. Kelpius died in 1708, after which the community is thought to have disbanded, though several may have remained hermits into the 1740s.

PIETIST COMMUNALISM

Both the Labadists and the circle of scholars around Zimmerman and Kelpius may be included by some scholars within expansive definitions of the beginnings of Pietism—the deeply influential movement of Protestant renewal originating in central Europe in the late seventeenth century and emphasizing individual Bible reading, meeting in small groups for mutual edification and living a Christian life in pious practice.[18] After 1700, a striking number of traditions of communal Protestantism emerging in the trans-Atlantic world were forged within this dynamic renewal movement, and its evolving attitudes to spiritual inspiration, a coming millennium and a discerned sense of God's will for a gathered community of believers.

Definitions of 'Pietism' are certainly contentious. Some historians still maintain that the term should apply strictly to the religious renewal in Lutheran regions of Europe initiated by Philipp Jakob Spener after the devastating confessional conflicts of the late Reformation, and extending

[17] Francis Burke Brandt, *The Wissahickon Valley within the City of Philadelphia* (Philadelphia: Corn Exchange National Bank, 1927), pp. 84–95.

[18] Johannes Wallmann 'Kirchlicher and radikaler Pietismus: Zu einer kirchengeschichtlichen Grundunterscheidung' [Church and Radical Pietism—toward a Basic Distinction] in Wolfgang Breul et al. (eds), *Der Radikale Pietismus: Perspektiven der Forschung* (Göttingen: Vandenhoeck & Ruprecht, 2010), pp. 19–44; Douglas Shantz, *An Introduction to German Pietism* (Baltimore: Johns Hopkins University Press, 2013), pp. 150–1; Hartmut Lehman, 'Zur Definition des "Pietismus"', in *Zur Neueren Pietismusforschung*, ed. Martin Gerschat (Darmstadt: Wissenschaftliche Buchgesellschaft, 1977), pp. 82–90.

into the eighteenth century.[19] Spener sought to enliven confessional Protestantism through 'conventicles' or small groups of accountable members, a theology of heartfelt affection and conviction drawn from Luther's writings, and a distinct expectation of a better future.[20] Other scholars acknowledge a wider definition of Pietism as a 'transnational and transconfessional phenomenon' enlivening diverse denominations well beyond the boundaries of Germany and Scandinavia by comparable means, and reflecting, according to Martin Brecht, a 'crisis of piety rooted in the difficulties the Reformation churches experienced in realizing Christian life and activity'.[21] As Simeon Zahl has observed, 'Pietism existed wherever the question of Christian praxis was raised over and against the strict confessionalism that characterized Protestant orthodoxy after the Reformation'.[22] Pietism, in other words, was the attempt to renew Protestantism as a way of 'doing' Christianity, as disciplined, active belief rather than simply membership of a church institution or subscription to declared dogmas. Pietism was, above all, a commitment to Christian practice rooted in inner experience in the present, looking not to past doctrinal differences, but to a coming future revealing the purposes of God.

---

[19] See Johannes Wallmann, *Philipp Jakob Spener und die Anfänge des Pietismus*, rev. ed. (Tübingen: Mohr, 1986); idem., 'Pietas contra Pietismus. Zum Frömmigkeitsvertändnis der Lutherischen Orthodoxie', in Udo Sträter (ed.), *Pietas in der Lutherischen Orthodoxie* (Wittenberg: Hans Luft, 1998), pp. 6–18. In extensive and sharply critical reviews of recent studies of Pietism, Wallmann further argues that the broadening of the concept of Pietism so blurs the contours of church history that Pietism as a movement is no longer definable and distinguishable from other movements. Johannes Wallmann, 'Eine alternative Geschichte des Pietismus. Zur gegenwärtigen Diskussion um den Pietismusbegriff', *Pietismus und Neuzeit*, 28 (2002), 30–71.

[20] Shantz, *Introduction to German Pietism*, pp. 86–91.

[21] Martin Brecht quoted in Carter Lindberg, 'Introduction', in Carter Lindberg (ed.), *The Pietist Theologians: An Introduction to Theology in the Seventeenth and Eighteenth Centuries* (Oxford: Blackwell, 2005), p. 3. Brecht's implementation of this broad conception of Pietism in the first volume of the *Geschichte des Pietismus* is, according to Wallmann, a 'false start': Johannes Wallmann, 'Fehlstart. Zur Konzeption von Band 1 der neuen "Geschichte des Pietismus"', *Pietismus und Neuzeit*, 20 (1994), 218–35. For Brecht's reply see, Martin Brecht, 'Zur Konzeption der Geschichte des Pietismus. Eine Entgegnung auf Johannes Wallmann', *Pietismus und Neuzeit*, 22 (1996), 226–29. The issue is really whether Pietism is a concept of a particular period of history or an a-historical, typological concept. Johannes Wallmann, '"Pietismus"—mit Gänsefüsschen', *Theologische Rundschau*, 66 (2001), 462–80; see 464, 478–80.

[22] Simeon Zahl, *Pneumatology and the Theology of the Cross in the Preaching of Christoph Friedrich Blumhardt* (London: T&T Clark, 2010), p. 17.

'Radical' Pietism has traditionally denoted strands specifically within German popular Protestantism which were either 'separatist' in organization—meeting outside the established Lutheran Church—or 'heterodox' in theology, departing from orthodox Protestant beliefs.[23] Many radical Pietists were both separatist and heterodox.[24] Small group conventicles, mostly in southwest Germany, tended to generate leading figures who would denounce the worship and practices of established religious authorities and gather their own separate followings in rigorous, intensive meetings outside of conventional church oversight.[25] Most such figures claimed a form of inspiration from the Holy Spirit or access to prophetic insight in their interpretation of the Bible and leadership. Many radical Pietists not only interpreted biblical prophecies of an imminent messianic age in particular ways, but also anticipated humanity's restoration to an original androgynous state known before the Fall of Adam and Eve—distinctive ideas drawn from the writings and interpretative traditions of Jakob Böhme, the sixteenth-century mystic who influenced Zimmerman and Kelpius as well as the English Philadelphian Society in the 1690s.[26]

The Ephrata community in Pennsylvania, which originated in the 1720s among a group of German separatists from the Palatinate region near Heidelberg, was deeply influenced by Böhme's ideas and millennial prophecy, and yet further demonstrated how radical Pietist experiments in communal disciplines could lead, by a circuitous route, back to practices lost with the destruction of Catholic monasticism. Ephrata's founder, Conrad Beissel, appears at one stage to have hoped to join Kelpius's Society of the Woman in the Wilderness, until he learned it had been disbanded.[27] Back in Germany, Beissel had moved in various conventicle circles before choosing to migrate across the Atlantic in 1720. On arrival in America, Beissel became involved with a group called the Schwarzenau Brethren, whose teachings against infant baptism earned them the label *Neu-Täufer*—new Baptists or 'Dunkers'—to distinguish them from older

[23] Shantz, *Introduction to German Pietism*, pp. 147–78.

[24] Many scholars now stress the porosity of the boundary between 'church Pietists' and radicals. Hans Schneider, *German Radical Pietism*, transl. Gerald T. Macdonald (Lanham, MD: Scarecrow Press, 2007); Breul et al. (eds), *Der Radikale Pietismus*.

[25] Shantz, *German Pietism*, pp. 154–8.

[26] Ariel Hessayon and Sarah Apetrei, *An Introduction to Jacob Boehme: Four Centuries of Thought and Reception* (New York: Routledge, 2014).

[27] Jeff Bach, *Voices of the Turtledove: The Sacred World of Ephrata* (University Park: Pennsylvania State University Press, 2003), p. 10.

Anabaptist traditions.[28] Increased persecution by Lutheran authorities had led these German Brethren to move initially from Beissel's home region to the Netherlands, then on to Pennsylvania a year before Beissel's own crossing.

Beissel subsequently claimed his own direct prophetic inspiration from God, and gathered a following among this Brethren group in the Philadelphia region, advocating a disciplined life of celibacy, and preaching on the imminent approach of a millennial age. Withdrawing west, Beissel and his supporters eventually split from other German Brethren in 1728, and four years later, Beissel stated his intention to become a hermit, at a site named Ephrata. In time, several hundred followers gathered in a community of shared goods, work and worship around Beissel's hermitage on the Cocalico Creek. The community's buildings echoed those of medieval German monasteries, though the stated theological purpose of communal property was to imitate the first Christian church in Jerusalem and appropriately prepare for the Millennium.[29] Most members were celibate, known as 'solitary sisters' and 'solitary brethren'. Others lived in family groups known as 'Householders'. Habits were worn, and the monk's tonsure was even adopted by men. Devotional activities included calligraphy and manuscript illumination, as well as a rich tradition of choral music and hymnody. Living conditions and bodily disciplines were harsh. Little food was permitted, meals were silent and communal worship took place at Ephrata during the day and night, leaving only short periods for sleep. From about 1770, the community began to dwindle through lack of new converts or immigrant adherents, though several buildings were still inhabited in 1800.

The branch of eighteenth-century Pietism commonly known as the Moravians—the reorganized *Unitas Fratrum*, or Czech Unity Brethren movement, descended in part from the fifteenth-century followers of Jan Hus—adopted forms of communal labour and property in a number of their scattered settlements across the Atlantic world for several decades. Count Nikolaus Ludwig von Zinzendorf originally welcomed religious refugees onto his family estate in Saxony, on the present border between

---

[28] The Pietist origins of the *Neu-Täufer* and their distinction from Anabaptists were debated during the 1960s in response to new studies of the Mennonite tradition which recognized their opposition to Pietism. For a useful summary of this debate, see Bach, *Voices of the Turtledove*, pp. 28–9.

[29] See Chap. 3, p. 45.

Germany and the Czech Republic, in 1722. Within 5 years, the settler community had adopted the name Herrnhut and a constitution drawn up by Zinzendorf.

From the 1730s, the Moravians became strikingly outward-looking, launching a series of missionary initiatives to slave groups in the Caribbean, indigenous populations in North America, and further programmes for planned settlements of artisan trades and schooling in Europe. The first communal settlement to be consciously planned was 'Herrnhaag', close to a Marienborn community in the Wetterau region near Frankfurt, begun in 1738 on the estate of the religiously tolerant Count Ysenburg-Büdingen.[30] By 1741, on the opposite side of the Atlantic, Moravian missionaries who had initially settled in Georgia had moved north to Pennsylvania. Here they built first Bethlehem, 60 miles north of Philadelphia, then nearby Nazareth, along lines dictated by the Herrnhaag plan. From the 1750s, a further series of small communities were established in central North Carolina, called 'Wachovia'.[31] In Britain, three communal settlements were founded at Fulneck near Leeds in 1744, Ockbrook in Derbyshire by 1750 and Dukinfield near Manchester around 1755 (moved to nearby Fairfield in 1785).[32] Zeist, in the central Netherlands, was also laid out in 1746, a decade after the first Dutch Moravians established their own 'Herrendijk'.[33] Numerous other settlements were laid out in yet further parts of Europe before the end of the century, including Gracehill in Ireland in 1765 and Christiansfeld in southern Denmark in 1773—though these later towns post-dated the period when shared property was observed.

Communal ownership of property was a central facet of what was called the 'General Economy' maintained in many Moravian settlements between the 1730s and early 1760s. All Moravian communities were divided into

[30] Hans-Walter Erbe, *Herrnhaag: Eine religiöse Kommunität im 18. Jahrhundert* (Hamburg: F. Wittig, 1988). Herrnhaag was abandoned by the Moravians between 1750 and 1753, after a new Count Ysenburg-Büdingen demanded the community reject Zinzendorf's leadership.

[31] Leland Ferguson, *God's Fields: Landscape, Religion, and Race in Moravian Wachovia* (Gainesville: University Press of Florida, 2011).

[32] Colin Podmore, *The Moravian Church in England 1728–1760* (Oxford: Oxford University Press, 1998).

[33] A useful overview of the development of Moravian settlements appears in Felicity Jensz, *German Moravian Missionaries in the British Colony of Victoria, Australia* (Leiden: Brill, 2010), pp. 20–1.

'choirs' by age, gender and marital status, for both living and work arrangements. No wages were paid; housing, food, clothing and other items were provided on the basis of need, meaning the produce of agricultural and manufacturing labour was more easily collectivized. In the case of the Pennsylvania and North Carolina communities, Donald Durnbaugh has suggested that the sharing of labour and its product was never intended to be permanent, but 'was the most efficient way to establish newcomers in a frontier situation'.[34] By the 1760s, communalism had therefore outlived its pragmatic purpose in the American context. Craig Atwood has alternatively argued that Bethlehem's 'complete commune where labo[u]r and other resources were shared' during the 1740s and 1750s may be read as 'an expression of Moravian religious ideals'. This complexly intertwined earthly circumstances and activities with perceptions of what heaven was like, meaning Moravians 'attempted to live together in a foretaste of paradise'.[35] Moravians believed their earthly community reflected, through the presence of the Holy Spirit among them, a 'heavenly community', and so communal life anticipated the harmony of heaven. Certainly, the wide-scale adoption of the General Economy in diverse localities on both sides of the Atlantic suggests it had a compelling consistency with the beliefs common to all Moravians, and was not merely a localized response.

The circumstances of the decline of the General Economy appear nonetheless to have varied, and did not follow a single diktat, though in the case of Herrnhaag in central Germany, the entire settlement was closed by a new, less tolerant Count Ysenburg-Büdingen.[36] From the 1750s onwards, most Moravian settlements sought to downplay their more overt particularities against the backdrop of surrounding church and social climates, whether in Lutheran Germany, or Anglican and Methodist regions of England, or Quaker-influenced eastern Pennsylvania.

Towards the end of the eighteenth century, 'separatist' forms of Pietism gained greater popularity in Württemberg to the south of the earlier Moravian settlements around Frankfurt and Beissel's Palatinate region. George Rapp, a weaver from Iptingen, had a series of religious experiences in the 1780s and 1790s which led him out of the established Lutheran Church of the Duchy of Württemberg, and into private conventicle

---

[34] Durnbaugh, 'Communitarian Societies in Colonial America', pp. 28–9.

[35] Craig D. Atwood, *Community of the Cross: Moravian Piety in Colonial Bethlehem* (University Park, PA: Pennsylvania State University Press, 2004), p. 3.

[36] Atwood, *Community of the Cross*, pp. 16–17.

meetings with neighbours animated by reading the Bible, Luther's works and probably some Böhme mysticism. Rapp's popularity and disobedience of church rules alarmed the local authorities, though his decision to lead several hundred followers to settle in America in 1804 owed more to Rapp's prophetic interpretation of contemporary events in Europe than fear of persecution. By 1805, perhaps 800 members of Rapp's Harmoniegesellschaft, or Harmony Society, had gathered under Rapp's leadership in western Pennsylvania, where they set about building their first community—'Harmony'. Here community of property was immediately introduced, a step which guaranteed a degree of common purpose useful to the clearing, planting and building work required in the frontier context, yet which was also a development from some patterns of land-use back in Württemberg.[37]

In time, community of property was, like groups before them, explicitly linked by the Harmony Society to reproducing the social conditions of the earliest Christians, and also the state of things anticipated in the Christian Millennium. In 1822, Rapp's adopted son wrote that by adopting the community of goods, the Harmony Society 'laid the foundation and plan for a New periode, after the Original Pattern of the primitive church described in the 2 & 4 Chapter of the Acts'.[38] The same letter continued,

> ... there being only and solely such people in Harmonie which are brought up and prepared for the Kingdom of God, it is reasonable that all individual property should be prohibited, for in the Kingdom of God no person possesses ought of anything as his own, but all things in Common.[39]

Within 10 years, the town of Harmony had recreated much of the pattern of the German *Dorf*, surrounded by fields and pasture, with mills, workshops, tannery, church and a renowned brewery.

Celibacy was made an additional feature of life in the Harmony Society in 1808. Contemporary evidence suggests that Rapp linked this practice to his reading of Paul's advice against marriage to the Corinthians—a teaching

---

[37] See Chap. 5, pp. 119–20.

[38] Frederick Rapp to Samuel Worcester, 19 Dec 1822 in Karl Arndt (ed.), *A Documentary History of the Indiana Decade of the Harmony Society 1814–1824*, 2 vols (Indianapolis: Indiana Historical Society, 1975–78), 2:512.

[39] Frederick Rapp to Samuel Worcester, 19 Dec 1822 in Arndt (ed.), *Documentary History of the Indiana Decade*, 2:514.

commonly linked to the apostle's own eschatological outlook.[40] Jakob Böhme was also influential, as Böhme's writings linked the fallen nature of humanity to sexuality, and predicted a sexless millennium, when all would be restored to some kind of androgynous virginity. These views justified the adoption of celibacy in the present, as, like communal property, it better prepared individuals for their anticipated millennial existence.[41]

In 1814, after 10 years at Harmony, the entire Society moved west to southern Indiana, to build another communal settlement—New Harmony on the Wabash River. Then in 1824, the community repeated the process by moving east again, this time to found Economy on the Ohio River, back in Pennsylvania. Through such enterprises and related disciplines, George Rapp tightened his control over the community, reserving all decisions to himself and his inner circle until his death in 1847. Under this leadership, a significant cultural life of music, literature, gardening and high craftsmanship flourished alongside the accumulation of spectacular communal wealth.

The renown of Rapp's Harmonist migrants in America gradually filtered back to Württemberg, through correspondence networks and other trans-Atlantic exchange. Between 1816 and the late 1840s, a number of further Pietist groups left Europe to establish communal settlements in North America. These included an alternative separatist tradition from villages in southern Württemberg near Rottenacker who settled in Zoar, Ohio, in 1817. The principal preacher of this Society of Separatists, Joseph Bäumeler, never wielded the same charismatic control as Rapp, and made particular use of Quakers in London and Philadelphia to reach and secure their land in Ohio, rather than organizing the Atlantic crossing alone.[42] After a year the society introduced 'a community of goods and effort', apparently to save the community from collapse, though they subscribed to a theology closely comparable to that of the Harmonists. Zoarites anticipated the imminent return of Christ to usher in the millennial age, and

[40] 1 Cor. 7:29. Karl Arndt, *George Rapp's Harmony Society 1785–1847*, second edn (Cranbury, NJ: Associated University Presses, 1972), p. 97.

[41] Andrew Weeks, *Böhme: An Intellectual Biography of the Seventeenth-Century Philosopher and Mystic* (Albany: State University of New York Press, 1991), pp. 114–21. For Separatist views on marriage, see Charles Nordhoff, *The Communistic Societies of the United States* (London: J. Murray, 1875), pp. 104–8.

[42] Eberhard Fritz, 'Roots of Zoar, Ohio, in Early 19th Century Württemberg', *Communal Societies*, 22 (2002), 27–44. See also, the second part of this article in *Communal Societies*, 23 (2003), 29–44.

consciously viewed themselves as a separated people, practising a 'pure' ascetic Christianity, including celibacy in many cases.[43] Like the Harmonists before them, the material outworking of these beliefs, with its corollaries of concentrated, purposeful work with no wage-related incentives, produced substantial collective wealth. As none of these communities had wages to pay, they rapidly accrued capital for buildings and machinery, thus enjoying a notable economic advantage over the individual system of family farms and domestic hand manufacture in most regions of the United States before 1850.

The Community of True Inspiration, or 'Inspirationist' movement, was a branch of radical Pietism considerably older than the Harmony Society or Rottenacker Separatists, having first grown and then declined in the early and mid-eighteenth century. Inspirationists gathered in small, loosely organized bodies of believers in the same Wetterau and Palatinate region as some Moravians and the Brethren associated with the Ephrata community in Pennsylvania. Related bodies were established to the south into Switzerland, to the west nearer France, and to the east in Saxony. Inspirationists recognized *Werkzeuge* ('instruments' believed to be inspired by the Holy Spirit) who would travel regularly between these local groups, but imposed little in the way of formal structure or communal direction.

A revival within the Inspirationist movement after 1817 produced a very different approach among a new generation of *Werkzeuge*. Outlying Inspirationist bodies in the Palatinate, as well as much further afield, were encouraged to move to the Wetterau, where they settled on former Moravian estates in the region, including Herrnhaag, and sites of Catholic monasticism. A degree of communal practice emerged among the Inspirationists in these new settings, at each stage endorsed and directed by the inspired 'testimonies' of the leading *Werkzeuge*, Christian Metz. Both these European initiatives and the eventual decision to emigrate collectively to the United States in the 1840s were essentially framed by an Inspirationist belief in the divine guidance of their group—they obeyed prophetic direction. When the Inspirationists established the Eben-Ezer community near Buffalo, New York, and adopted full community of property, they were therefore not only following a pragmatic path for communal cohesion in straitened circumstances, and following biblical precedent from Acts, but further following a belief that this was how God intended their group to live. This was revealed to the Spirit's instrument.

[43] K.M. Fernandez, *A Singular People* (Kent, OH: Kent State University Press, 2003).

Dissention certainly occurred, yet Metz ultimately made commitment to common property a test of faith—faith in the God revealed by inspiration. From 1850, over a thousand members of the community migrated west together to continue their communal practice at Amana in Iowa.[44]

Pietism wielded a significant influence in popular religion beyond the borders of German-speaking Europe in the first half of the nineteenth century, especially in Lutheran regions of Scandinavia. In Norway, the itinerant preaching of Hans Nielsen Hauge produced an extensive conventicle movement—some members of which migrated to New York State in the 1820s, then on to the Fox River region in Illinois in the 1830s, where they appear to have experimented briefly with shared property.[45] During the 1840s, a Swedish separatist body centred around the prophetic figure of Eric Jansson, resolved to leave Europe together for North America, and also acquired land in Illinois. In Sweden, the 'Janssonists' rejected the rites of the established Lutheran Church much like the Harmonists and Zoarites had in Württemberg. Common property appears to have been adopted on the eve of departure for America, as 'a common fund was necessary if all should obtain sustenance and transportation across the Atlantic', one of their descendants recalled, leading them to follow 'the example of the first Christians at Jerusalem by selling their possessions and forming a common treasury'.[46] Over a thousand Janssonists sailed for America in 1846–47, though within a year barely half this number were on their Illinois settlement called Bishop Hill, after a large number of deaths and desertions. Despite Jansson's own violent death in 1850, Bishop Hill grew and prospered in its communal arrangements for a decade, before dissolving in 1861.[47]

As this succession of Pietist groups migrating to America in the early decades of the nineteenth century demonstrates, the western side of the

[44] The Eben-Ezer to Amana migration features in S. Scott Rohrer, *Wandering Souls: Protestant Migrations in America, 1630–1865* (Chapel Hill: University of North Carolina Press, 2010), pp. 194–214.

[45] *History of La Salle County, Illinois*, 2 vols (Chicago, 1886), 1:454. For more on this group, see Chap. 7, p. 176.

[46] The oral history of Bishop Hill descendants is reported in Philip J. Stoneberg, 'The Bishop Hill Colony', in *History of Henry County, Illinois*, ed. H.L. Kiner (Chicago: Pioneer, 1910), p. 630.

[47] Paul Elmen, *Wheat Flour Messiah: Eric Jansson of Bishop Hill* (Carbondale: Southern Illinois University Press, 1976); Jon Wagner, 'Eric Jansson and the Bishop Hill Colony', in Pitzer (ed.), *America's Communal Utopias*, pp. 297–318.

Atlantic became much the more popular continent for the practice of Protestant communalism. In some parts of Europe, if Protestant bodies sought to found distinct settlements for themselves, local laws of landownership could stand in the way of shared ownership. Pietists who remained in Württemberg, for instance, had to issue shares or otherwise raise funds to establish settlements within the boundaries of conventional individual property-holding, as they did at Korntal and Wilhelmsdorf in 1819–24.[48]

It is noteworthy that a further strain of German-speaking Pietist communalism emerged within the borders of the United States, though still the product of Atlantic migrations: the communities led by Wilhelm Keil.[49] Keil was born in Prussia, and emigrated to the United States in his mid-twenties in 1836. At this age he appears to have held various Pietist beliefs, influenced by the distinct *Erweckung* or religious revival in northern Germany that gathered strength during the 1820s. Settled in Pittsburgh, Keil was drawn into local revivalist Methodism, became a preacher, then had a series of mystical experiences in the early 1840s, which he interpreted in apocalyptic terms. Keil's expectations of an imminent millennium closely paralleled the contemporary speculations of William Miller, who calculated the Second Coming would occur in 1843, then 1844.[50] By 1844, Keil himself had a sizeable group of followers, almost exclusively German-born immigrants, among whom were a breakaway faction of the Harmony Society that had left Rapp's Economy community some years before.[51] It is unclear how far these former Harmonists influenced Keil to propose setting up a communal settlement to await the Millennium, but not long after, Keil's group settled on land in northern Missouri and called their community 'Bethel'.[52] Over time, Keil's pattern of leadership mirrored Rapp's style and effect, overseeing a highly productive colony which maintained traditions of German folk music. After 10 years, Keil even repeated Rapp's career by directing his followers further west to begin

[48] Samuel Koehne, 'Pietism as Societal Solution: The Foundation of the Korntal Brethren (*Korntaler Brüdergemeinde*)', in Jonathan Strom (ed.), *Pietism and Community in Europe and North America: 1650–1850* (Leiden: Brill, 2010), pp. 329–51. Korntal and Wilhelmsdorf are discussed further in Chap. 5, p. 126.

[49] David Nelson Duke, 'The Evolution of Religion in Wilhelm Keil's Community: A New Reading of Old Testimony', *Communal Societies*, 13 (1993), 84–98.

[50] Duke, 'The Evolution of Religion in Wilhelm Keil's Community', 87–9.

[51] Arndt, *George Rapp's Harmony Society*, pp. 539–41.

[52] Robert J. Hendricks, *Bethel and Aurora: An Experiment in Communism as Practical Christianity* (New York: Pioneer Press, 1933).

a new community—in Keil's case, Aurora, in Oregon. However, Bethel was not sold, and remained a working community administered by Keil's deputies for some decades after.[53]

AMERICAN COMMUNALISM AND THE ATLANTIC WORLD

Almost every instance of German and Scandinavian Pietist communalism to cross the Atlantic retained its vernacular language, limiting the appeal of joining for most Anglophone Americans. For a period this left a wide field of recruitment largely clear for the Shakers—the mission-minded variety of English-speaking Protestant communalism which established itself on the American continent in the late eighteenth century.

The 'Shaking Quakers', or United Society of Believers in Christ's Second Appearing as they called themselves, originated in the northwest of England, and initially set themselves apart from other forms of English Protestantism by their small, separatist-like meetings and dramatic movements in worship, rather than any distinct attitude to property or celibacy. Over time, this Lancashire and Cheshire grouping came to revere the leadership of Ann Lee, a Manchester working woman who reported visions and prophecies during her lifetime. Shaker theology suggests some familiarity with Jakob Böhme's mysticism and movements of spiritual inspiration in radical German Pietism, though it would be a stretch to argue Shakerism was simply a branch of Pietism in an English idiom, as alternative Quaker roots and other local influences seem likely.[54]

After two small parties of Shakers migrated to North America in 1774 and 1775, and most settled together on land in the Hudson Valley north of New York, Ann Lee's claims to inspiration and prophetic insights were promoted by herself and other itinerant preachers in neighbouring New England, then western territories. Converts were directed to confess publicly all previous sins, and take up a strict, disciplined and now celibate life alongside other Shaker believers, set apart from 'the world'. Shakers looked towards the purity and perfection of a divinely-ordained future, and during the 1780s moved towards an understanding of their life together

---

[53] James Kopp, *Eden within Eden: Oregon's Utopian Heritage* (Corvallis: Oregon State University Press, 2009), pp. 39–50.

[54] Clarke Garrett, *Origins of the Shakers: From the Old World to the New World* (Baltimore and London: Johns Hopkins University Press, 1998), pp. 145–8.

in 'union' related closely to the realization of this new dispensation.[55] By 1790, six years after the death of Ann Lee, a number of American Shaker farm groups had adopted the 'doctrine of having all things in common'; and by 1794, Shakers had consolidated into ten New England and New York communities, scattered through Maine, New Hampshire, Massachusetts, Connecticut and the Hudson Valley. A further six communities were founded in Kentucky, southern Ohio and western Indiana by 1810.

In an authoritative study of Shaker history, Stephen Stein has suggested that the sect's expansion westwards in the early 1800s acted as a catalyst for a more formal theological justification for communalism presentable to new recruits.[56] Community of property and celibacy came to be viewed as the marks of a final dispensation of God in human history, when all sin would be overcome. The teachings and spiritual experiences of Ann Lee were by now conceived as the means by which this final millennial dispensation was brought about, allowing some to experience facets of the new age through following Lee's messianic path in the present. Shaker self-sufficiency and separation—of the sexes and from a sinful world—were understood to reach into this dispensation and enable the living of a perfected Christian life by Shakers as if the millennial age had arrived.

During the nineteenth century, Shaker communities totalling several thousand members became a familiar feature of the American agricultural, economic and religious landscapes. The material success of the communities and the consistent quality of manufactured goods and produce were frequently remarked on. Many visitors were further drawn to observe and comment on Shaker styles of worship. The contemporary reputation of the Shakers reached right across the Atlantic world.

Between the 1820s and 1850s, English-speaking American interest in communal living and shared property extended beyond the distinctive kinds of Christian groupings discussed so far, into a wider social reform movement associated with the earliest forms of socialism.[57] This too had a trans-Atlantic dimension to its origin and spread, as Robert

[55] Stephen A. Stein, *The Shaker Experience in America* (New Haven: Yale University Press, 1992), pp. 25–31.

[56] Stein, *Shaker Experience*, pp. 70–1.

[57] Arthur Bestor, *Backwoods Utopias: The Sectarian and Owenite Phases of Communitarian Socialism in America, 1663–1829* (Philadelphia: University of Pennsylvania Press, 1950; second edn, 1970); Robert P. Sutton, *Communal Utopias and the American Experience: Secular Communities* (Westport, CT: Praeger, 2004).

Owen, Charles Fourier and Etienne Cabet—the particular early socialist theorists who each gained or established some kind of following in
America—were Europeans. While Protestant thought, practices and personal commitments may be traced among the memberships of several
socialist communities in the early nineteenth century, such communities
are commonly categorized as examples of 'secular communalism', principally because their theorists, and a vocal proportion of their inhabitants,
avowedly rejected a single religious foundation for their communities.[58]

The sporadic growth in enthusiasm for 'Owenite', 'Fourierist' and
other theories of communal life in the second quarter of the nineteenth
century, as well as the reputation of Shaker and some Pietist settlements,
may have sowed some seed of sympathy for communalism among a far
wider collection of American Christian traditions. An extensive survey of
recognized 'communes' established in the United States in the 1830s and
1840s indicates many short-lived communities of property with traceable
Protestant beliefs—frequently of a heterodox variety—in New York State
and New England, as well as further west in Ohio and Indiana.[59] Such settlements ranged from Zion Hill in New York, associated with the prophetic
leader Robert 'Matthias' Mathews, to individual bodies calling themselves
'United Christians' in Berea, Ohio, 'The Family' in Kirtland, Ohio and the
'Congregation of Saints' in Lexington, Indiana. Each of the latter three
bodies were secessionist groups from local Methodist, Disciples of Christ
and Baptist churches respectively, and each gathered themselves briefly on
communal farmland, apparently seeking to recapture the social arrangements of the primitive church.[60] Some among the 'Hicksite' tendency
of American Quakers were involved in community founding in the early
1840s.[61] In New England, in the same period, both the Brook Farm and

[58] J.F.C. Harrison, *Robert Owen and the Owenites in Britain and America: The Quest for the
New Moral World* (London: Routledge & Kegan Paul, 1969), pp. 107–8; Carl Guarneri,
'The Associationists: Forging a Christian Socialism in Antebellum America', *Church History*,
52:1 (1983), 36–49.

[59] Foster Stockwell, *Encyclopaedia of American Communes, 1663–1963* (Jefferson, NC:
McFarland, 1998), pp. 233–6.

[60] Paul Johnson and Sean Wilentz, *The Kingdom of Matthias: A Story of Sex and Salvation
in 19th-Century America* (New York: Oxford University Press, 1994); R.A. Gilruth, 'The
Community of United Christians at Berea, Ohio, in 1836' (PhD thesis, Princeton University,
1941); *Counties of La Grange and Noble, Indiana, Historical and Biographical* (Chicago:
Battey, 1882), pp. 268–9. For more on The Family at Kirtland, Ohio, see Chap. 7, p. 166.

[61] See Beinecke Rare Book and Manuscript Library, Yale University, A.J. Macdonald
Collection of Utopian Materials, *c.*1840–65, ff. 271–92. Thomas Hamm, *God's Government*

Hopedale communities, which were linked to Unitarian and Universalist varieties of Massachusetts Protestantism, considered themselves to be realizing 'Practical Christianity'.[62] In addition, an expanding circle of 'Bible Communists' gathered first in Vermont then in upstate New York around the 'Perfectionist' preacher, John Humphrey Noyes, over the course of the 1840s. Bible Communists eventually formed the Oneida community in 1849, which practised 'perfectionism' in the light of the millennial age they believed already inaugurated around them. Oneida maintained shared property arrangements until 1881.[63]

Each of these distinctive communities is invariably considered a product of the social and religious context of early nineteenth-century America. Rarely, if ever, are their emergence or development set upon a broader canvas of trans-Atlantic religious exchange, principally because it can seem that the factors at play in their growth and decline were then particular to the United States—whether the expansive possibilities of 'freedom's ferment' towards the western land frontier and in pockets of the industrializing northeast, or the precise dynamics of American Protestantism in the era.[64] In like manner, the notable rise of Mormonism—the Church of Jesus Christ of Latter-day Saints—and its own early communal settlements, are typically studied with close reference to contemporary circumstances and conditions in the United States around 1830.

Mormonism emerged out of western New York, where its founding prophet, Joseph Smith Junior, resided, though the movement soon linked into popular Protestant 'Restorationist' and revivalist traditions spanning several regions further west. This facilitated a rapid spread into Ohio, then to Missouri and Illinois within just a few years. In locations including Kirtland, Ohio (where they incorporated the converted Family community), Far West, Missouri and Nauvoo, Illinois, the Latter-day Saints practised forms of communalism which involved the newly founded church

Begun: The Society for Universal Inquiry and Reform, 1842–1846 (Bloomington: Indiana University Press, 1995), pp. 31–56.

[62] Sterling Delano, *Brook Farm: The Dark Side of Utopia* (Cambridge MA: Harvard University Press, 2004); Edward K. Spann, *Hopedale: From Commune to Company Town, 1840–1920* (Columbus OH: Ohio State University Press, 1992).

[63] Oneida Community, *Bible Communism: a compilation from the annual reports and other publications of the Oneida Association and its branches* (Brooklyn, NY: 1853); Spencer Klaw, *Without Sin: The Life and Death of the Oneida Community* (New York: Allen Lane, 1993).

[64] Alice Felt Tyler, *Freedom's Ferment: Phases of American Social History to 1860* (Minneapolis: University of Minnesota Press, 1944).

assuming ownership of believers' property, together with responsibility for its assignment back to individuals as 'stewards'. This method of distribution was inspired by specific revelations received by Smith pointing towards the need for equality among believers and a wider vision of a holy city where none would suffer poverty. While these early settlements could not last long, as local opposition repeatedly moved Mormon populations on, communal ideas persisted among the Latter-day Saints, surviving the eventual migration to Utah, and experiencing a revival in various cooperative and communal schemes devised in the later decades of the nineteenth century. These ideas remained linked to Mormon expectations of what the imminent millennial age would be like. Among the many converts who migrated across the Atlantic to join the Mormon 'Zion' before and after 1850, prior millennial convictions often laid the groundwork for journeys into Mormon communalism.[65]

COMMUNALISM IN THE BRITISH ATLANTIC BEFORE 1850

In Britain, where many early Mormon converts came from, the period between 1800 and 1850 witnessed perhaps the most intensive proliferation of dissenting Protestant bodies in the nation's history.[66] The success of Mormon missionaries in the late 1830s and after appears to have drawn deeply on this pool of popular dissent and its eschatological culture centred on a coming millennium.[67] Despite a range of British-born millennial movements emerging in the period—some of which bear close comparison with trans-Atlantic radical Pietists and American groups detailed so far—very few adopted full communal property.

The 'Southcottian' movement, which recognized a series of modern prophets receiving 'divine communications' not unlike the testimonies of

---

[65] Grant Underwood, *The Millenarian World of Early Mormonism* (Urbana: University of Illinois Press, 1993); Philip Taylor, *Expectations Westward: The Mormons and the Emigration of Their British Converts in the Nineteenth Century* (Ithaca, NY: Cornell University Press, 1966).

[66] This proliferation was unwittingly measured and recorded in a unique religious census carried out in 1851: Horace Mann, *Census of Great Britain, 1851. Religious Worship in England and Wales. Abridged from the Official Report* (London: George Routledge, 1854). A classic statistical study of the period is Alan D. Gilbert, *Religion and Society in Industrial England: Church, Chapel and Social Change, 1740–1914* (London: Longman, 1976).

[67] Underwood, *Millenarian World of Early Mormonism*, pp. 127–38; J.F.C. Harrison, *The Second Coming: Popular Millenarianism, 1780–1850* (London: Routledge, 1979).

Inspirationist *Werkzeuge*, established an institutional focus for its previously dispersed movement in Ashton-under-Lyne, east of Manchester, in the 1820s.[68] Several hundred Southcottians, some with Methodist backgrounds, migrated to Ashton, and a number of buildings were constructed or acquired within the Lancashire mill-town, including shops and houses. It is unclear how these were owned or inhabited. Yet, the evidence of the prophecies reported at the time indicates that John Wroe (a successor of Joanna Southcott, the founding prophet of the tradition) believed he was receiving visionary insight into the nature of future millennial living, and so directed his following to live as a community in ways which foreshadowed or prefigured the approaching New Jerusalem.[69] While Southcottian millennialism crossed the Atlantic in the early 1840s, it was another 50 years before the tradition developed communal settlements in America—in Detroit and Benton Harbor, Michigan.[70]

A further body of millennial belief in early nineteenth-century Britain, the Catholic Apostolic Church associated with the Scottish preacher Edward Irving and wealthy London banker Henry Drummond, displayed no outright tendency towards communalism. 'Irvingites' nevertheless generated a complex system of tithing and offerings to their church from any income derived from property, as 'all … earthly possessions are God's property'.[71]

One considerably smaller radical Protestant group in Britain who did adopt community of goods in the 1840s was the 'Community of the Son of Man', also called the Agapemone or 'abode of love', in Somerset. This group was founded in 1846 by Henry Prince, previously ordained in the Anglican ministry, and a provocative evangelical preacher in the Somerset region.[72] Prince was dismissed from his position in the established Church around 1842, but set up as an independent revivalist preacher for several years, offering an apocalyptic message of imminent judgement and the

[68] Philip Lockley, *Visionary Religion and Radicalism in Early Industrial England* (Oxford: Oxford University Press, 2013), pp. 103–24.

[69] Lockley, *Visionary Religion*, pp. 118–23.

[70] Philip Lockley, 'Missionaries of the Millennium: Israelite Preachers in the English-speaking World, 1823–1863', *Journal of Religious History*, 37:3 (2013), 369–90.

[71] C.J.T. Bohm quoted in C.G. Flegg, *Gathered Under Apostles: A Study of the Catholic Apostolic Church* (Oxford: Oxford University Press, 1992), pp. 180–6.

[72] Timothy C.F. Stunt, 'Prince, Henry James (1811–1899)', *Oxford Dictionary of National Biography*, Oxford University Press, 2004 (http://www.oxforddnb.com/view/article/37864, accessed 28 July 2015).

return of Christ, and declaring himself a prophet. During 1846, pockets of 'Princites', who considered themselves members of an Elect exempt from the coming judgement, gathered together at Spaxton, in southwest Somerset. Here, about 60 of them gave over their considerable collective wealth to Prince's control and built a chapel, a banqueting hall, houses and gardens. Life in community was intended to be as comfortable and leisurely as possible, reminiscent of the Oneida community in New York in its attitude to earthly sin and the possibility of perfection.[73] This theology implied that aspects of the millennial age were believed to be already realized for a select body of believers.

The millennial and adventist speculation which was fairly widespread within British evangelicalism in the early nineteenth century has been considered 'a symptom of Romanticism'—the cultural sensibility expressed in poetic, literary and artistic interests in not only the sublime and spectacular within nature, but also the grand sweep and drama of history.[74] For other early Victorians, Romanticism encouraged an imagining of the past more than an apocalyptic future, leading to a radical change in attitude to medieval and ancient history. Monasticism, in particular, came to be viewed with far less Protestant suspicion, and cast in a new light by some confronting the treatment of the poor in emerging industrial cities. A common reflection was that the poor had been better off in the Middle Ages, cared for by a network of religious houses providing education and relief for the sick and hungry. Lord John Manners, a radical Tory MP and poet, advocated a return to feudal paternalism, declaring in 1841 that 'nothing but monastic institutions can Christianise Manchester'.[75]

Manners was sympathetic to the Oxford Movement, or Tractarians—the group of Oxford scholars who set themselves the task of reasserting the Catholic inheritance of the Church of England in the 1830s and early 1840s. Tractarian scholarship reflected a Romantic idiom in its effort to reach back into history for an authoritative theology—in their case to the patristics era and the religious thought generated by the earliest age of Christian monasticism. Tractarian ascetic practices drew on this and subsequent periods of church history, asserting an affinity between Anglican

---

[73] Dennis Hardy, *Alternative Communities in Nineteenth-Century England* (London and New York: Longman, 1979), pp. 134–9.

[74] David Bebbington, *Evangelicalism in Modern Britain: A History from the 1730s to the 1980s* (London: Routledge, 1989), pp. 80–5.

[75] Quoted in Charles Whibley, *Lord John Manners and His Friends*, 2 vols (Edinburgh: Blackwood, 1925), 1:107.

methods of pursuing holiness and Catholic and Orthodox traditions. The inner logic of these efforts led to a revival of monastic communities of shared property in the Church of England.[76]

The leading Tractarian, John Henry Newman, devised a plan for a small male 'monastic house' close to Oxford in 1840, which was brought to fruition on a small scale before Newman notoriously converted to Roman Catholicism in 1845.[77] In the latter year, the first Anglican community for women was established—the Park Village community, or Sisterhood of the Holy Cross, near Regent's Park in London.[78] A further series of 'sisterhoods' were organized within a short space of time: the Community of Saint Mary the Virgin began in Wantage in 1846; the Society of the Most Holy Trinity in Devonport, near Plymouth, in 1848. Related houses soon opened in Bristol and Bethnal Green in East London. The beginnings of the Community of Saint John the Baptist at Clewer near Windsor, better known as the 'Clewer Sisters', lay in an initiative in 1849, with the Order formally commenced in 1852.[79] For a period, male communities formed as less formal associations of clergy living under a shared devotional rule. The Brotherhood of the Holy Trinity began in this way in Oxford in 1845; likewise the Brotherhood of St James at Tamworth, near Birmingham, and the Society of the Holy Cross in London in 1855.[80] Communities varied in the demands they made on their members' property, with some initially allowing an annual contribution to a common fund rather than the complete surrender of all private capital.[81] Yet by the 1860s, as plans for the Society of Saint John the Evangelist (the Oxford 'Cowley Fathers') were drawn up, the discipline of 'what the world would call self-denial and poverty' through the giving up of personal property was explicitly intended.[82]

Anglican communalism had a brief trans-Atlantic dimension in the 1840s, some decades before English Orders expanded into North America

---

[76] A.M. Allchin, *The Silent Rebellion: Anglican Religious Communities, 1845–1900* (London: SCM, 1958), pp. 52–6.

[77] Anson, *Call of the Cloister*, pp. 30–43.

[78] Susan Mumm, *Stolen Daughters, Virgin Mothers: Anglican Sisterhoods in Victorian Britain* (London: Leicester University Press, 1999), p. 3.

[79] Allchin, *Silent Rebellion*, pp. 71–3; Mumm, *Stolen Daughters, Virgin Mothers*, pp. 3–8.

[80] Allchin, *Silent Rebellion*, p. 186. For other short-lived lay and clerical 'brotherhoods' in the period, see Anson, *Call of the Cloister*, pp. 50–1.

[81] Allchin, *Silent Rebellion*, p. 89.

[82] R.M. Benson, quoted in Allchin, *Silent Rebellion*, p. 193.

in the 1870s, and further, longer-lasting American societies were founded.[83] The Oxford Movement's *Tracts for the Times* began appearing in American editions in 1839, and were well received by the substantial section of the American Episcopal Church sympathetic to High Church traditions.[84] In 1840, just as Newman was planning his community near Oxford, a group of ordinands at General Theological Seminary, New York, devised a plan for a mission settlement of unmarried clergy, 'yielding implicit obedience to the Rules of the Community ... and holding property in common'.[85] Accepting an invitation to settle in Wisconsin, from 1841 the group slowly established the Noshotah Community, on a site some miles inland from Milwaukee. Over several years, the monastic and communal character of the settlement appears to have faded, as the founding 'brothers' left to marry or undertake church work elsewhere; though the land remained in Episcopal Church hands, and eventually hosted a seminary.[86] From 1847, another group of young priests from New York, calling themselves the Society of the Holy Cross, moved to North Carolina to aid an educational institution called Valle Crucis, named after a medieval monastic community in Wales. The nascent brotherhood was considered deeply suspect in the region, and was wound up soon after a North Carolina senator launched an attack on the local bishop for countenancing a subversive 'Monastic Order, a Society within the Church, composed of persons bound ... by the vows of celibacy, poverty and obedience'.[87]

CONCLUSION: MAPPING THEOLOGIES OF COMMUNALISM

Anglican monastic communalism clearly grew from substantially different roots of Christian thought and practice compared with other examples of Protestant communal property before 1850. Anglican monasteries and convents were consciously reconnecting their branch of Protestantism with a theological culture preserved in the Catholic and Orthodox Christian worlds—a culture of communal living and bodily disciplines that evolved from early Christianity in the Near East. The origins of Christian monasticism are variously traced in ascetical movements in Egypt, Syria

---

[83] Anson, *Call of the Cloister*, pp. 531–79.
[84] Anson, *Call of the Cloister*, p. 532.
[85] Anson, *Call of the Cloister*, pp. 532–3.
[86] Anson, *Call of the Cloister*, p. 535.
[87] Senator George Badger, quoted in Anson, *Call of the Cloister*, p. 537.

and Palestine in the fourth century (which may have superseded martyr-dom as a demonstrated public commitment to Christian faith), as well as a persisting critique of property-ownership and valorizing of poverty in the early church.[88] Over centuries, the holding of property in common, the renunciation of sex and family life, and obedience to an overseer, became recognized components of cohesive Christian communities, underpinned by a theology which cast such restrictions as, counter-intuitively, a means of individual freedom for the service of God and others. In most instances, then, monasticism was a way of living seen to facilitate a church's concep-tion of a fully Christian life, in an earthly present, and towards a temporal horizon reaching beyond death, into eternity.

Most of the numerous other traditions of Protestant communalism in the trans-Atlantic world between 1650 and 1850 appear to have devel-oped alternative theological bases for their practice of shared property. The Labadist communities in the seventeenth-century Netherlands, Maryland and Surinam may well have borrowed many of their harsh disciplines from older monastic asceticism; yet the Ephrata community in eighteenth-century Pennsylvania, even though it reproduced so many aspects of medieval monastic life—tonsures, habits, choral music and illustrated manuscripts—was structured by a radically dissimilar theology centred on belief in a coming millennial age. Several trans-Atlantic communities and traditions may seem to have first adopted communal property as simply a pragmatic decision in challenging circumstances—from the Shakers in the eastern United States to migrating Janssonists in Sweden. However, each unquestionably grounded their practice, before or soon after, in theology—a particular understanding of how holding property in com-mon related to God, or God's intention for their group and the world.

Beyond the ancient Christian traditions of monasticism, three theologi-cal frameworks may be discerned across the Protestant communal groups with traceable beliefs in this chapter. The key distinction between these frameworks would seem to involve a group's eschatology—or how they believed their community related to either an imminent millennial future or a yet broader conception of God's intervention in, and intention for, the world.

---

[88] The classic study of early Christian asceticism is Peter Brown, *The Body and Society: Men, Women and Sexual Renunciation in Early Christianity* (New York: Columbia University Press, 1988). On property, see Peter Garnsey, *Thinking about Property: From Antiquity to the Age of Revolution* (Cambridge: Cambridge University Press, 2007), pp. 59–106.

One evidently popular framework endorsing communalism centred on belief in an imminent millennium or age equated with the reign of the Kingdom of God on earth. This might be predicted to be coming soon from biblical interpretation or the insight or calculations of a prophetic leader. The adoption of communal property was, in turn, conceived to be a form of meaningful preparation in the present for this millennial age in the near future. Several radical Pietist communities demonstrated this theological approach, including Ephrata, the Harmony Society, the Separatists of Zoar and probably the Harmonist-influenced communities led by Wilhelm Keil. Because there was believed to be no personal property in the Millennium, these groups demonstrated in some sense their faith in the Millennium's approach, by living now as they expected to in the coming age. In like manner, influenced by the sexual theology of Jakob Böhme, celibacy was also adopted so that members of Ephrata, the Harmony Society, and some Separatists, could prefigure the sexless, androgynous existence anticipated for humanity when restored from the Fall in the Millennium. The late seventeenth-century Philadelphian Society and Society of the Woman in the Wilderness, also influenced by Böhme, appear to have linked their shared hope of a coming Kingdom to modes of community. Some aspects of early Mormon communalism also reflected a comparable anticipation of a revealed future. The British millennial tradition of Southcottians further related its communal practices to foreshadowing the way of life envisioned in the Millennium.

A second framework encouraging communalism bore significant similarities to this first cluster of beliefs, with a critical difference. Within this theology, millennialism remained a central trope, yet it might be said that the 'timetable' had changed: the messianic age or new dispensation overcoming sin and the Fall was understood to have already commenced in some way. Examples of this belief are apparent across diverse communities, including Gerrard Winstanley's Diggers, the Shakers, the Oneida Bible Communists and the Somerset Agapemonites. While Winstanley viewed the adoption of common property and recognition of the land as a common treasury as evidence of the new age being realized around him, the Oneida community and Agapemonites were to some degree more exclusive in viewing themselves as perfected, without sin and enjoying the benefits of the Millennium before others did. Shaker theology more clearly evolved over a considerable period, yet the idea of earthly history being in a process of transition into a new sinless dispensation, which Ann Lee herself had helped signpost and bring about, formed a cornerstone of belief. 'Christ's Second Appearing' attested in the Shakers' official name was bound up with interpretations of Ann Lee's prophetic inspiration and ministry. For Shakers, their life in community—celibate and without possessions—signified and embodied the millennial dispensation which Lee's life inaugurated. To avoid ownership of property, like avoiding sex, was in effect a discipline about avoiding sin.

The third and final theological framework leading to communalism was looser and more expansive in its perspective. Like the other two frameworks, it centred on eschatological ideas, only less in the traditional sense of eschatology as 'last things'—death, judgement or the 'end times'. In many periods of Christian history, eschatology is now recognized to have been concerned with how the divine is envisaged 'breaking in', disrupting the existing order of things in the present or bringing the vision of heaven into closer proximity to Earth.[89] In the case of the Moravians, life together in community was intimately bound up with the Moravian understanding of how the divine order of things in heaven could be reflected in an earthly social order. An intensive belief in the work of God's Spirit within believers—conceived as a transformational divine 'breaking in' to this world—drew the Moravian everyday experience into close relation to a heaven imagined as the embodiment of harmony. The General Economy's detaching of effort within 'choirs' from the gain of individual wealth was designed to encourage collective harmony and not discord.

Among other groups, the role of prophetic inspiration directing the adoption of communal property was decisive. Christian Metz, principal 'instrument' among the Community of True Inspiration, made clear at each stage of the tradition's progression towards full community of goods that this was the divine will for the gathered body of believers. Joseph Smith's revelations were received in a similar light by early Mormons; as were the New York prophet Matthias's commands at Zion Hill. Eric Jansson styled himself as a prophetic leader, weighting his orders to his Swedish following to institute a common treasury with the authority of a communication from God.

Jansson's Bishop Hill colony was one of many communal groups to have acknowledged the influence of the communalism of the first Christians in Jerusalem described in Acts 2 and 4. A number of such groups have

---

[89] A recent, valuable study taking its cue from this broader definition of eschatology is Martin Spence, *Heaven on Earth: Re-imagining Time and Eternity in Nineteenth-Century British Evangelicalism* (Eugene, OR: Pickwick, 2015).

already been categorized as belonging to the first framework of millennial belief, including Ephrata, the Harmony Society and Separatists of Zoar. For them, the Millennium they expected was signposted in the life of the early church, just as it was elsewhere in biblical prophecies, and in their own collective practices. Yet, for other communal traditions, who did not articulate as precise a millennial theology, the precedent of Acts 2 and 4 could hold an alternative theological meaning: communal property was the divine intention for human society realized in the initial period after the eschatological events of the life, death and resurrection of Christ and coming of the Holy Spirit. This intention remained a prospect and a sign of pure, uncorrupted, spirit-filled Christianity. In this case, a group's eschatological beliefs could be closely tied up with an understanding of the messiah's *first* rather than second coming, and the prospect of a new divine order of society indicated by the New Testament and the continuing inspiration of the Spirit in history.

For groups of Christians seeking explicitly to 'restore' New Testament Christianity in early modernity, communal property held this appeal. Among the sixteenth-century Anabaptists, the diverse secessionist groups on the American frontier in the early nineteenth century and, to a degree, the Hicksite Quakers, Brook Farm and Hopedale communities, sharing property as Christians was a means of demonstrating the realization of an ideal going back to the original divine disruption of the coming of Christ. This, in the end, meant the end of private property was just as much an outworking of their eschatology as more millennialist varieties of Protestant communalism.

CHAPTER 3

The Ephrata Community in the Atlantic World

Jeff Bach

The Ephrata Community was a monastic, communal society founded by Georg Conrad Beissel in 1732 in the sparsely settled Conestoga River region of present-day Lancaster County, Pennsylvania. Beissel had arrived in North America 12 years earlier from mid-western Germany. After living 1 year in Germantown, serving as a weaver's apprentice, Beissel moved to the Conestoga region in 1721, seeking a solitary religious life. Writing in 1756 to a friend named Griess in Mannheim, Germany, Beissel described himself remaining 'in an unceasing longing of the heart to enjoy the love of my God', and so 'thought I would forsake people'.[1] In a moment, he claimed to have suddenly 'glimpsed the light beam of divine friendship', and all 'misery fell away at once'. Beissel explained the goal of his hermit's life from this vision: 'Before I understood, the entire region was illumined by this same heavenly light and afterward it spread to almost all American provinces ... [and to] various nations and languages of the peoples.'[2] Beissel would later take credit for starting a religious awakening

---

[1] Lamech and Agrippa [Jacob Gaas and Peter Miller] (eds), *Chronicon Ephratense* (Ephrata: [Drucks der Bruderschaft], 1786), p. 17. Translation mine. The passage is quoted verbatim from [Conrad Beissel], 'Brief an Freund Griess in Mannheim', in [Conrad Beissel] (n.d.), 'Conrad Beissel Letter Book', Free Library of Philadelphia, B. Ms. 22, ff. 251–2.

[2] Lamech and Agrippa, *Chronicon*, p. 17.

J. Bach
Elizabethtown College, Pennsylvania, USA

© The Editor(s) (if applicable) and The Author(s) 2016   39
P. Lockley (ed.), *Protestant Communalism in the Trans-Atlantic World, 1650–1850*, DOI 10.1057/978-1-137-48487-1_3

that drew together a communal settlement around his hermitage, which he would name 'Ephrata'.

Beissel's words, quoted in 1786 in Ephrata's internal history, *Chronicon Ephratense*, point to the complex connections the Ephrata community had in the Atlantic world, from its beginnings and until late in the eighteenth century. Indeed, the Ephrata community is best understood within the network of personal acquaintances, correspondents, printed religious material, even music and folk art that connected continental Europe and colonial North America, by way of Britain, and the Caribbean. The few historians of Ephrata in the past have seen it as an isolated sect[3] or an 'American counter-culture commune'.[4] Ephrata stands out in fuller detail when viewed in the ongoing connections between the community and its ties across the Atlantic. Correspondence and some publications from Ephrata to Europe attracted new members and raised awareness of the community. Visitors to Ephrata spread its reputation. Even conflicts within the community and with external antagonists had connections to religious, social and political issues that spanned the Atlantic in the eighteenth century. The full significance of Ephrata is only to be interpreted in its Atlantic context.

Conrad Beissel's religious views formed in Germany from the writings of the sixteenth-century German visionary, Jakob Böhme, and to some extent the late seventeenth-century disciples of Böhme in England—the Philadelphian Society, led by John Pordage and Jane Lead. Ultimately Beissel formed a communal group of mostly German and Swiss settlers with some English-speaking members. Beissel recruited new members through writing back to Europe, evangelizing tours in immigrant settlements in America, and securing indentured ship passengers. The new adherents increased the membership, added economic resources and provided labour. Although Beissel may have desired life as a religious hermit far from Europe, he propagated connections in the Atlantic world that nourished a nascent communalism at Ephrata.

---

[3] Oswald Seidensticker, *Ephrata, eine amerikanische Klostergeschichte* (Cincinnati, OH: Mecklenborg and Rosenthal, 1883); Julius F. Sachse, *German Sectarians of Pennsylvania: 1708–1742, 1742–1800*, 2 vols (Philadelphia, 1899–1900).

[4] E.G. Alderfer, *The Ephrata Commune: An Early American Counterculture* (University of Pittsburgh Press, 1985). A similar view, somewhat derivative from Alderfer, comparing Ephrata to America's first 'hippie commune', appeared in Mark Matthews, *Droppers: America's First Hippie Commune, Drop City* (Norman, OK: University of Oklahoma Press, 2010), pp. 134–47. Both these works contain errors.

The name 'Ephrata' appeared first in print in 1736, referring to the place where Rachel, the wife of biblical patriarch Jacob, died in childbirth. Beissel interpreted her death to mean the suffering from renouncing marriage and sexual relations to live in celibacy. Members typically referred to their community as *das Lager der Einsamen* or 'the camp of the solitary'.[5] Outsiders often called them *Beisselianer* or Beisselians, after their founder, or *Siebentäger*, meaning Sabbatarians. The community flourished most spectacularly between about 1745 and 1755, with about 300 adherents, including married families known as householders. The community diminished rapidly after Beissel's death in 1768 and the last vowed celibate sisters died by 1813. The householders reorganized the congregation as the German Seventh Day Baptists in 1814. A much smaller daughter community, Snow Hill, flourished into the nineteenth century.

Evidence uncovered as recently as the 1990s reveals that the sisterhood at Ephrata, known as the Roses of Sharon, had some financial autonomy, paying for repairs in their dormitory and receiving payment services such as spinning yarn.[6] Archaeological explorations have yielded fragments of earthenware vessels with letters scratched into the bottom surfaces after firing, which may be personal initials denoting ownership.[7] This evidence, along with documentary evidence of some privately-owned dwellings at Ephrata suggests that Beissel's group may not have maintained full community of goods throughout all its history.[8] However, the shared housing, shared labour and shared dining of most of the celibate members, and many aspects of a shared economy, point to a largely communal group, and a distinct tradition of Protestant communalism.

EPHRATA ORIGINS

Ephrata's beginnings are rooted in Protestant religious networks of the Atlantic world well before 1732. Georg Conrad Beissel (also spelled Beusel) was born 1 March 1691 in Eberbach in the Electoral Palatinate

---

[5] Lamech and Agrippa, *Chronicon*, p. 54.

[6] Alan G. Keyser, 'Michael Müller/Miller of Cocalico Township Lancaster County and His "Debt Book"', *Journal of the Historical Society of the Cocalico Valley*, vol. 20 (1995), 40, 44–5, 65. The journal will be cited hereafter as *JHSCV*.

[7] Stephen Warfel, *Report of Archaeological Investigations* (Harrisburg: Pennsylvania Historical and Museum Commission, 1994), p. 18.

[8] Ezechiel Sangmeister, *Leben und Wandel des in GOTT ruhenten Ezechiel Sangmeisters: Weiland Einwohner von Ephrata*, 6 parts (Ephrata, 1825), translated by Barbara Schindler in *JHSCV*, vols 4–10 (1979–85). This evidence is given in vol. 9 (1984), 56, 59.

of the then Holy Roman Empire.[9] Orphaned by the age of eight, he was apprenticed to learn baking from a brother. His journeyman years took him to Mannheim and Strasbourg. Later he worked in Heidelberg for a baker named Prior. In 1715 Beissel experienced a religious conversion in private meetings of a group of local Pietists who introduced him to the writings of Jakob Böhme.

Harassment from authorities for his religious activities pushed Beissel out of Heidelberg around 1717 or 1718 to a tiny village, Düdelsheim, belonging to the small principality of Ysenburg-Büdingen.[10] Here Beissel lived with another baker, Jacob Schatz, who was a member of the Community of True Inspiration, founded in 1714 in nearby Himbach by Eberhard Ludwig Gruber and Johann Friedrich Rock.[11] The area around Düdelsheim had also been home to another new religious group: the Schwarzenau Brethren, nicknamed *Neu-Täufer* or New Anabaptists, founded in 1708.[12] They had a congregation in Marienborn in Ysenburg, but were expelled in 1715 for conducting adult baptism by immersion.[13] They moved to Krefeld in the Rhineland in 1715, before Beissel arrived in Düdelsheim, but their influence was not forgotten.

In 1720, Beissel left Düdelsheim and emigrated with three travelling companions to Pennsylvania—a common destination for migrants from German lands since the 1680s. Beissel certainly made use of trans-Atlantic connections, as he landed at Boston in October 1720, and immediately made his way to Germantown, Pennsylvania.

Germantown had been founded in 1683 by Daniel Pastorius, acting on behalf of the Frankfurt Land Company—an economic venture by a group of early Pietist separatists who had withdrawn from the established Lutheran Church in Frankfurt. Pastorius had led a group from Krefeld with Mennonite backgrounds but who had adopted the Quaker faith.

---

[9] Sangmeister, *Leben und Wandel, JHSCV*, vol. 10 (1985), 75.

[10] Jeff Bach, *Voices of the Turtledoves: The Sacred World of Ephrata* (University Park: Pennsylvania State Press, 2003), pp. 13–14. This biographical information about Beissel is based on printed and manuscript letters by Beissel and *Chronicon Ephratense*.

[11] See Chap. 6.

[12] The largest denomination descended from this tradition today is the Church of the Brethren.

[13] Donald F. Durnbaugh, *European Origins of the Brethren* (Elgin: Brethren Press, 1958), pp. 160, 167, 171, 177, 185–8. These are court records of the baptisms and the order of expulsion.

The following year Johannes Kelpius's small group of German dissenters arrived in Germantown, and began a form of communal living along the Wissahickon Creek. Kelpius's group held Böhmist views, anticipated Christ's return and judgment and wrote hymns. Kelpius maintained correspondence links with Böhmists in the Philadelphian Society in England and with acquaintances in Germany.[14] Thus Germantown already represented the intersection of British Quakers, German Mennonites and Pietist separatists in Pennsylvania before Beissel's arrival.

According to the *Chronicon Ephratense*, Beissel intended to join the Kelpius group, only to discover that its young leader had died by 1708.[15] Beissel may have had other reasons for making the trans-Atlantic crossing: economic opportunities in Pennsylvania, together with William Penn's promise of religious liberty, attracted Beissel, like many other poor German immigrants in the early decades of the eighteenth century.[16] In Germantown Beissel apprenticed himself to Peter Becker, a former citizen of Düdelsheim and minister among a group of Schwarzenau Brethren recently arrived in Germantown from Krefeld in 1719. The Brethren had not yet resumed meetings for worship.

Beissel remained with Becker one year and then moved in 1721 to the region of the Conestoga River, 60 miles northwest of Germantown. He lived in a cabin shared with friends.[17] Sometime in 1721, Beissel travelled with Isaac van Bebber, a Mennonite, to visit the remnant of the Labadist community at the Bohemia Manor community in present-day Cecil County, Maryland.[18] By this date, community of goods had been abandoned by these followers of Jean de Labadie, and the two dozen

---

[14] Johannes Kelpius, *The Diarium of Magister Johannes Kelpius*, trans. and ed. by Julius Friedrich Sachse (Lancaster, PA: Pennsylvania German Society, 1917), pp. 29–31, 33, 75–9. See also Levente Juhász, 'Johannes Kelpius (1673–1708): Mystic on the Wissahickon', in Maria Caricchio and Giovanni Tarantino (eds), *Cromos Virtual Seminars (2006). Recent Historiographical Trends of British Studies (17th–18th Centuries)*, p. 1. http://cromohs. unifi.it/seminari/juhasz_kelpius.html (accessed 16 December 2011).

[15] Lamech and Agrippa, *Chronicon*, pp. 10–12.

[16] Aaron S. Fogelman, *Hopeful Journeys: German Immigration, Settlement, and Political Culture in Colonial America, 1717–1775* (Philadelphia: University of Pennsylvania Press, 1996), pp. 4–11.

[17] Lamech and Agrippa, *Chronicon*, pp. 11–13. The friends were Jacob Stuntz, George Stieffel, Simon Koenig and Henry van Beber.

[18] See Chap. 2, p. 13

or so members were aging. What impression the visit made on Beissel is unknown.[19]

In the autumn of 1722, the Schwarzenau Brethren renewed their activity in Pennsylvania. Peter Becker led preaching tours and on Christmas Day 1723 they baptized six new members in the Wissahickon Creek, inaugurating the first Brethren congregation in the New World. In November 1724, Peter Becker preached in the Conestoga region where Beissel lived, and the 33-year-old Conrad Beissel now stepped forward to receive baptism after Becker's sermon.[20]

The Brethren organized a new congregation that day at Conestoga, and chose Beissel to serve as their preacher. By the time of his baptism, Beissel had explored a wide variety of religious views among disciples of Jakob Böhme, the Inspirationists and the diverse opinions to be found in Germantown. Beissel soon began to elaborate his own distinctive theology in his preaching, leading to formal separation from the Schwarzenau Brethren. He taught his congregation to worship on Saturday—the seventh day—rather than on Sunday. The seventh day represented the eternal Sabbath of the fast-approaching millennium that Beissel expected soon, a hallmark of his teaching.[21] He also preached superiority of celibacy. Taking the step to rebaptize some of his supporters, Beissel formally departed the Brethren, and soon established the nucleus of what would become a communal settlement.[22]

A GROWING AMERICAN COMMUNITY

A small, informal community of some celibate Beissel followers first formed in the late 1720s on the land of one supporter, Hans Rudolf Nägele, one of the first Mennonite ministers in Lancaster County. While not living in

---

[19] T.J. Saxby, *The Quest for the New Jerusalem: Jean de Labadie and the Labadists, 1610–1744* (Dordrecht: Martinus Nijhoff, 1987), p. 308. Saxby notes that the Labadists no longer practised a formal community of goods by 1721 and that the community was in advanced decline.

[20] Lamech and Agrippa, *Chronicon*, pp. 17–21.

[21] Cunrad Beysell [sic], *Mystyrion Anomias: The Mystery of Lawlesness: Or, Lawless Antichrist Discover'd and Disclos'd*, trans. M[ichael]. W[ohlfahrt] (1729), pp. 20–3. No copy is known of the German version, reportedly printed in 1728.

[22] No copy of the German copy survives of the 1729 treatise on celibacy, *Die Ehe das Zuchthaus fleischlicher Menschen* (Marriage: The Prison of Carnal People). See also Bach, *Voices of the Turtledoves*, pp. 32–3.

a fully communal economy yet, small clusters of about two or three celi-bates lived together in shared cabins.[23] In 1732, Conrad Beissel abruptly withdrew from the congregation and moved about 8 miles north to the banks of Cocalico Creek. There he occupied a small cabin already built by one of his followers, Emmanuel Eckerlin, then squatting on land that the Germans called *Koch-Halekung* (later diminished to Cocalico), from the place-name used by the Delawares (the Lenni-Lenape tribe), meaning 'the den of serpents'.

Beissel clearly sought a hermit's life, but members of his congrega-tion had other ideas. By autumn 1732, Martin Bremer, Samuel Eckerlin (oldest brother of Emmanuel) and Jacob Gass had followed him to the Cocalico and built dwellings.[24] In the subsequent winter, two sisters, Anna and Maria Eicher, also followed. They had lived as celibate women in the original Nägele settlement. The small group built a cabin for the sisters across the creek from the men's cabins. In due course, further celibate members moved to the banks of the Cocalico, and householder married families established farms surrounding the small cluster of cabins for the celibates.

From 1734 to 1735, the community built a common bakehouse, a common storehouse, another house for single men and finally the first monastic dormitory, named 'Kedar'.[25] With small *Kammern*, or monastic cells on the ground floor for men and similar cells on the third floor for women, the floor in-between featured a *Saal*—a hall or meeting room—for worship and love feasts. By fully adopting communal living, Beissel wanted to imitate the church in Acts 2.[26] Growing communal space was paralleled by an expansive approach to recording and promoting Beissel's religious teachings: a book of mystical maxims was printed by the com-munity in 1730, and two small hymnals were also produced in 1730 and 1732.

From 1735 until about 1756—the outbreak of the Seven Years War—the Ephrata community generally grew in membership and buildings, while developing its printing enterprises, a unique style of musical compo-sition and a highly ornamented calligraphy known as *Fraktur*. In the early

---

[23] Sangmeister, *Leben und Wandel, JHSCV*, vol. 4 (1979), pp. 26–9.

[24] Lamech and Agrippa, *Chronicon*, pp. 53–4.

[25] Lamech and Agrippa, *Chronicon*, pp. 53–4, 62–4.

[26] Irenici Theodicäi, *Zionitischen Stiffts Ier Theil* (Ephrata: Drucks der Bruderschaft, 1745), p. 114. Irenici Theodicäi is the Hellenized form of Beissel's spiritual name, Friedsam Gottrecht, meaning 'Peaceable and Right with God'.

1740s, the community prospered economically, even while dealing with an external challenge from rival Protestant communalists in Pennsylvania— Moravians—and an internal challenge, as Beissel's authority and control of the community were threatened by two brothers, Israel and Samuel Eckerlin.

After the first monastic dwelling, Kedar, was completed, construction projects continued with almost one new building each year until 1746. These included the *Bäthaus*, or house of prayer, added on to Kedar. In 1738, members built a separate monastic house for the celibate men named Zion, and the following year a second monastic house for the sisters.[27] A worship house, or *Saal*, was attached to Zion at this time. In 1741 Beissel ordered the construction of a new worship building for the householders, 'Peniel'. The name, meaning 'the face of God', referred to the location where Jacob wrestled with God and received a blessing (Gen 32:30). In a letter written in 1741, Beissel described 'Peniel' as having an allegorical meaning for the 'renunciation of all things', including wealth and marriage, in order to obtain God's blessing.[28] In 1743, a large monastic dormitory known as 'Hebron' was added onto Peniel, enabling some householder married couples to take up celibate living in Hebron. Most, however, opted to return to a conventional pattern of married life on nearby farms by 1745.

In 1745, Beissel ordered a new dormitory with a meetinghouse for the brothers, called 'Bethania', to be built in the meadow near Cocalico Creek. Beissel then reorganized the brothers previously living in 'Zion'— called the Zionitic Brotherhood—and made them the Brotherhood of Bethania, placing them in the new house in 1746. Zion was then used for the weekly Sabbath worship service for the whole community. The Ephrata sisterhood was reorganized as the Order of the Roses of Sharon in 1745, and Peniel became their place of worship, known simply as the *Saal*.

The reasons for this flurry of construction are not fully known.[29] The *Chronicon* claimed that more space was needed because of a growing membership. Archaeologist Steven Warfel has pointed out the function of control that Beissel exercised in ordering new buildings. An eighteenth-century contemporary, Christopher Sauer the elder, claimed that Israel

---

[27] Lamech and Agrippa, *Chronicon*, pp. 90–1, 100–1, 108, 128, 133–5, 157, 165–6. These passages describe the various communal buildings.

[28] Irenici Thedoicäi, *Zionitischen Stiffts Ier Theil*, p. 250.

[29] For a fuller discussion, see Bach, *Voices of the Turtledoves*, pp. 118–24, 130–9.

Eckerlin was the driving force in the building campaign. Another possible interpretation is that the building projects helped to integrate new members into shared communal work. Whatever factors contributed to the building projects, they created a communal space out of a small collection of hermit cabins.

BELIEFS AND RITUALS

Monastic dwellings and the formation of brotherhoods and sisterhoods in the Pennsylvania landscape can seem like the importing of European Catholicism to the New World. Yet Conrad Beissel built his religious worldview from distinctive traditions of Protestant mysticism, and the ritual life of Ephrata was adapted from Pietist practices common among the Schwarzenau Brethren.

Beissel's theology was clearly shaped by elements of Jakob Böhme's 'theosophy' as transmitted by Johann Georg Gichtel, the publisher of Böhme's works from the 1680s. Drawing from Böhme, Beissel believed that God was androgynous, possessing male and female characteristics in perfect balance. Like Böhme, Beissel personified the female aspect of God as the Holy Virgin Sophia, or Heavenly Wisdom. Beissel interpreted the male characteristic of God as wrathful, and the female characteristic as loving.[30] Beissel believed that the first human, Adam, was created androgynous, possessing both female and male characteristics in perfect balance.[31]

Beissel's central theological problem was the question of evil, human sin, and the need for redemption. He saw human evil arising from Adam's

[30] Beissel presented his most systematic attempt to explain his theology in the so-called *Wunderschrift* ('Miraculous Writing') published in its most complete form in 1773 after his death. See Friedsam Gottrecht [Conrad Beissel], *Deliciae Ephratenses, Pars I* (Ephrata: Typis Societatis, 1773), pp. 1–47. For a second German printing with a few slight changes in vocabulary, see [Conrad Beissel], *Göttliche Wunderschrift* (Ephrata: [Typis Societatis], 1789). The *Chronicon Ephratense* refers to a *Wunderschrifft* that Beissel wrote after an illness around 1741, and identifies that work as the 'Dissertation'. Curiously, an English translation by Peter Miller was published in 1765; however, it is faulty at a few points. See [Conrad Beissel], *A Dissertation on Man's Fall* (Ephrata, 1765). No copy of a version printed prior to 1765 is known. For a brief discussion of the three versions, see Bach, *Voices of the Turtledoves*, pp. 37–8.

[31] Beissel mentioned 'heavenly Wisdom' as the true spouse of Adam in 1728. See [Beysell] (sic), *Mystyrion Anomias*, pp. 20–1. He wrote a detailed letter sometime before 1745 detailing his views on divine gender, the separated genders in sinful humanity and Christ's restoration of spiritual androgyny in Irenici Thedoicäi, *Zionitischen Stiffts Ier Theil*, pp. 183–95.

sexual desire for a mate when he saw the animals reproducing.[32] With this sin of desire, the Holy Virgin Sophia departed from Adam and God created the woman, Eve, intending that the couple would still be androgynous. When Adam ate from the tree of the knowledge of good and evil, the couple fell into the second sin. Sexual desire unleashed the fiery male desire to dominate over women.[33]

Only a twofold conversion could reverse the effects of the twofold sin, for Beissel. The first conversion came as a person tried to live a totally good life. Such efforts would lead to despair and the relinquishing of all hope of doing good deeds. At this point a person passed through the so-called 'mystic death', to enter a second conversion where Christ and Sophia effected a spiritual rebirth and forgiveness. Christ and Sophia restored spiritually the primordial androgyny, thus ending sexual desire. Such believers were baptized by threefold immersion in the names of the Trinity, signifying their rebirth and the restitution of spiritual androgyny through Sophia and Jesus Christ.[34] The practice of celibacy followed. Ironically, given Beissel's view of Sophia's role in redemption, he still made women at Ephrata subordinate to male leaders.[35]

The Ephrata community developed a complex ritual life, derived primarily from the Schwarzenau Brethren, but with Beissel's unique interpretations. Baptism by threefold immersion was much like the practice of the Brethren.[36] Unlike the Brethren, Beissel allowed for multiple rebaptisms, as a sign of renewal or at the request of a member. He also developed proxy baptism on behalf of the dead.[37] Members of the Ephrata occasionally practised a ritual of anointing the sick with oil and praying for healing.[38]

---

[32] Friedsam Gottrecht, *Deliciae Ephratenses, Pars I*, pp. 12–13. For a fuller discussion of Beissel's religious thought, see Bach, *Voices of the Turtledoves*, pp. 25–47.

[33] Friedsam Gottrecht, *Deliciae Ephratenses, Pars I*, pp. 14–17.

[34] Friedsam Gottrecht, *Deliciae Ephratenses, Pars I*, pp. 16–18, 26–30.

[35] Friedsam Gottrecht, *Deliciae Ephratenses, Pars I*, pp. 19–21.

[36] Irenici Theodicäi, *Zionitischen Stiffts Ier Theil*, pp. 80, 116–17, 125. For a description of the manner of baptizing, see the comments by the Swedish Lutheran provost, Israel Acrelius, who visited Ephrata in 1753. Israel Acrelius, *A History of New Sweden, or the Settlements on the Delaware River*, trans. William M. Reynolds, reprinted in Felix Reichmann and Eugene E. Doll, *Ephrata as Seen by Contemporaries: Proceedings of the Pennsylvania German Folklore Society*, vol. 17 (Allentown, PA: Schechters, 1953), p. 70.

[37] Lamech and Agrippa, *Chronicon*, pp. 148, 163–5, and for baptism for the dead see p. 103.

[38] Lamech and Agrippa, *Chronicon*, p. 120.

Ephrata's communion ritual was known as the love feast, and consisted of a time of examination and repentance, a simple meal shared by all participants, followed by feet-washing, culminating in the communion of unleavened bread and the cup, symbolizing Christ's body and blood given on the cross for the redemption of human sin. Love feasts, or agape meals, were a named event common to diverse forms of trans-Atlantic Pietism, including Methodism, though not all groups considered them to be eucharistic rituals like the German Brethren and Ephrata. Love feasts were held frequently at Ephrata, sometimes two or three times a month. The celibate orders might hold their own love feasts, or a householder family might sponsor a love feast and invite only select guests. The community also held general love feasts for all members, sometimes on the anniversary of a member's death.

Accounts of Ephrata love feasts survive from two different visitors to Ephrata with trans-Atlantic connections. Israel Acrelius, a provost in the Lutheran Church in Sweden, visited Ephrata in 1753.[39] He noted that at communion, Beissel alone distributed the elements of bread and wine from a special table behind the chair where he preached in the centre of the meetinghouses at Zion, Saron and Bethania. Communicants came forward to receive the sacramental elements.[40] Acrelius also reported that feet-washing was sometimes practised as a hospitality ritual when guests arrived at Ephrata.[41]

Charles Mifflin, a Philadelphia merchant and son of a Quaker originally from Wiltshire in England, described a love feast which he attended while living at Ephrata in 1769.[42] Mifflin resided briefly at Ephrata to improve his German for business in Pennsylvania and beyond. A householder couple hosted the love feast for celibate brothers and sisters. Upon entering, each sister kissed the wife and each brother kissed the husband, a ritual greeting observed often among Ephrata members known as the holy kiss. Feet-washing followed, in which the husband washed each of the feet of

---

[39] Reichmann and Doll, *Ephrata as Seen by Contemporaries*, pp. 52–77.

[40] See the description by Acrelius in Reichmann and Doll, *Ephrata as Seen by Contemporaries*, pp. 54–57.

[41] Lamech and Agrippa, *Chronicon*, pp. 215, 254, and Acrelius in Reichmann and Doll, *Ephrata as Seen by Contemporaries*, pp. 61, 72.

[42] For the entire account, see Bach, *Voices of the Turtledoves*, p. 79. Charles Mifflin letter to his father, 29 November 1769, in University of Michigan, William L. Clements Library, Mifflin Family Papers, unpaginated manuscript. I credit Michael Showalter for calling these letters to my attention.

the brothers, while another brother followed with a towel to dry their feet. The wife of the household and another celibate sister did the same among the women. After a meal of beef soup and slices of bread, the members received the communion of bread and cup. Singing and preaching accompanied the ritual actions.

The celibate members sometimes observed unique rituals for their monastic vocation, such as wearing a tonsure, which began in 1738. About this time Beissel also introduced monastic white habits and new spiritual names were given to the celibates.[43] Beissel chose the name Friedsam Gottrecht, meaning 'Peaceable, Right with God'. He also adopted the title of 'Father', which aroused some resistance.

Worship and prayer alternated with work at Ephrata, although they had no fixed liturgy. Worship services included hymn-singing, prayer and Beissel's preaching. The celibates often rose for *Nachtmette*, a worship service around midnight. *Die Rose*, a manuscript account of the Order of the Roses of Sharon, written by the sisters after 1745, described a rather exact daily schedule, permitting one meal per day in the evening. After this the sisters practised choral singing or their *Fraktur*-ornamented lettering. Saturdays were devoted entirely to rest, worship and prayer. Whether the sisters observed this schedule precisely, and whether the brothers matched it, is unknown. By the 1750s, the Ephrata community began to relax some of their asceticism, according to the Swedish observer, Israel Acrelius.

The *Fraktur* art and the music were two forms of Ephrata's material culture that represented their religious beliefs and their continued connection with Europe. Both forms first appeared in the late 1730s as the community stabilized and grew.

Fraktur was defined by Donald Shelley as a form of lettering imitating the Gothic font found in Pennsylvania German manuscripts.[44] He demonstrated similarities between Ephrata's *Fraktur* and early modern German and Swiss lettering books, which Don Yoder has further confirmed.[45] Cynda Benson pointed out similarities between decorative elements in

[43] Lamech and Agrippa, *Chronicon*, pp. 72–3.

[44] Donald A. Shelley, *The Fraktur-Writings or Illuminated Manuscripts of the Pennsylvania Germans*, Proceedings of the Pennsylvania German Folklore Society, vol. 23 (Allentown: Schechters, 1961), pp. 21–3.

[45] Don Yoder, 'The European Background of Pennsylvania's Fraktur Art' and 'The Fraktur Texts and Pennsylvania-German Spirituality', in Cory M. Amsler (ed.), *Bucks County Fraktur* (Publications of the Pennsylvania German Society 33; Kutztown: Pennsylvania German Society and Bucks County Historical Society, 1999), pp. 15–61.

European textile patterns and illustrations in Ephrata's *Fraktur*.[46] Ephrata members were the first to create this text art, and it was introduced in 1736.[47] While some celibate brothers produced *Fraktur* pieces, the sisters achieved the most sophisticated work.

The Ephrata scriveners created four main categories of text art: large and small placards with devotional texts for the cells of celibate members, manuscript music books for the choirs, book plates showing ownership, and a work known as *The Christian's ABC* (*Der Christen ABC*).[48] This latter work, dated 1751, was a unique book with two entire upper-case alphabets with highly ornamented letters, followed by lower-case letters and numerals. Thirteen large wall placards survive in the collection at the Ephrata Cloister Museum. The placards helped to define the sacred space for worship in the meeting houses and for prayer in the sleeping chambers. The music books served the needs of the choirs. Some books were created as gifts. The most exquisite example was the sisters' music book created in 1751 for Mother Maria Eicher, abounding in floral images, doves and one portrayal of Christ's crucifixion (Fig. 3.1). The depictions of the natural world in such lettering patterns and decorative images expressed an aspect of Ephrata beliefs: the artists were anticipating the paradise they believed they would experience in an approaching divine consummation and millennial age.

The second type of material culture that expressed the transfer of religious influences across the Atlantic was their music. Conrad Beissel, celibate women and men, and some householders wrote hymn texts, producing their first hymnal in 1730. Beissel also composed hymn tunes and harmonization from the early 1740s. In 1747 he published his rules for composition as the preface to the second large hymnal at Ephrata, *Das Gesäng der einsamen und verlassenen Turtel-Taube* (The Song of the Solitary and Forsaken Turtledove).[49] Böhmist numerology influenced his unusual harmonic sequences and categories of servant notes and master notes. His preface was the first musicological treatise published in America.

---

[46] Cynda L. Benson, 'Early American Illuminated Manuscripts from the Ephrata Cloister' (PhD thesis, University of Kansas, 1994), pp. 66–70, 99–100, 125–9.

[47] Lamech and Agrippa, *Chronicon*, p. 64. The first pieces were supposedly used to adorn the prayer house (*Bäthaus*) attached to Kedar.

[48] For a fuller discussion of the range of Ephrata's *Fraktur* and their symbolic imagery, see Bach, *Voices of the Turtledoves*, pp. 141–69.

[49] [Ephrata Community], *Das Gesäng der einsamen und verlassenen Turtel-Taube Nemlich der Christlichen Kirche* (Ephrata: Drucks der Brüderschaft, 1747), pp. 5–13.

Fig. 3.1   Manuscript illustration from Ephrata hymnal, *Zionitischer Weyrauchs-Hügel* (*c*.1745). Courtesy of Earl H. and Anita F. Hess Archives and Special Collections, Elizabethtown College, Elizabethtown, Pennsylvania

The community created thousands of texts and hundreds of tunes, mostly for four voices, but some for six to eight voices.

Through their hymnody, Ephrata's influence notably travelled back to Europe. Konstanze Grutschnig has demonstrated that the Radical German Pietist, Christoph Schütz, praised the spiritual insight of the hymns from Ephrata, incorporating several hymn texts and the preface from Ephrata's 1732 hymnal, *Vorspiel der neuen Welt* (Prelude to the New World) into the third volume of his comprehensive hymnal, *Des Geistlichen Würtz[,] Kräuter[,] und Blumen Gartens, oder Universal-Gesangbuchs* (The Spiritual Spice, Herb and Flower Garden, or Universal Hymnal), printed in 1740.[50] Through these hymn texts, Beissel's religious thought travelled back to Europe and circulated in radical Pietist circles there.

A COMMUNITY IN AN ATLANTIC NETWORK

The Ephrata community's flourishing in the middle decades of the eighteenth century was dependent on a trans-Atlantic network of recruitment for new members. Beissel attracted converts with preaching tours among recent migrants already in America, and through a correspondence network reaching back to Europe.

A notable example of Beissel's recruiting from European immigrant settlements in Pennsylvania was his success in the Tulpehocken settlement in present-day Lebanon County, north of Ephrata. Beissel visited Tulpehocken in 1735, and converted the community's erudite pastor, Peter Miller, trained at Heidelberg University. Miller would later oversee the publication of many of Beissel's writings on the community's press. He also translated the massive Dutch Anabaptist martyrology, *Het Bloedig Toneel* (Martyrs Mirror) into German in 1748–49, producing a 1200-page book—the largest printed work produced in the American colonies by this date. Several members of Reformed and Lutheran background also followed Miller from Tulpehocken to join Ephrata, including Conrad Weiser,

---

[50] Christoph Schütz, *Des Geistlichen Würtz-, Kräuter- und Blumen-Gartens, oder Universal-Gesangbuchs Dritten Theil* (Homburg vor der Höhe: Johann Philipp Helwig, 1740). The *Vorrede* appears on the six leaves preceding the hymns that begin on p. 1. See Konstanze Grutschnig-Kieser, *Der Geistliche Würtz-, Kräuter- und Blumen-Garten: ein radikalpietistisches 'Universal-Gesang-Buch'* (Göttingen: Vandenhoeck & Ruprecht, 2006), pp. 150–6. I am grateful to Dr Grutschnig-Kieser for calling this to my attention during her doctoral research.

a skilled interpreter of aboriginal languages who assisted in treaty negotiations with native peoples.[51]

Beissel had some limited success recruiting English settlers to Ephrata during a preaching tour in the French Creek area of Chester County in 1745 and 1746. Several English families and some single people came to Ephrata, one of whom, Israel Seymour, married a former celibate sister from Ephrata and moved to South Carolina to found an English-speaking congregation with Ephrata beliefs. Although the French Creek members were few in number, their descendants were present at Ephrata well into the nineteenth century. The French Creek recruits illustrate a rare instance of a German-speaking communal group mixing language and cultural backgrounds, while also producing a small but successful extension in a distant outpost.[52]

Beissel recruited new followers from Europe through letters to his family and wider acquaintances during most of his life. Beissel's only surviving published letter with a date and destination was addressed to a 'beloved sister in the Lord' in Basel, Switzerland, in 1733. Admonishing her to let her self-will be broken and attain spiritual rebirth, he encouraged the sister and her associates to flee 'Sodom and Gomorra'—a veiled metaphor for the fallen established Churches and perhaps Europe in general.[53] Beissel prophesied doom for Europe and the flowering of true Christian faith like a lily blooming in America.[54]

Although the exact recipients are not named in the 1733 letter, in 1736 the Thoma family came to Pennsylvania from Niederdorf in the district of Waldenburg in Basel Canton.[55] Margareth, the mother, and her daughters Catherina and Anna, and son, Hans Jacob, entered the Ephrata community and all except for Anna died there. Durst (Theodorus), Margareth's husband, and two sons, Martin and Durst Junior, did not enter the community but settled at present-day Schaefferstown, remaining active in the German Reformed congregation there.[56]

---

[51] Lamech and Agrippa, *Chronicon*, pp. 57–61. Weiser left Ephrata in 1742, returning to the Lutheran Church. One of his daughters married Henry Melchior Mühlenberg, a Lutheran minister sent by Pietist leaders at Halle in 1742 to organize the Lutheran Church in America and halt the advances of sectarian groups like the Brethren and Ephrata.

[52] Lamech and Agrippa, *Chronicon*, p. 168. 'Moravians also recruited some English-speakers'.

[53] Irenici Theodicäi, *Zionitischen Stiffts Ier Theil*, pp. 98, 102.

[54] Irenici Theodicäi, *Zionitischen Stiffts Ier Theil*, p. 98.

[55] Lamech and Agrippa, *Chronicon*, pp. 138–40.

[56] Leo Schelbert, 'On the Power of Pietism: A Documentary on the Thommens of Schaefferstown', *The Historic Schaefferstown Record*, 18:4 (1984), 47–54.

The Thoma family was very wealthy: their assets were valued at £3497 in Basel currency at their departure. While Durst Thoma gave economic reasons in a petition to leave Waldenburg in 1735, religious reasons were also clearly a factor, as Leo Schelbert has demonstrated. The pastor at Waldenburg suspected Margareth and Catharina Thoma of Pietist activities in 1732, because they had abstained from communion at church and were reportedly attending forbidden devotional meetings in homes.[57] An Ephrata death register further noted that Catharina had 'suffered much persecution in Switzerland'.[58]

Anna Thoma also sent communication from Ephrata back to Europe. In 1743 she wrote a letter to Hieronymus d'Annone, the pastor who came to Waldenburg after her departure. She described the contemplative life that she, her mother and sister shared in the sisters' monastic house, Kedar.[59] In 1767, her brother, Martin, and his family returned to Switzerland.[60] Anna herself left Ephrata in 1771, three years after Beissel's death, but remained in Pennsylvania, marrying an elderly, wealthy, wine merchant in Philadelphia, Johannes Wister (or Wüster). She died in 1778. The marriage may well have been one of convenience to support Anna as the economic support for the aging sisters at Ephrata declined, and Wister had provided financial support for other elderly members of the community before. His wealth accumulated through international trade and his generosity to members at Ephrata further illustrate how Ephrata was not an isolated cloister in the Pennsylvania wilderness, but tied into the dynamic economics of the Atlantic world in this period.

Other Swiss families came to Ephrata, such as the Kellers, who came from Rothenflüh, outside Basel, the birthplace of Margareth Thoma, and her daughter Catherina. Peter Schumacher joined the brotherhood and signed over a tract of land to them. Benedict Jüchlie, a wealthy man from Bern who travelled on the same ship as the Thoma family, donated land and provided funds for the community to purchase a grist mill on the Cocalico.[61] The *Chronicon* reported that Jüchlie intended to return to Switzerland, supposedly to retrieve part of his inheritance to use for

---

[57] Schelbert, 'On the Power of Pietism', 49.

[58] Jeff Bach, 'The Death Registers of the Ephrata Cloister', in *JHSCV*, vol. 21 (1996), 38.

[59] Schelbert, 'On the Power of Pietism', 60. The letter is in the papers of Hieronymus d'Annone in the Universitätsbibliothek Basel F II, No. 921. The translation is by Hedwig Rappolt.

[60] Schelbert, 'On the Power of Pietism', 63.

[61] Bach 'Death Registers', 34.

purchasing a printing press, but died in Philadelphia in 1741. A proportion of his estate was entailed to Ephrata, further showing how Ephrata's connections to Europe brought financial assets, and not just members, into the Pennsylvania communal group.

Beissel's correspondence with family members remaining in the Palatinate region of Germany, and associating with further bodies of Protestant dissent, likewise led to recruits for Ephrata. A key figure in this was Beissel's elder brother, Johann Peter Beissel, a shoemaker who moved from Eberbach to Gimbsheim with his wife, Eva Magdalena, around 1720.[62] In 1742, Conrad wrote to Peter in Gimbsheim, recalling how they were 'remnants of the relatives and natural father's house', and yet had now been 'born in a new brotherhood from the one and true father'.[63] Beissel prophesied doom on the Electoral Palatinate and warned his brother to flee with his family from 'Sodom, Egypt and Babel' before the coming judgment of Christ.[64]

Like Margareth Thoma in Switzerland, Peter Beissel was involved with a new, suspect religious movement already stirring in Gimbsheim. Helmut Schmahl has traced this group in documents written by a Catholic priest serving Gimbsheim and neighbouring Alsheim, Father Hess. Hess complained to regional officials in Alzey in 1741 about a new 'sect' in Gimbsheim,[65] who abstained from holy communion and from having their children baptized. They also rejected secular authority—common forms of behaviour in separatist Pietism. Hess further claimed that they met in small groups in their homes, studying the Berleburg Bible—a popular edition of the Bible among Radical Pietists. They reportedly read 'die güldene rooss' [sic], referring to *Die Güldene Rose* by a German Pietist, Christoph Schütz, whose book was also popular at Ephrata.

---

[62] Annette K. Burgert, *Brethren from Gimbsheim in the Paltinate to Ephrata and Bermudian in Pennsylvania* (Myerstown, PA: AKB Publications, 1994), pp. 7–8. The date is based on Burgert's citation for the confirmation entry of Peter's daughter, Anna Elisabetha, who was confirmed in 1720.

[63] Irenici Theodicäi, *Zionitischen Stiffts Ier Theil*, p. 92. The date is based on Beissel's note that the letter was written 27 years after the beginning of his new Christian life, or 27 years since his conversion in 1715, thus 1742.

[64] Irenici Theodicäi, *Zionitischen Stiffts Ier Theil*, pp. 85, 92.

[65] Helmut Schmahl 'Radikalpietisten in der atlantischen Welt: Die Auswanderung der Gimbsheimer "Erweckten" an Ephrata/Pennsylvania in den Jahren 1749 und 1751', *Mitteilungsblatt zur rheinhessischen Landeskunde*, new series, 7 (2005), 21–2.

The Reformed minister in Gimbsheim, Pastor Beer, joined Father Hess in requesting an ecclesiastical investigation of the group's leaders, Heinrich Lohmann and Jacob Kimmel. The group was fined 258 guilders—which Schmahl calculates to be more than twice the average annual income in the village. They protested the fine, but ultimately acquiesced and attended communion at the Reformed Church the following Easter. After both Father Hess and Pastor Beer died suddenly in 1743, rumours spread that the Pietists had prayed for their accusers' deaths.[66]

The Gimbsheim group soon moved temporarily to Count Zinzendorf's Moravian communal settlement at Herrnhaag and then to Gelnhausen, home of Johann Friedrich Rock, a co-founder of the Inspirationists.[67] Yet, Ephrata was the ultimate refuge for the Gimbsheim believers. Two years after Beissel's brother died in 1747, the first members immigrated to Pennsylvania, with the Ephrata community paying their passage.[68] The poorer members emigrated first, including Peter Beissel's widow and three of their children, among them a Peter Beissel the younger. According to Schmahl, Heinrich Lohmann and Jacob Kimmel were considerably wealthier than the Beissel family and paid their own passage to Ephrata with some other members in 1751. For dissenters from Europe, Ephrata was truly a refuge.

While the Gimbsheim group made a good addition of like-minded members and a good labour source to work off the passage costs paid by Ephrata, Beissel also saw in Lohmann a potential challenge to his leadership. Beissel encouraged Lohmann to move with Jacob Kimmel and other Gimbsheim families to York County in 1751 to form a daughter congregation. They settled on the Bermudian Creek near a large settlement of Schwarzenau Brethren and several Reformed Protestant families. Some of the single Gimbsheim members stayed in the celibate orders at Ephrata, including Beissel's nephew, Peter Beissel and two nieces.

Common to the migration stories of many Germans sailing to North America in the eighteenth century was the indenture system: poorer Germans, as well as some other Europeans, afforded their passage across the Atlantic by having it paid for them. They then indentured themselves, committing to work for several years in America. After their debt was paid, the migrant was free to work for themselves. Ephrata recruited indentured

---

[66] Schmahl, 'Radikalpietisten in der atlantischen Welt', 23.
[67] On the Inspirationists, see Chap. 6.
[68] Lamech and Agrippa, *Chronicon*, p. 187. For the year of Peter Beissel's death, see Burgert, *Brethren from Gimbsheim*, p. 8.

passengers with the help of at least one agent in Philadelphia—Wilhelm Jung. Jung sent Anton Hellenthal and Ezechiel Sangmeister to Ephrata in 1748, the latter of whom became a harsh critic of Beissel. In his autobiography, *Leben und Wandel*, Sangmeister heaped scorn on Beissel and the community for hypocrisy, drunkenness and sexual immorality, while indulging in self-pity for his own hardships.[69] While Sangmeister rejected Beissel's leadership and the community's ritual life, he held the same Böhme-derived beliefs about an androgynous God and celibacy, as well as observance of the seventh-day Sabbath, and expectations of the end times. In the early 1750s, Sangmeister left Ephrata for a secession community in Virginia, though he would return for a period in the 1760s to gather further allegations against Beissel.

Artefacts recovered during archaeological explorations at Ephrata between 1994 and 2001 demonstrate the community's trans-Atlantic connections in material culture, showing the effects of Beissel's networks of communication and recruitment. Stephen Warfel, a state archaeologist, led a team that pieced together recovered ceramic fragments to restore over two dozen ceramic vessels primarily for domestic use.[70] Some of the plates and pots revealed styles typical of late seventeenth- and early eighteenth-century construction. Warfel found evidence of European-made ceramics, including combed-slip earthen ware, tin-glazed earthenware and Westerwald stoneware. They also recovered fragments of later styles of redware and more refined creamware and pearlware, introduced later from Europe. Warfel interpreted the ceramic evidence to suggest that initially Beissel's group retained objects reflecting an older style of domestic ware, but that ongoing trade and new members brought objects of later European origin and style into the community.[71] Beissel did not create an isolated communal group in the Pennsylvania wilderness but one that flourished through and because of its trans-Atlantic ties.

CONFLICTS AND ATLANTIC CONNECTIONS

Ephrata's Atlantic connections factored into several conflicts for the community, both internal and external, both religious as well as political.

---

[69] Ezechiel Sangmeister, *Leben und Wandel, Dritter Theil* (Ephrata: Joseph Baumann, 1826).

[70] Stephen G. Warfel, *Historical Archaeology at Ephrata Cloister: A Report on the 1994 Investigations* (Harrisburg, PA: Commonwealth of Pennsylvania, 1995), p. 15.

[71] Warfel, *Historical Archaeology at Ephrata Cloister*, pp. 20–1.

Perhaps the most consistent external challenge to Ephrata came from the Moravians, particularly in 1742 and 1743, after the efforts of the Moravian leader, Count Nikolaus Ludwig von Zinzendorf, to organize a series of unity meetings (or synods) among the German-speaking religious groups in Pennsylvania. The Ephrata community, Mennonites and members of the Brethren, as well as various other separatists, participated. Ephrata soon withdrew, as did the Mennonites and the Brethren, due in part to differences over adult baptism, but also resistance to Zinzendorf's perceived dominating role. Some Moravians and members of Ephrata nevertheless exchanged visits between Bethlehem and Ephrata, 60 miles apart, seeking to understand each other better. One Ephrata celibate brother, David Lessle, decided to join the Moravians in 1742 and travelled back to Europe to the Herrnhaag settlement in Hessen. Within 2 years, Lessle had decided to return to Ephrata, but grew ill on the journey in 1744 and died at sea, aged 29. Among his last words, he was reported to have called out, 'O! Efratha, Efratha, you dear Efratha: O my dear mother, and my dear sister!'[72]

Count Zinzendorf himself visited Ephrata twice in 1742. However, neither Zinzendorf nor Beissel would go to see the other while Zinzendorf was there, so the two men never met.[73] Polemical battles subsequently broke out between the two groups in 1743. Beissel accused Israel Eckerlin, Ephrata's main representative in the 1742 unity meetings of showing too much sympathy for the Moravians. Beissel demanded that Israel write a treatise against them. Johannes Hildebrand, an older member, wrote two other similar treatises.[74] Hildebrand claimed that the Moravians had no concept of the spiritual rebirth since they did not prioritize celibacy.[75] Ephrata declared that the Moravians were therefore a 'fallen' church. The Moravians in turn wrote against Beissel's community, calling them instruments of the devil.[76]

---

[72] Bach, 'Death Registers', p. 33.

[73] Lamech and Agrippa, *Chronicon*, pp. 126–7.

[74] Lamech and Agrippa, *Chronicon*, pp. 128–9. The anti-Moravian tracts were often bound with a document printed in 1743 that served as the community's confession of faith, *Mistisches und Kirchliches Zeuchnüß der Brüderschaft in Zion* (Germantown: C[hristoph] Saur, 1743).

[75] Johannes Hildebrand, *Wohlgegründetes Bedencken der Christlichen Gemeine in und bey Ephrata Von dem Weg Der Heiligung* (Germantown: Christoph Saur, 1743).

[76] [Author unknown], *Ein Schreiben der Herrnhutischen Gemeine aus ihrer Conferentz an Mstr. Johann Hildebrand in Ephrata* ([Germantown]: [Christoph Saur], 1743).

Similarities and differences fed the bitterness between the two groups. They disagreed vehemently over adult baptism and on the significance of celibacy or marriage. Yet both groups shared a commitment to communal living and a strong devotion to Christ's wounds and suffering.[77] It is likely that the strong charisma of their two leaders played a part in preventing cooperation, along with the reality that they were competing for converts in much the same population pool. Although Pennsylvania was the primary scene, the conflicts between Ephrata and the Moravians spanned the Atlantic, as their literature against one another reached audiences in Germany and Switzerland.

The married couple Jean-François Reynier (also spelled Jan-Franz Regnier) and his wife, Maria Barbara Reynier (née Knoll) together illustrate the long-standing interconnections between Ephrata and the Moravians, while Maria Barbara was also a central witness in Ezechiel Sangmeister's allegations intended to discredit Beissal in his later years. Jean-François, originally from Vevey in Switzerland, first visited Ephrata as a single man, and attempted to join the celibate brothers in 1734.[78] He wrote that the extreme ascetic living sent him mad (*rasend wurde*), so he left Ephrata for the early Moravian settlement in Georgia. In 1739, Reynier crossed the Atlantic back to Germany, and married Maria Barbara in 1740 at the Moravian settlement in Marienborn, close to Herrnhaag. The Moravians sent them immediately to Surinam in South America, and afterwards to St Thomas in the Caribbean. The Reyniers subsequently moved to Bethlehem, Pennsylvania. After 1743, however, they left Bethlehem and the Moravians, moving to York County, settling where Ephrata's daughter congregation from Gimbsheim would soon relocate. In 1762, the Reyniers moved to live at Ephrata, though they withdrew in 1765 and settled in Georgia for the rest of their lives.[79]

Although the Reyniers purchased a small house in Ephrata in 1762, they soon separated to live in celibacy. Not long after this, Maria Barbara reported to Ezechiel Sangmeister Conrad Beissel's apparent nocturnal

---

[77] Lamech and Agrippa, *Chronicon*, p. 123.

[78] Johann Frantz Regnier, 'Das Geheimnis der Zinzendorfischen Sekte, oder eine Lebens-Beschreibung Johann Franz Regnier', in Johann Philip Fresenius, *Bewährte Nachrichten von Herrnhutischen Sachen*, vol. 1 (Frankfurt am Main and Leipzig, 1748), pp. 357–61. See also Lamech and Agrippa, *Chronicon*, p. 55.

[79] Aaron Fogleman, *Two Troubled Souls: An Eighteenth-Century Couple's Spiritual Journey in the Atlantic World* (Chapel Hill, NC: University of North Carolina Press, 2013), pp. 74, 85, 96, 108, 147, 176, 184, 215, 220–32.

sexual exploits in the sisters' house. One night Maria Barbara 'saw Conrad in a form like a shadow, coming in at my window'. She further alleged that he 'fell upon me and mixed himself with me more tenderly and with better feeling than ever with my husband'.[80]

Aaron Fogleman has interpreted Maria Barbara Reyneir's report to mean she literally 'saw' Conrad Beissel coming through her window, and 'welcomed him as he crawled into her bed' to have sex with her. Reyneir then used this attention to advance her standing in the community.[81] However, Sangmeister's account of Reyneir's story requires greater caution. The text indicates Beissel was 'like a shadow' (*wie einen Schatten*), and Reyneir made no mention in her report to Sangmeister that she welcomed Beissel into her bed. Sangmeister also quoted her as saying that after the alleged sexual encounter, she did not know 'if such a thing could happen by means of magic'.[82] While Reynier may have implied that she had sexual intercourse with Beissel, her words may just as well imply that she had a 'magical' encounter with a shadowy likeness of him that produced a satisfying sensation, but no physical contact with a bodily person. In the world of common people in the eighteenth century, encounters with magical likenesses of people could be very 'real', even if they were not physically tangible. Although Sangmeister accused Beissel of multiple sexual trysts with the sisters, the vocabulary of magic allows for wider interpretations than just a literal one. Fogleman's valuable study of the Reyniers has nevertheless shown how this couple's trans-Atlantic lives embodied the connections and concerns at work in varieties of popular Protestant religion in the age, with a notable role played by Ephrata.

Ephrata's greatest internal struggle in the mid-eighteenth century centred on Israel Eckerlin and his oldest brother, Samuel. In 1741, Israel became the head of the brothers' order, the Zionitic Brotherhood. Between 1741 and 1745 the two brothers led an economic expansion that began with the purchase of the grist mill on Cocalico Creek in 1741, paid for by Benedict Jüchlie's funds from Switzerland. The Eckerlin brothers also established a saw mill, linseed-oil mill and fulling mill. The milling

---

[80] '[S]o sahe ich den Conrad in Gestalt wie einen Schatten, zu meinem Fenster herein kommen, fiel auf mich drein und verischte sich mit mir, mehr empfindlicher und wohlthuender als mit meinem Mann jemalen' (translation mine). Sangmeister, *Leben und Wandel, Dritter Theil*, pp. 51–2.

[81] Fogleman, *Two Troubled Souls*, pp. 227–9.

[82] '[I]ch nicht wußte ob so was durch die Magia geschehen könte' (translation mine). Sangmeister, *Leben und Wandel, Dritter Theil*, p. 52.

enterprises bustled as an important economic centre on the Pennsylvania frontier. In 1743 Israel sought to bring householder couples into celibate life in a new dormitory, Hebron, persuading some of them to sign over their land to the community, further increasing the community's wealth. While Israel saw Beissel as a kind of father figure, the Prior of the Zionitic Brotherhood also wished to take over leadership of the entire community from Beissel. A sense of Israel's ambition may be gauged by his decision to order a large bell, imported specially from England, with an inscription honouring the 'venerable man Onesimus'—Israel Eckerlin's adopted Ephrata name.[83]

In the summer of 1745 the power struggle ruptured the community. Beissel expelled Israel, Samuel and their youngest brother, Gabriel Eckerlin, from the community, and much of the community turned against them. That autumn the three Eckerlin brothers and another celibate brother, their friend Alexander Mack Jr, left to start a new community named Mahanaim on the New River in southern Virginia. Some disgruntled Ephrata families followed soon afterward. However, the Eckerlin community was abandoned around 1749 due to Indian hostilities. Alexander Mack, Jr returned to the Brethren in Germantown, the group that his father had organized in 1708.

The Eckerlin brothers next moved into southwestern Pennsylvania, negotiating with the Delaware tribe for protection. Upon the advice of the Delawares, they settled along the Cheat River near present-day Kingwood, West Virginia, around 1752. Samuel purchased about 4000 acres, including the rich, level land that is still known today as Dunkard Bottom ('Dunkers' and 'Dunkard' being derogatory names for the Brethren in America because of their mode of baptizing by immersion). Samuel also purchased 140 acres of land, known as Sandy Hook, along the northern portion of the Shenandoah River near the present town of Strasburg, Virginia. A small group of disaffected Ephrata members settled here along with Ezechiel Sangmeister.

From about 1752 until 1757 Samuel, his brothers and a household servant, Johann Schilling, farmed and hunted at their outpost on the Cheat River. Samuel sold furs back in the East, staying at Sandy Hook for periods of time. Israel, however, almost constantly wrote lengthy diatribes against Beissel, sending them with Samuel to Ephrata.

---

[83] The bell only arrived after Israel left Ephrata, and was subsequently sold. It is now displayed in Grace Lutheran Church in Lancaster, PA.

While Israel fuelled the old battle with Beissel, much larger hostilities soon broke out, pitting native peoples and settlers, French and the British colonial powers against one another. The flames of the Seven Years War literally overtook the outpost of German pacifists on the Cheat River. In 1757 a small group of Mohawk raiders and a French soldier captured Israel, Gabriel and Johann Schilling. The attackers burned the Eckerlins' cabin and buildings and took the brothers and Schilling captive. Samuel was spared because he was away selling furs. The Indians kept Schilling, but sold Israel and Gabriel to the French at Fort Duquesne. The two brothers were taken to Montreal and later to Quebec, where they either died or were sent captive to France. Schilling escaped from his captors in 1761 and returned to Pennsylvania to tell his story, which the Ephrata Chronicle recorded.[84]

One further, almost innocuous, religious conflict challenged Beissel just before the outbreak of the Seven Years War. Around 1755 a certain Brother Ludovici (Ludwig) from Altona near Hamburg, Germany led a group of followers to Lancaster County.[85] The *Chronicon* reported that Ludovici held some beliefs similar to Ephrata, such as communal living, adult baptism and celibacy. Yet he was allegedly a disciple of Christian Wolff, a rationalist professor at Halle from 1706 until his suspension in 1723, and then recalled in 1740.

After Ludovici's group settled on Pequea Creek in Lancaster County, he and Beissel engaged in controversy through correspondence.[86] Beissel's letters reveal how aware he was of the different contexts for religious dissent in Europe and America. He wrote to Ludovici that a religious awakening in Germany differed from awakenings in America. Beissel pointed to the power of the established churches to suppress and eliminate any new dissenting movement. Citing imagery from the book of Revelation

---

[84] Lamech and Agrippa, *Chronicon*, pp. 199–201. See also Klaus Wust, *The Saint-Adventurers of the Virginia Frontier: Southern Outposts of Ephrata* (Edinburg, VA: Shenandoah History Publishers, 1977), pp. 13–39.

[85] Lamech and Agrippa, *Chronicon*, p. 204. See James E. Ernst, *Ephrata: A History* (Proceedings of the Pennsylvania German Folklore Society 25; Allentown, PA: Schechter, 1961), pp. 303–5. Ernst created for the first time the claim that Ludovici and his followers were Labadists from Altona. This is impossible because the last few Labadist members effectively disbanded with the sale of their Wieuward estate in 1727. The last Labadist 'speaker' (preacher) died in 1744, marking the end of the movement. See Saxby, *Quest for the New Jerusalem*, pp. 327–30. See also Ernest Green, 'The Labadists of Colonial Maryland (1683–1722)', *Communal Societies*, 8 (1988), 119–20. Green followed Ernst's suggestion that Ludovici was a Labadist.

[86] Lamech and Agrippa, *Chronicon*, p. 205.

that described attacks by a dragon against Christians, Beissel noted that Pennsylvania was 'not ruled with the power of the dragon and the great beast, [but] rather stands with its judgments under the saints', thus making it possible that 'the priestly and virginal race is sought' and can flourish.[87] Although Ludovici probably posed little real danger of luring members away from Ephrata, the correspondence shows how Beissel could still leverage the differences in the governing structures to reinforce Ephrata's identity and its potential appeal to immigrants.

During the middle decades of the eighteenth century, Beissel and the Ephrata community navigated the currents of internal conflict over leadership and economic expansion, external conflict with rival religious groups from Europe and overarching political struggles between world powers and native peoples in the American colonies. Each of these struggles tied Ephrata in various ways to political, religious and social forces spanning the Atlantic. Through all of the upheaval, Beissel steered a course that kept most of the celibate community dedicated to his view of communal religious life, maintaining pacifism in war while waging polemical battles with rivals.

LATER YEARS AND DECLINE

After the Eckerlins were expelled, the Ephrata community achieved some of their greatest accomplishments in material culture from 1745 to 1755. Beissel's reassertion of leadership in the community encouraged its members, at least for a time, to express their faith more confidently through their unique music, art, poetry and religious publications. Until the outbreak of the Seven Years War in 1756, Ephrata grew in numbers, developed more complex communal architecture and became yet more creative in both music and art—the *Fraktur*. Yet despite the Ephrata community surviving the crisis with the Eckerlins, the seeds were still sown for future crises which hastened its decline.

Between 1762 and 1770, further conflict erupted over who would succeed the aging Beissel as leader and a dispute over ownership of the property. Three contenders vied to succeed Beissel: Christian Eckstein, who

---

[87] Lamech and Agrippa, *Chronicon*, p. 205. The compiler of the *Chronicon* cited here from Beissel's lengthy letters to Ludovici in 1755 and 1756. See [Conrad Beissel], 'Letterbook' (Free Library of Philadelphia), pp. 45–50, 92–106, 111–36, 172–4. The letter book at the Free Library has one additional letter, dated '22nd of the 7th month 1755' not found in the book at the Historical Society of Pennsylvania.

received the authoritative backing of one of the original sisters, Mother Maria Eicher[88]; Peter Miller, the former Tulpehocken pastor[89]; and a third candidate, George Adam Martin, a relative newcomer to Ephrata, who was Beissel's own choice. Martin had only begun to associate with Ephrata around 1762, when he was expelled for unknown reasons from the ministry of a Brethren congregation at Conewago, York County.[90] Martin, originally from Landstuhl in the Palatinate, had also been a member of Miller's congregation in Tulpehocken in 1735.[91]

The three-way power struggle at Ephrata intensified in August 1764 when Samuel Eckerlin returned to Ephrata from his Sandy Hook settlement, accompanied by its small group of former Ephrata members, including Ezechiel Sangmeister. Eckerlin was the only signatory to the communal deed who still acknowledged his part in the deed, and returned to press his claim to the property, potentially unseating the community from their land.[92] This final conflict with Beissel resulted in Maria Eicher losing her influence, Christian Eckstein moving away from the community in 1767 (he returned in 1777) and George Adam Martin settling at Antietam, a new daughter congregation in present-day Franklin County. Peter Miller ultimately prevailed as the new leader at Ephrata after Beissel's death in 1768. Samuel Eckerlin's land claim was resolved in 1770 with permission being granted for his supporters to live on Mount Zion and have a share of bread from the communal bakery.[93] The bitter struggle undermined the communal fabric of Ephrata and hastened its decline.

In the years after Beissel's death, the celibate community at Ephrata aged, decreased in number and greatly relaxed their lifestyle. The American Revolution brought the violence of trans-Atlantic power struggles to Ephrata, now a small and weakening community. George Washington requisitioned the Zion dormitory for a field hospital for sick soldiers from December 1777 to May 1778. About 260 soldiers were sent to Ephrata,

[88] Sangmeister, *Leben und Wandel*, in *JHSCV*, vol. 9 (1984), p. 60; and vol. 10, p. 11.

[89] Sangmeister, *Leben und Wandel*, in *JHSCV*, vol. 10 (1985), p. 39.

[90] Donald F. Durnbaugh, *The Brethren in Colonial America* (Elgin: Brethren Press, 1963), p. 185. Durnbaugh cites Morgan Edwards's *Materials toward a History of the American Baptists Both British and German*, published beginning in 1770. Edwards did extensive personal research for his history and gathered probably the most reliable information about George Adam Martin.

[91] Lamech and Agrippa, *Chronicon*, pp. 207–8.

[92] Sangmeister, *Leben und Wandel*, in *JHSCV*, vol. 9 (1984), p. 7.

[93] Sangmeister, *Leben und Wandel*, in *JHSCV*, vol. 10 (1985), pp. 54–5.

and almost 60 died there.[94] A few Ephrata members died from disease while caring for the wounded. Two biological brothers of the Gorgas family defied the community's teaching about peace and fought in the Revolution.

The last three celibate sisters of the Roses of Sharon died by 1813. The congregation of householders reorganized the church as the German Seventh Day Baptist Church in 1814. By this time, few understood Beissel's writings, and no one could sing in the style of the Ephrata choirs. The daughter monastic community at Snow Hill lasted almost the entire nineteenth century, with around 30 celibates for a long period. The last two celibate members there died in 1894 and 1895. Another congregation of German Seventh Day Baptists formed in Salemville in Bedford County and survives today, although it never had celibate orders.

Conrad Beissel's longing to enjoy solitude and salvation in the American wilderness gave rise to a communal settlement that was neither an isolated European sect nor the product of New World religious freedom. The Ephrata community of the eighteenth century arose and flourished amid religious and cultural influences from both Europe and America. Beissel's followers accomplished remarkable feats as creators of the Germanic folk art known as *Fraktur*, creators of unique music and printers of the largest book in the American colonies. As Ephrata flourished and then declined, complex religious, social, political and economic ties that bound people to both Europe and the Americas connected Ephrata to a larger world. Ephrata is best interpreted in the context of networks, contests for power and the wider concern to construct cultural meaning in the Atlantic world.

---

[94] Clarence E. Spohn, 'The Myths Surrounding the Ephrata Cloister and the Revolutionary War Era', *JHSCV*, vol. 27 (2002), 32, 37.

CHAPTER 4

Believers in Two Worlds: Lives of the English Shakers in England and America

Christian Goodwillie

At Manchester, in England,
This blessed fire began,
And like a flame in stubble,
From house to house it ran.

('Mother' from Millennial Praises *(Hancock MA, 1813).)*

In the fall of 1822, a young man visited the flourishing Shaker settlement at Watervliet, New York. The visitor, whose name is not recorded, generated particular excitement in the community, as he declared himself to be from Manchester in England, and born in Toad Lane—the very street where Ann Lee, the founder of American Shakerism, had lived 50 years before. For most Believers (as Shakers called themselves), at Watervliet and their other 18 communities in the United States, Toad Lane was an almost mythic location, linked only in distant memory to the original English Shakers who brought their beliefs across the Atlantic.

C. Goodwillie
Hamilton College, Clinton, New York, USA

© The Editor(s) (if applicable) and The Author(s) 2016
P. Lockley (ed.), *Protestant Communalism in the Trans-Atlantic World, 1650–1850*, DOI 10.1057/978-1-137-48487-1_4

In 1774, a party of nine Shakers had sailed to America. Accompanying Ann Lee were her husband Abraham Stanley, her brother William Lee, her niece Nancy Lee, James Whittaker, Mary Partington, John Hocknell, his son Richard Hocknell and James Shepherd. Led by 'Mother' Ann Lee, they and two smaller Shaker migrations in following years came to America to escape religious persecution, and also to spread their beliefs. Their faith was nevertheless transformed by the immigration experience, and further refined in the crucible of revolutionary New York and New England. The result was a religion in which the volatile spiritual impulse was distilled and captured within a new practical hierarchy—the manifestation of Shakerism as a Protestant communalism that persists to this day.

In 1822, the Shakers were in the midst of a public relations battle with several apostates. Shaker leaders were scrambling to counteract questions about the integrity and morality of their English forebears, and launched a vigorous publishing campaign issuing books based on the oral histories of aged converts who had embraced the faith in the 1780s. In works such as *A Summary View of the Millennial Church* (published in 1823), *The Testimony of Christ's Second Appearing* (first published in 1808 and 1810, but revised in 1823), *Testimonies of the Life, Character, Revelations, and Doctrines ... of Mother Ann Lee* (1816) *and Testimonies concerning the Character and Ministry of Mother Ann Lee* (1827) the American Believers sought to collect the stories and received wisdom of the founders of their faith. Serving variously as compiler, editor, author and consultant for each of these publications, Brother Seth Youngs Wells of Watervliet was thrilled to meet the young stranger from Manchester, and described the encounter in a manuscript letter to the Shaker Ministry at New Lebanon, New York:

He was a very sensible intelligent pretty young man as I have seen ~~of the world~~ for many years. His feelings became much attached to Believers, and as he was going back to England he offered to do us any service in his power—I thought it a good time to search the Records for Mother's & Father William's ages, and also to make some other particular inquiries; but my main object in this, was to see what could be raked up by our enemies hereafter, if they should be disposed to try; for I felt satisfied as to the facts without sending there to enquire. The result of his enquiries, was, that the most diligent search was made in the Records without any success—their names were not there.[1]

---

[1] Western Reserve Historical Society, Cleveland, Ohio, Shaker Collection (hereafter OClWHi) IV:A-78, Seth Youngs Wells to Ministry, New Lebanon, New York, 20 May 1823.

As Brother Wells was realizing, the records of Shakerism's beginnings were scant—and they remain so. Believers wrote virtually nothing about their English founders before 1803.[2] Even while four of the original English émigrés remained alive and in the faith after 1803, they offered only a few brief testimonies to oppose apostates. Mere fragments of the lives of the English Shakers and, most importantly, the sayings and stories of Mother Ann Lee and the First Elders, were gathered by 1808, when the living link to the original generation was growing ever more tenuous.

This essay presents the most comprehensive existing study of the lives of the English Shakers and their faith as lived in England and America. Those who travelled with Mother Ann in support of her gospel mission built with her a religious tradition dedicated to the eradication of personal and social evil, so inaugurating a millennial vision through a commitment to communal equality and the practice of celibacy. While Ann Lee's life has been the subject of numerous studies authored by both Shakers and outsiders, far less has been written about those who made the trans-Atlantic journey beside her. Surveying a wide variety of sources yields heretofore-uncollected information about these Believers in the two worlds of Europe and America. It further illuminates their roles in disseminating Shakerism, as well as their ultimate fate—for some among the Believers, for others in 'the World'.

THE WARDLEY SOCIETY AND SHAKER ORIGINS

The Shaker movement is commonly acknowledged to have begun when James and Jane Wardley, tailors, separated from a group of Quakers in Bolton in Lancashire in 1747. All early English Shakers lived in this Lancashire and Cheshire region. The Wardleys were just two among many reformers, schismatics and mystics caught up in widespread regional religious ferment. A century earlier in 1647, George Fox travelled often here, leaving Quaker Meetings dotting the countryside.[3] By the mid-eighteenth century, the Methodist movement was also gaining momentum here,

---

[2] Hancock Shaker Village Collection, ID no. 6140a, Daniel Goodrich, Sr, 'The Rise and progress of the church', 1803.

[3] For Fox's visit, and much more on early Quaker activities in Lancashire, see Benjamin Nightingale, *Early Stages of the Quaker Movement in Lancashire* (London: Congregational Union of England and Wales, 1921), p. 10.

and Moravians preached throughout Cheshire.[4] Even remnants of the French Prophets—a radical French Protestant sect that arrived in London in 1706—itinerated through the region, bedevilling such luminaries as Charles Wesley.[5] Later Shakers explicitly named most of these sects as ancestors in their spiritual lineage.

Almost nothing is known of the Wardleys or their origins outside of later Shaker accounts. Shaker Daniel Goodrich Senior, an early American convert, wrote that the people who gathered in 1747 'ware or had been of the Denomination called Methodiss [sic]'.[6] The *Summary View* states that the Wardleys were endowed with the same spirit that guided the French Prophets, and that James 'was greatly gifted in public speaking'.[7] They rejected all creeds, worshipped with extreme physical enthusiasm, heard confessions of sin, and testified that the second appearing of Christ was at hand, ideas also later expressed in Shaker practice. American Shaker apostate Thomas Brown, writing significantly later, claimed that Jane Wardley was called 'Mother' by her followers, though this is not substantiated in any Shaker-published sources.[8]

The Wardleys held meetings at Bolton and Manchester. They eventually moved to Manchester, residing with a wealthy bricklayer named John Townley and his wife on Canon Street, a major thoroughfare in the town. Although evidence in genealogical databases indicates that Mrs Townley's name might have been Mary, it is not given in Shaker sources, a fate sadly common to many of the spouses of early Believers.[9] Shakers

[4] For first-hand accounts of the growth of Methodism in Lancashire see S.R. Valentine, *John Bennet and the Origins of Methodism and the Evangelical Revival in England* (Lanham, MD: Scarecrow Press, 1997); Joseph Edmund Hutton, *A Short History of the Moravian Church* (London, 1895), p. 210.

[5] John Whitehead and Thomas Stockton, *The Life of the Rev. John Wesley* (Auburn and Buffalo [NY], [1844]), pp. 119–21. Shaker apostate Thomas Brown in *An Account of the People called Shakers* ... (Troy, 1812) claims that '[John] Partington and [John] Hocknell had both been noted men among the French prophets' (313), but this is not confirmed by any other source. John Lacy, one of the chief French Prophets, was nevertheless resident in Cheshire as late as the 1720s: John Lacy *The Spirit of Prophecy Defended*, ed. J. Ramsay Michaels (Boston: Brill, 2003), p. xxv. I thank David Newell for these references.

[6] Goodrich, 'The Rise and progress of the church'.

[7] Calvin Green and Seth Youngs Wells, *A Summary View of the Millennial Church* (Albany, 1823), p. 4. New Lebanon Shaker Alonzo Giles Hollister's copy of some of the English publications of the French Prophets is in the collection of the Western Reserve Historical Society, Cleveland, Ohio. However, it appears to have been acquired by him in 1892.

[8] Brown, *An Account*, p. 312.

[9] On John Townley's wife's name see n. 45.

stated, however, that she 'had great power and the gift of prophecy'. The Wardley Society during the 1750s is supposed to have numbered around 30 adherents.[10] The Wardleys did not travel to America with Ann Lee and her small band, and except for several suggested conversations in the collected memories, they rapidly disappear from the Shaker record.

THE LEES/LEES'S OF MANCHESTER

Multiple biographers—Shaker and non-Shaker—have told the story of Ann Lee, née Lees, the Shaker leader born on 29 February 1736, and its recapitulation exceeds the scope of this essay.[11] Some details, however, deserve re-examining, especially the role of Lee's extended family in the rise of Shakerism. Shakers most often used the surname 'Lee' when writing about their leader, but early English records give 'Lees' as her family name. Each were common and frequently confused or misspelled in the period, though they would have originally denoted being from 'Lees', a village east of Oldham, or 'Lee', a village south of Lancaster, or even 'Leeds' in Yorkshire. (Generally, when speaking of Ann Lee or her brother William, I will use Lee; otherwise I will use Lees for the rest of the English family.)

The Manchester constable's accounts covering the years when Shakers were active in the town contain interesting references to Lees family members. Online genealogical information has expanded research opportunities considerably. Even so, because the family names and first names were so common, identifying the correct Lees in records must be approached cautiously. The information presented below represents a careful assessment of the records, but in some cases is offered as informed speculation.[12]

[10] Benjamin Seth Youngs, *Testimony of Christ's Second Appearing* (Lebanon, OH, 1808), pp. 19–20.

[11] Calvin Green and Seth Youngs Wells, *Testimonies of the Life, Character, Revelations and Doctrines, of Our Ever Blessed Mother Ann Lee* (Hancock, MA, 1816), p. 2; Frederick Evans, *Shakers. Compendium of the Origin, History, Principles, Rules and Regulations, Government, and Doctrines of the United Society of Believers in Christ's Second Appearing* (New York, 1859); H.C. Blinn, *The Life and Gospel Experience of Mother Ann Lee* (East Canterbury, NH, 1901). The best modern biography of Ann Lee is Richard Francis, *Ann the Word: The Story of Ann Lee, Female Messiah, Mother of the Shakers, the Woman Clothed with the Sun* (New York: Arcade, 2000). Francis does an excellent job situating Ann Lee in her native Manchester and contextualizing her intellectual and spiritual development against events that occurred in Manchester during her youth.

[12] The first effort to assemble genealogical information about the Lees family was undertaken by William E.A. Axon who published a 'Biographical Notice of Ann Lee, a Manchester

Ann Lee's father was John Lee, a blacksmith.[13] The first extended history of the Shakers, the *Testimony of Christ's Second Appearing* (1808), identifies John Lee and his occupation, and names Ann's seven siblings: Joseph, James, Daniel, William, George, Mary and Nancy.[14] No mention is made of Ann's mother, seemingly an odd omission. Baptismal records for Ann Lee and her siblings reveal a mother's name in only one entry—that for her brother George, baptized on 26 March 1749—indicating she was also named Ann.[15]

Apostate Thomas Brown referred to Ann Lee's brother, and key follower, William Lee as being her 'half-brother'. Another apostate, William Haskett, repeated this claim, adding that it was the death of John Lee's first wife that prompted his daughter Ann to move back in with him to perform 'the duties of a housekeeper'.[16] Two burials are listed in the records of Manchester Parish Church (now Cathedral) for 'Ann wife to John Lees' on 8 October 1758 and 'Ann Wife of John Lees' on 5 May 1760.[17] Either of these women might have been the mother of Mother Ann Lee. Yet, among her family, William Lee was closest to Ann, and venerated by later Shakers, whose sources name him as the *natural* brother of Ann Lee, the fourth son of John Lee, and born in the town of Manchester around 1740. William Lee's age would certainly suggest he shared the same parents as Ann Lee (unless he was illegitimate, and there is no evidence for this). Four years younger than Ann, William was trained as a blacksmith by his father.

Prophetess and Foundress of the American Sect of the Shakers' in the Historic Society of Lancaster and Cheshire's *Transactions*, 27th session, 3rd Series, vol. 3 (1874–75), 51–76. Axon's work on the Shakers was included in his *Lancashire Gleanings* (Manchester, 1883), pp. 79–106.

[13] A record for the apprenticeship of 'James son of John Henthorne' to 'John Lees of Manchester Blacksmith' on 3 September 1747 was located on Ancestry.com, UK, Register of Duties Paid for Apprentices' Indentures, 1710–1811 (database online). John Lees is also named as a blacksmith on some baptismal records of his children.

[14] Youngs, *Testimony* (1808), pp. 21–2.

[15] Ancestry.com. Lancashire, England, Baptisms, Marriages and Burials, 1538–1812 (database online). Original data: Lancashire Archives, Preston; Lancashire Anglican Parish Registers. Definitive baptismal records have not been located for James, Daniel, and Mary Lees. However, 'James Son of John Lees of side of Greenacres [?] by Anne his Wife' was baptized at Oldham on 27 August 1749. Oldham, eight miles northeast of Manchester, was home to the Whittaker family.

[16] William Haskett, *Shakerism Unmasked, or the History of the Shakers* (Pittsfield, MA, 1828), p. 15; Brown, *An Account*, pp. 268 and 314.

[17] Ancestry.com. Manchester, England, Baptisms, Marriages and Burials, 1573–1812 (Cathedral) (database online).

An early researcher, William Axon, published a baptismal record dated 9 October 1743 for 'William s[on] of John Lees, blacksmith'.[18] William married a woman named Betty and had at least one son named Joseph. Manchester Parish Church records show that on 15 June 1766 'Joseph son of William & Betty Lees' was baptized.[19] Amazingly, the 1822 visitor to Watervliet wrote back to Seth Youngs Wells informing him that Betty and Joseph were still alive, aged 82 and 60 respectively. They were interviewed, but 'he knew nothing of any consequence, and she but very little'.[20]

Despite their pacifist beliefs, Shaker sources never failed to report that William Lee was an officer of horse, in the King's Royal Guard and served in the noted regiment called the Oxford Blues.[21] Perhaps reiteration of this military past highlighted his dramatic change of heart in embracing Shakerism, and gives poignant context to his passive endurance of violent abuse suffered for his beliefs.[22] Thomas Brown wrote that Lee's wife Betty was unfaithful to him while he was away in the service and 'had a child by another man; after which he entirely forsook her'.[23] If this were true, it might account for why Betty and Joseph Lees had so little information to share with their young Mancunian interviewer in 1822. It was perhaps following this infidelity that William Lee, 'gaily dressed', but in spiritual distress, visited his sister Ann who was already a follower of the Wardleys. She reportedly 'reproved him for his pride, and convinced him of the wickedness of his life. He immediately threw off his ruffles and silks, and put his hands to work and his heart to God.' Following the Wardley's practice he 'confessed [his] sins all over town'.[24]

---

[18] Axon, 'Biographical Notice of Ann Lee', 51. I have been unable to locate this record through ancestry.com. However, another record exists dated 4 April 1742 for the baptism of 'William son of John Lees' at the Manchester Cathedral. Lancashire, England, Baptisms, Marriages and Burials, 1538–1812 (database online). Original data: Lancashire Archives, Preston; Lancashire Anglican Parish Registers.

[19] Ancestry.com. Lancashire, England, Baptisms, Marriages and Burials, 1538–1812 (database online). Original data: Lancashire Archives, Preston; Lancashire Anglican Parish Registers.

[20] Seth Youngs Wells to Ministry, New Lebanon, New York, 20 May 1823. OClWHi IV:A-78. Brown, *Account* (p. 331) claimed that William had two children, something mentioned in no other source until the 1816 *Testimonies*. Brown may have relied on an oral account.

[21] Cursory searches in British military records have not located William Lees, but more work remains to be done to document his military service.

[22] Green and Wells, *Testimonies*, p. 333.

[23] Brown, *Account*, p. 331.

[24] Green and Wells, *Testimonies*, pp. 334–5.

William Lee's conversion 'raised the enmity of his neighbors and acquaintances, who opposed and persecuted him'. 'At one time', the 1816 *Testimonies* recorded, 'there came a mob and followed him into his father's house; and, in a rage, they struck him over his head, with a fire-hook, and fractured his skull'.[25] William worked in a large blacksmith shop with customers regularly coming and going. Following his conversion he would reportedly not look at them, 'but chastised every turn of my eye that was not after God'. Often, he was so weary that he wished to sit upon his anvil to rest, but dared not for he felt his soul was 'upon a needle's point, and therefore kept my hands to work, and my soul in continual labor to God'. He suffered extreme physical ailments by the time he lived in America, including an illness that caused him to 'vomit large mouthfuls of clear fresh blood'.[26]

Shaker sources agree that in September 1758 Ann Lee joined the Wardley Society, whose teachings thus far did not preclude marriage or sexual intercourse.[27] The marriage register of Manchester Parish Church for 5 January 1762 records 'Abraham Standerin, blacksmith, and Ann Lees, married.'[28] Standerin, whose last name has long-vexed Shaker research-ers, was variously recorded as Abraham Standerin, Standley, Stanley and Standevin.[29] He worked for John Lees.[30] Two men, James Shepherd and Thomas Hulme, witnessed the wedding ceremony.[31] The union of Ann and Abraham yielded four children. According to Shaker records these

[25] Green and Wells, *Testimonies*, pp. 335–6.

[26] All quotations from Green and Wells, *Testimonies*, pp. 336–7.

[27] Youngs, *Testimony* (1808), p. 22; Green and Wells, *Testimonies*, p. 4; and Green and Wells, *Summary View*, p. 7. Brown, *Account*, p. 312, gives the date as 1757.

[28] The original of this source has not been digitized and is quoted here from Axon, 'Biographical Notice of Ann Lee', p. 53. Another source simply gives 'Abraham Standerin & Ann Lees'. Ancestry.com. Lancashire, England, Marriages and Banns, 1754–1936 (database online). Original data: Lancashire Archives, Preston; Lancashire Anglican Parish Registers.

[29] The last name is recorded Standerin in the original manuscript, and mis-transcribed as Standevin in some electronic sources. Most Shaker sources give it as Stanley (*Testimonies*, 1816; *Summary View*, 1823) or Standley (*Testimony*, 1808). Brown (*Account*, 1812) and Haskett (*Shakerism Unmasked*, 1828) use Standley.

[30] Youngs, *Testimony* (1808), p. 22.

[31] James Shepherd's name is spelled three ways in the sources: Shepard, Shephard and Shepherd. Documents extant in his hand give it as Shepherd. I have chosen to conform to his own rendering. Green and Wells in the 1823 *Summary View* (p. 11) refer to there being two Shakers called James Shepherd: one who remained in England, and one who came to America. It remains unclear whether the Shepherd who witnessed Mother Ann's wedding also sailed to America with her.

perished in infancy, although one daughter supposedly lived to the age of six.[32] The burial of a daughter 'Elisabeth dau[ghter] of Abraham Standley' on 7 October 1766 is recorded in the Manchester church register.[33] The names and details of the other three children are unknown.

THE WHITTAKERS OF OLDHAM

James Whittaker, who travelled from England to America with Ann Lee, was one of the most respected and valued Shaker leaders. The *Testimonies* record that 'as he was brought up in the gospel, from his childhood, he possessed a remarkable degree of purity'.[34] Whittaker was born in Oldham on 28 February 1751, son of Jonathan Whittaker and a woman named Ann. Shaker sources claim that her last name was Lee—'probably some distant relation of Mother Ann'.[35] Marriage records from Oldham alternatively show that on 11 June 1738 'Jonathan Whittaker of Sholver moor Maried Anne Whitehead of Whetstone hill Spinster.'[36] Sholver Moor farm lies three miles northeast of the centre of Oldham. Jonathan, born about 1713, and Anne, born about 1717, had at least six children in addition to James.[37]

James Whittaker's mother Ann was a follower of James and Jane Wardley but his father Jonathan was initially not. Young James accompanied his mother to Wardley Society meetings. The *Testimonies* contains conflicting accounts of his relationship with Ann Lee, who was 15 years older. One account says that 'in early youth, he was placed under the care of Mother Ann'. However, the same work quotes Whittaker declaring during her imprisonment in 1772 that he 'was young at that time and had but little acquaintance with Mother; but I had a remarkable feeling for her'.[38] Drawn from later Shaker memory, the details of these accounts

---

[32] Youngs, *Testimony* (1808), p. 20; Green and Wells, *Summary View*, p. 6.

[33] Ancestry.com. Manchester, England, Baptisms, Marriages and Burials, 1573–1812 (Cathedral) (database online). Original data: Manchester Cathedral, Manchester, Anglican Parish Registers.

[34] Green and Wells, *Testimonies*, p. 369.

[35] Green and Wells, *Testimonies*, p. 353.

[36] Ancestry.com. Manchester, England, Baptisms, Marriages and Burials, 1541–1812 (database online). Original data: Manchester Libraries, Manchester, Anglican Parish Registers. Images produced by permission of Manchester City Council.

[37] http://trees.ancestry.com/tree/9737979/person/-751706416 (accessed 25 March, 2015).

[38] Green and Wells, *Testimonies*, pp. 52, 353.

seem unreliable. In 1772, Whittaker was 21 years old, and if he had been attending the small Wardley Society meetings with his mother, he would have been better acquainted with Ann Lee than indicated. An undated and religiously inflected account tells of a more lasting commitment. While walking with Mother Ann in England, the story goes, Whittaker

> ... felt the heavens open, and the manifestations and givings of God fell upon him, in so marvellous a manner, that his soul was filled with inexpressible glory; and he felt such an overflowing of love to Mother that he cried out, 'As the Lord liveth, and as my soul liveth, I will never leave thee, nor forsake thee.' and that Mother, then and there promised him the bishoprick.[39]

Whittaker's bond with Ann Lee became so strong that apostate Thomas Brown claimed that Whittaker and William Lee openly competed for the secondary place beside her.[40]

A weaver by trade, James Whittaker seems to have been the only literate early English Shaker leader. No writings survive from either Ann or William Lee, apart (ironically given her later view of marriage) from Mother Ann's X mark in the marriage register. Conversely, Whittaker's surviving letters are lengthy and skilfully written. He was also a gifted public speaker, and served as the primary preacher for the Shakers in America. Many members of the Whittaker family embraced the teachings of the Wardleys and, subsequently, of Ann Lee; however, only James made the journey to America with her. Whittaker's letters back to his family in England chastised them for rejecting the gospel, and expressed his desire that they, and others who stayed behind, would again gather with him in America.

THE HOCKNELLS OF CHESHIRE

John Hocknell is perhaps the most underappreciated of the English Shakers. A 'John Hocknall', son of John and Mary, was baptized on 27 January 1722 at Marbury, Cheshire (see Fig. 4.1).[41] According to a later statement by his children, John's father was poor and hired him out as a servant to a wealthy man, whose daughter he eventually

---

[39] Green and Wells, *Testimonies*, p. 354.

[40] Brown, *Account*, p. 324.

[41] Ancestry.com. England, Select Cheshire Bishop's Transcripts, 1598–1900. Hocknell's personal Bible, held in the Western Reserve Historical Society in Cleveland, Ohio, confirms 1822 as his birth year.

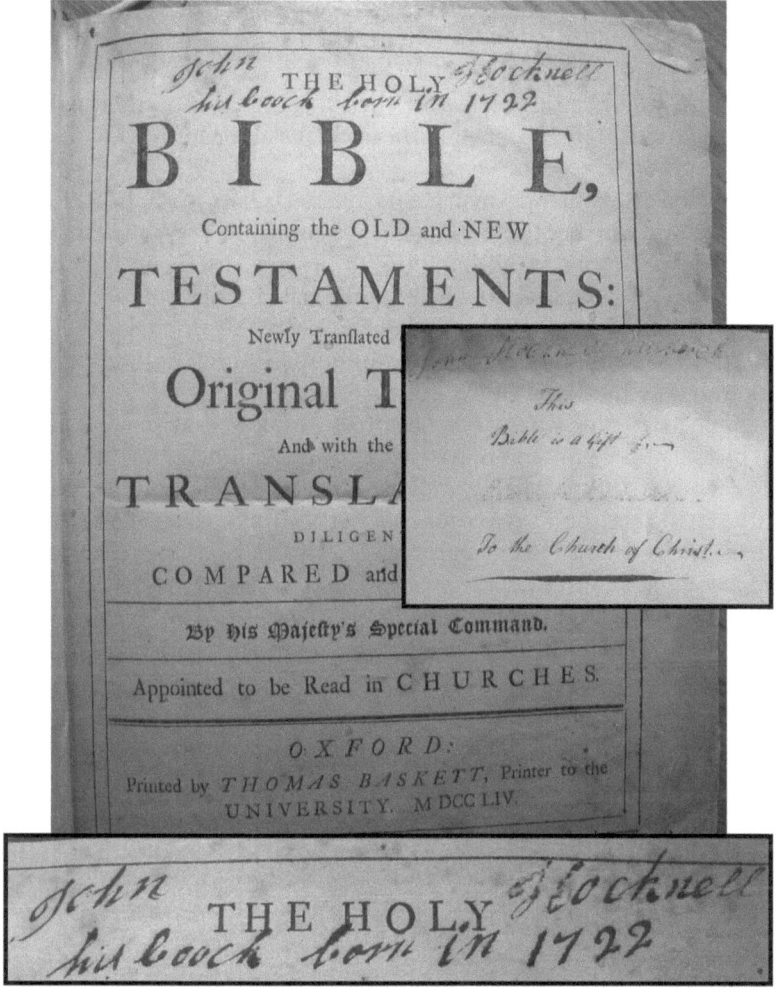

Fig. 4.1   John Hocknell's Bible. This probably crossed the Atlantic with Mother Ann Lee in 1774. He inscribed it with his name, as well as his consecration to the 'Church of Christ', an early name for the Shakers. Courtesy of Western Reserve Historical Society, Cleveland, Ohio

married. His bride's dowry established John on 'a handsome property'.
They had six children, one of whom was a son named Richard. When
Hocknell's wife died, her father legally wrested control of the property
from John, and kept it in trust for the six children upon their majority.
This supposedly left Hocknell without financial means to care for them
in their minority.

Hocknell subsequently married Hannah Dickins on 5 June 1756 at
Lower Peover in Cheshire.[42] Hannah was also from a wealthy family, and
John Hocknell again found himself well situated. John and Hannah had
four further children Mary (b. 1759, often called Molly), Anna (b. 1762),
Francis (b. 1765) and William (dates unknown).[43] John Hocknell was
drawn to the Methodist movement within the Church of England in this
period, before he joined the Wardley Society in 1766.[44] According to his
daughter Mary, this latter decision greatly displeased Hannah, who with
her brothers had him committed to prison at Middlewich. After a trial,
Hocknell was released and eventually his family joined him in his faith.
Mary stated that John's sister was married to John Townley, with whom
the Wardleys lived.[45] If this was the case he may well have known the
Wardleys long before accepting their religious claims.[46]

---

[42] Ancestry.com. England, Select Cheshire Bishop's Transcripts, 1598–1900. Two baptismal records in this same collection exist for women named Hannah Dickins, both from Lower Peover, Cheshire; one is dated 2 February 1719, the other 14 June 1732. Shaker records sourced for the Cathcart Index of Shakers at the Western Reserve Historical Society in Cleveland, Ohio, give Hannah Hocknell's birthdate as 18 October 1723 (a specific source for this information is not given).

[43] Canterbury Shaker Village Archive, no. 244, 'Account of Elder Hocknell's family & the disposal of his property, as stated by Mary, Anna & Francis Hocknell'. I thank David Newell and Renee Fox for sharing this document with me.

[44] Youngs, *Testimony* (1808), p. 20. Haskett, *Shakerism Unmasked* (p. 20) gives 1771 as the date that Hocknell joined the Wardley Society.

[45] Youngs, *Testimony* (1808), p. 20. Records of marriages on Ancestry.com show a number of instances where a John Townley wed a woman named Mary in mid-eighteenth century Lancashire and Cheshire, but none of the Marys has a surname even close to Hocknell.

[46] Francis, son of John and Hannah Hocknell was baptized at Swettenham, Cheshire, on 15 September 1765 according to Ancestry.com, England, Select Cheshire Bishop's Transcripts, 1598–1900. By her own account Mary Hocknell was born on 19 July 1759, although the Cathcart Index at OClWHi states Mary (Molly) Hocknell was born 12 July 1758; see *A Review of Mary Dyer's Publication, Entitled 'A Portraiture of Shakerism'; Together with Sundry Affidavits, Disproving the Truth of Her Assertions* (Concord, NH, 1824), p. 62. The Cathcart index also states Anne Hocknell was born 8 March 1762 and Francis Hocknell was born 1 September 1765. There is no entry for Richard.

Mary Hocknell stated that she was born in Cheshire, and Anna and Francis were both born, and/or baptized, in Swettenham, Cheshire.[47] Mary said that her father took her to live with Ann Lee and William Lee at their father John Lee's house in Manchester when she was nine years old (roughly 1768). Of all the original families connected with the Wardley Society and Ann Lee, the Hocknells proved the most steadfast in their faith. It was their wealth which enabled the early Shakers to traverse the Atlantic multiple times and secure property in America. All but one of them remained Believers and witnessed the transformation of a small enthusiastic sect in England to a large and respected communal religious society in the United States.

THE PARTINGTONS OF CHESHIRE

The Partington family lived in Mayor-town or Meretown, Cheshire, according to Shaker sources, which is most likely today's Marton. Marton lies 25 miles due south of Manchester. The Partington home was used for Shaker meetings beginning around 1766 for Believers travelling from Manchester to visit the Hocknells, who lived at Swettenham just four miles further west.[48] John Partington had at least one child—a daughter Mary, born 3 August 1755.[49] In time, Mary became one of Ann Lee's closest companions. The identity of John's wife is unknown, and no mention is made of her in Shaker sources. Apostate Amos Taylor's account, published during Mother Ann's lifetime, claimed that John Partington was 'formerly a Baptist preacher in England'.[50] Baptists had been active in Cheshire from the 1650s, but Shaker accounts make no mention of this, or any, prior religious affiliation for Partington.[51]

With the Hocknells and Partingtons joining the Wardleys, Townleys and Lees, the core group of traceable English Shaker membership was

---

[47] Francis, *Ann the Word*, p. 37, states that the Hocknells probably lived in Kermincham, but does not give a source or rationale for this speculation.

[48] Youngs, *Testimony* (1808), p. 20.

[49] Mary Partington's birthdate and place are given in OClWHi III:B-12, 'Names, ages, and places of birth of those gathered into the Church beginning in 1787'. I thank Glendyne Wergland for this reference.

[50] Amos Taylor, *A Narrative of the Strange Principles Conduct and Character of the People Known by the Name of Shakers Whose Errors Have Spread in Several Parts of North-America* (Worcester, MA, [1782]), pp. 14–15.

[51] David Douglas, *History of the Baptist Churches in the North of England, from 1648 to 1845* (London, 1846), p. 21.

complete. The ferment of this group's activities in the late 1760s and early 1770s would result in a change of leadership, as well as violent confrontations with civil and ecclesiastical authorities.

A Mother in Manchester

During the 1760s the Shakers entered a new and publicly disruptive phase. Evidence of this survives in a newspaper article from 1769, which may have first appeared in an English paper, but was also carried—portentously—in an American newspaper, the *Virginia Gazette*:

> Our correspondent at Manchester writes a very strange account of a religious sect who have lately made a great noise in that town. They took their rise from a prophet and prophetess who had their religious ceremonies and tenets delivered to them in a vision, some years ago. They hold theirs to be the only true religion, and all others to be false. They meet constantly three times a day, at the house of someone of their society, and converse in their own way about the scriptures, a future state, other sects of religion, &c. until the moving of the spirit comes upon them, which is first perceived by their beginning leisurely to scratch upon their thighs or other parts of their bodies; from that the motion becomes gradually quicker, and proceeds to trembling, shaking, and screeching in the most dreadful manner; at the same time their features are not distinguishable, by reason of the quick motion of their heads, which strange agitation at last ends in singing and dancing to the pious tunes of Nancy Dawson, Bobbin Joan, Hie thee Jemmy home again, &c. These fits come upon them at certain intervals, and during the impulse of the spirit they disturb the whole neighbourhood for some considerable distance, and continue sometimes whole nights in the most shocking distortions and commotions, until their strength is quite exhausted, from which uncommon mode of religious worship they have obtained the denomination of Shakers.[52]

The house mentioned here may have been that of John Townley—where the Wardleys had been located—or the home of John Lees. Shaker meetings were by then held at both houses. Believers recalled a story told by Mother Ann of all the windows in John Townley's house being broken by a rock-throwing mob.[53]

[52] *Virginia Gazette*, 9 November 1769.
[53] Green and Wells, *Testimonies*, p. 60.

Around the time of this newspaper account, a fundamental shift was occurring in the hierarchy of the Shakers. Until this point, the 'spiritual light' received by James and Jane Wardley had secured their leadership. Ann Lee had been just another member of their society in the 1760s, though during this time she underwent 'deep mortification and suffering, her flesh wasted away and she became like a skeleton'. This physical suffering was taken to be an outward manifestation of inner spiritual change as she strove for 'light and understanding'. The culmination of this ordeal was a revelation received while confined in '*Bedlam*, or the *Mad-house*' in 'about 1770', according to some Shaker sources. This was the Manchester Infirmary, a hospital where she had once worked as a cook, and Mary Hocknell recalled this ordeal occurring before she lived with Mother Ann, which was around 1768. These conflicting details make dating Ann Lee's first imprisonment—and her crucial revelation—problematic. Upon her release Lee shared with her fellow Shakers 'that manifestation of God by which the *man of sin* was revealed'. This was the revelation that sexual intercourse caused mankind's fall. The only way to restore humanity to the Edenic state, she declared, was through confession of sins (which the Wardleys encouraged) and permanently forsake 'the flesh'.[54] Forsaking was not simply cessation of sexual relations, it also entailed rejecting non-Believer family members and the levelling of family relationships. From this moment, Ann Lee became Mother Ann Lee, or 'Ann the Word', for the indwelling logos, or Word of Christ within her. Her greater light made her leader of the Shakers.

At about this time, evidence of the Wardleys' Shaker involvement disappears. Although no source mentions a schism within the society, it is possible that the new claims and demands made by Ann the Word exceeded the dedication of the Wardleys and perhaps others. The Shakers, under new leadership, held enthusiastic meetings. So enthusiastic that on Sunday 12 July 1772 they brought the attention of a mob led by a church-warden. This may have been the meeting recalled by Mary Hocknell when

---

[54] Youngs, *Testimony* (1808), p. 23. Green and Wells in their *Summary View*, p. 9, state that this revelation was received while she was in prison for profaning the Sabbath. However, their chronology seems muddled as this occurred in 1772. Edward Deming Andrews cites a letter written by Seth Youngs Wells to the New Lebanon Ministry on 25 April 1822 for this information regarding Mother Ann's imprisonment from Mary Hocknell; *The People Called Shakers* (New York: Dover, 1963), p. 299. The original of this letter has not been located. A letter of the same date written by Wells to the New Lebanon Ministry in the collection of the Western Reserve Historical Society does not contain this information.

'church-officers and spies had been, previously, placed in the streets, as watchmen, under a pretence [sic] of preventing people from violating the sabbath'. While Shakers worshipped in the attic of John Lees's house, the authorities accosted 11-year-old Mary demanding she reveal the whereabouts of William Lee. She eventually escaped her interrogators and fled to John Townley's house on Canon Street.[55] The constables paid 24 people for apprehending five Shakers, and all were supplied with ale. The following day, two Shakers were 'committed to the House of Correction', John Lees and Ann Stanley—Mother Ann. On 23 July each was sentenced to one month's imprisonment for assault. James Whittaker attended Ann Lee in prison, strengthening his bond with his spiritual mother by administering milk and wine through a pipe stem thrust through the keyhole of her cell door.[56]

Ann Lee had further run-ins with the authorities, this time for provocative behaviour in churches. According to constable accounts, on 30 May 1773, 'Ann Lees a shaker' was 'apprended [sic] for disturbing the Congregation in the old Church' and imprisoned for 2 days.[57] The *Manchester Mercury* of 20 July 1773 records that John Townley, John Jackson, Betty Lees and Ann Lees were fined 20 pounds each (a substantial sum) for 'going into Christ Church, in Manchester, and there wilfully and contemptuously, in the time of Divine service, disturbing the congregation then assembled at morning prayers'. Early Ann Lee biographer William Axon speculates that non-payment of this fine resulted in a further two-day stint in jail for Mother Ann, as the constable accounts for 28 July 1773 record 'attending Ann Lees two whole nights'.[58] The *Mercury* story is the last known reference to John Townley in association with Shakerism. The identities of Betty Lees and John Jackson are murky, though James Whittaker would write to a 'Betty Lees widow of Charles Lee' later from America.

Following this last English imprisonment, Shaker sources state that the 'testimony ceased in England', and Mother Ann received 'her mission and revelation of God in relation to America'. On 19 May 1774, aged 38,

[55] Green and Wells, *Testimonies*, pp. 60–1.

[56] Youngs, *Testimony* (1808), p. 24; Green and Wells, *Summary View*, p. 6; J.P. Earwaker, *The Constables' Accounts of the Manor of Manchester … from the year 1743 to the Year 1776*, 2 vols (Manchester, 1891), 2:227–9; Green and Wells, *Testimonies*, pp. 52–3.

[57] Earwaker, *Constables' Accounts*, 2:256.

[58] Axon, 'Biographical Notice of Ann Lee', p. 57. This issue of the *Manchester Mercury* is not available on the British Newspaper Archive so I have relied on Axon's transcription. Earwaker, *Constables' Accounts*, 2:265.

Lee sailed from Liverpool aboard the *Mariah*. Sailing with her, Abraham Stanley's age is unknown, William Lee was 34, James Whittaker was 23, Mary Partington was 18 and John Hocknell was 52. The ages of Richard Hocknell, Ann Lee's untraced niece Nancy Lee and James Shepherd are all unknown. Shepherd, whom Thomas Brown describes as a shoemaker, and Amos Taylor reported 'to have been a merchant in England', may have known Mother Ann and Abraham Stanley as far back as 1762, if it was he who witnessed their wedding.[59] After a difficult crossing, attended with the miraculous repair of a leaking hull in mid-ocean, the party arrived in New York Harbour on 6 August 1774.[60] They left many of their natural and spiritual relations behind them in England, but the fervency of their mission to spread the Shaker gospel carried them forth into the wilderness of upstate New York.

Little is known of the fate of John Townley as well as the Wardleys. The 1808 *Testimony* records that in the same summer of 1774 the Wardleys 'removed from John Townley's' into a rented house, and from there to an Alms-house where they died at an unknown date.[61] Townley likely separated from the Wardleys, but why he did not chose to sail with the other Shakers is unclear. The fate of Ann Lee's remaining family is also lost to history, as their names are too common in the region to establish an accurate family tree. John Lees, like John Townley, suffered persecution for following the faith of his daughter, yet did not follow her to America. There is no record that either Ann or William Lee ever attempted to contact their family once they reached America.[62]

EMIGRATION AND SETTLEMENT OF NISKEYUNA

Following their landing at New York, John Hocknell travelled up the Hudson River and leased land in the western part of the Manor of Rensselaerswyck. This was the estate, or patroonship, of the Van Rensselaer

---

[59] Brown, *Account*, p. 314; Taylor, *Narrative of the Strange Principles*, pp. 14–15. No corroborating evidence for either occupation has been traced.

[60] Youngs, *Testimony* (1808), pp. 24–5; the full passenger list of the *Mariah* first appears in Green and Wells, *Testimonies*, p. 8.

[61] Youngs, *Testimony* (1808), p. 25.

[62] The only subsequent entries concerning Lees family members (not necessarily from Mother Ann's family) in the *Constable's Accounts* are for 3 August 1773 'three Men attending George Lees for stealing Soldiers Linnen', and 1 November 1775 'John Lees [confined] upon Suspicion of Felony', Earwaker, *Constables' Accounts*, 2:266, 332.

family established in 1630. In 1774 it was under the administration of Abraham Ten Broeck on behalf of his nephew Stephen Van Rensselaer III, then only ten years old. Hocknell's original deed has not been located, but subsequent land-deeds show he held around 200 acres.[63] During this time Mother Ann resided in New York City, presumably with her husband, serving a family named Smith.[64] William Lee likely journeyed up river with Hocknell and found employment as a blacksmith in Albany with one Jesse Fairchild. James Whittaker found work as a weaver. John Hocknell returned to New York City and embarked for England in the fall of 1774 to retrieve his wife and other children.[65]

In New York, Ann Lee nursed her husband through a severe illness. Following his recovery he demanded that she 'live in the flesh with him', which she refused. The earliest sources do not give much detail on what exactly happened next, but the 1823 *Summary View* paints a colourful picture. Stanley apparently 'brought a lewd woman into the house ... and declared that, unless [Ann] would consent to live in sexual cohabitation with him, he would take that woman for his wife'.[66] It is reported that he did marry the woman, and it is at this point that Abraham disappears from the historical record. The Shakers claim he was a Believer when he sailed from England, but lost his faith in America.[67] The commencement of the revolutionary war complicates the record, as the British Army captured New York City in September 1776, and held it until evacuating in 1783. Stanley, like many British people, may have evacuated the city with the Loyalists, but, for the present, nothing is known of his fate.

During 1775, Ann Lee visited the Believers at Albany, and also received their visits in New York. John Hocknell landed at Philadelphia on Christmas Day 1775 with his family, including his daughter Anna and son Francis, but not his youngest son, William, who died during the voyage. John Partington, the father of Mary already in America, was also with Hocknell, reportedly with further members of his family—though their

[63] Dorothy Filley, *Recapturing Wisdom's Valley: The Watervliet Shaker Heritage, 1775–1975* (Albany: Albany Institute of History and Art, 1975), pp. 20–1.

[64] Youngs, *Testimony* (1808), p. 25.

[65] Green and Wells, *Testimonies*, p. 9; Mary Hocknell, [affidavit], *A Review of Mary Dyer's Publication ...*, pp. 62–4.

[66] Green and Wells, *Summary View*, p. 16.

[67] Green and Wells, *Testimonies*, pp. 8–9.

names and number are unknown.[68] From Philadelphia, the party journeyed north to be reunited with Ann Lee in New York, where she remained the Smith family's housekeeper, and perhaps already followed one of her most famous sayings: 'Clean your room well; for good spirits will not live where there is dirt. There is no dirt in heaven.'[69] In February 1776, while the Hudson River remained frozen, the Hocknells and Partingtons travelled over land to Albany, then returned to New York later in the year to collect both their belongings and Mother Ann. Together they made a final voyage north to take up permanent residence on their Rensselaerswyck tract, a wilderness called Niskeyuna. Here in September 1776, for the first time since May 1774, the Believers reunited as one body.[70]

John Partington leased a large 422-acre tract abutting John Hocknell's land, and the Believers set about constructing shelter.[71] A small log house was erected to house Ann Lee, William Lee, James Whittaker and James Shepherd.[72] Apparently the log house did not last long. As one later Shaker recounted, 'in the spring of 1776, while they were burning rubbish to clear the land, the sparks caught a sheep cot which was covered with straw and before it could be stoped [sic] the house took fire and burned down'.[73] The Hocknells maintained their own house, as did the Partingtons, where presumably the other Believers sheltered in the interim. In 1778, the group built 'the first dwelling house'. A surviving description records that 'they lived in this when people began to gather, the rooms were small, but 15 lay upon the floor in one room, some had one blanket to cover them, and nothing for a pillow but a chair turned down'.[74]

A 1779 tax list of Rensselarwyck gives John Partington as lessor for lands valued at £350. Scholars have conjectured that the entry adjacent to Partington's name may represent all Shaker land holdings, though this speculation stems from confusion over when precisely Shakers

[68] Canterbury Shaker Village Archives no. 244 'Account of Elder Hocknell's family'; Green and Wells, *Summary View*, p. 16.

[69] Green and Wells, *Testimonies*, pp. 8–9, 265.

[70] Green and Wells, *Summary View*, p. 16. The name Niskeyuna is spelled in a variety of ways in Shaker and non-Shaker sources, including Niskayuna, Niskauna, Nistageune and Nisqueunia.

[71] Filley, *Recapturing Wisdom's Valley*, pp. 20–1.

[72] Brown (apparently quoting Mary Hocknell), *Account*, pp. 46, 316.

[73] Library of Congress, Washington, D.C. (LCW), MS Shaker Collection, item 55, Rhoda Blake 'A Sketch of the Life and Experience of Rhoda Blake, also a Narrative of things which have taken place since 1808'.

[74] Blake 'Sketch'; OClWHi, I:A-20, 'Buildings at Watervliet', [*c*.1825], Watervliet, NY.

instituted communal property.[75] An affidavit from Shaker Timothy Hubbard, described as 'one of the first who visited Mother and the Elders at Watervliet' (the alternative name used for Niskeyuna after 1797), states, 'the Family that Resided [at Watervliet] before our acquaintance with them, as we were Informed, held their property they had here, as a Joint Interest'.[76] Certainly, early living arrangements indicate some pooling of resources. It would seem logical to assume that communal principles gradually took hold as a practicality, if not yet a fully fledged tenet of faith, during the establishment of the Niskeyuna/Watervliet settlement.

During 1779, despair reportedly overtook the small Shaker family; they felt 'alone in the world, [concluding] they must keep the way of God for themselves, & end their days without any further opening of the gospel'.[77] They had nonetheless made at least one convert in America already: a neighbouring farm woman named Eleanor Vedder.[78] At this time, the Shakers were unaware of a significant religious revival among Presbyterians and Baptists in the New York–Massachusetts border region, barely 35 miles east of Watervliet. In April 1780, they encountered it, as Tallmadge Bishop and Reuben Wight, two revivalists from New Lebanon, New York, stumbled on the Shaker settlement while travelling westward. Bishop and Wight were astonished to find people espousing a gospel message of salvation and spiritual rebirth already. They returned home and informed their neighbours of this 'new and strange religion'. When Bishop asked Mother Ann what he should say about the Shakers she replied, 'Tell them, that we are the people who turn the world upside down.'[79]

A meteorological phenomenon, the 'dark day' of 19 May 1780, increased the anxiety of the general populace. Following a thunderstorm, the sky was black as midnight at noon. Yale President Ezra Stiles wrote in his diary, 'About Ten o'clock A.M. a Darkness came on, which by Eleven

[75] Filley, *Recapturing Wisdom's Valley*, pp. 20–1.

[76] Green and Wells, *Testimonies*, p. 208; OClWHi, I:A-20, 'A Representation of Wiliam Scales Living in the West District of Ranseler Wyck', 1789.

[77] Green and Wells, *Testimonies*, p. 13.

[78] Calvin Green, 'Biographical Account of the Life, Character, & Ministry of Father Joseph Meacham', ed. Theodore E. Johnson, *Shaker Quarterly*, 10:1 (1970), pp. 26–7.

[79] Valentine Rathbun, *A Brief Account of a Religious Scheme: Taught and Propagated by a Number of Europeans ... Commonly Called, Shaking Quakers* (Harvard, MA, 1782), p. 4; Anna White and Leila S. Taylor, *Shakerism: Its Meaning and Message* (Columbus, OH, 1905), p. 99; Green and Wells, *Testimonies*, p. 318.

was perceived to be very unusual and extraordinary.' He continued: 'The Darkness became and continued so intense from a little before noon to near Two o'clock, as that persons could not read, and it became necessary to light up candles ... The inhabitants were thereupon thrown into perhaps unnecessary Consternation, as if the appearance was preternatural.'[80] For Ann Lee it was a sign, and she used the opportunity to reopen the testimony in America.[81] Her message resonated with the revivalists from the New York–Massachusetts border, and the settlement at Niskeyuna was soon crowded with prospective converts travelling to meet Mother Ann Lee and the Shakers.

Over the next 4 years, Mother Ann and the Elders (as the English male Shakers were called) are alleged to have experienced tribulation and suffering dwarfing anything they had experienced in England. Their strangeness as a people only added to the suspicion they received as recent English immigrants. As the war of independence raged, Americans viewed them as disloyal at best, treasonous at worst. When they began traversing the backwoods of an economically depressed New England, a region riven by political and religious turmoil, the Shakers frequently faced physical assaults and considerable hardships. Through this experience not only Ann Lee, but also William Lee, James Whittaker, John Hocknell and John Partington each became leaders, preaching their gospel in the face of often violent opposition and establishing its lasting presence in America. As Mother Ann's life has been so thoroughly documented, the remainder of this essay will focus predominantly on the American experience of the other English Shakers.

SHAKERS AND THE WAR OF INDEPENDENCE

During the spring of 1780 multitudes of people, including Presbyterian and Baptist ministers, travelled to Niskeyuna to visit Mother Ann and the Elders. The frequent visits to this small English group sequestered in the wilderness near Albany aroused suspicion from the revolutionary state government in the region. British General Burgoyne had been defeated three years earlier, but upstate New York, particularly the Schoharie and Mohawk Valleys, were still scenes of brutal partisan warfare. On 7 July

---

[80] For a general account of the day, see Cora E. Lutz, 'Ezra Stiles and the Dark Day', *Yale University Library Gazette*, 54:4 (1980), pp. 163–7.

[81] White and Taylor, *Shakerism*, p. 100.

1780, the 'Commission for Detecting and Defeating Conspiracies' investigated the Shaker David Darrow, caught driving sheep from New Lebanon
to Niskeyuna, and suspected of intending to 'convey them to the enemy'.
Darrow informed commissioners that due to his religious principles he
was 'restrained from taking up Arms in defence of the Country'. John
Hocknell (here rendered Hocknear) and David Meacham, a new convert
from New Lebanon, appeared to corroborate Darrow's testimony, and
declared that it was also 'their determined Resolution never to take up
arms and to dissuade others from doing the same'—the first record of
pacifist principles as a fundamental tenet of the Shaker faith. In response,
the Commission committed Darrow, Hocknell and Meacham to prison at
Albany.[82]

The conspiracies commission summoned 'James Partherton' from
Niskeyuna on 11 July 1780 who affirmed that he also was restrained
from taking up arms due to his religious principles. This must be John
Partington, unless he had an otherwise unknown son named James.
Partington gave surety for his good behaviour and declared himself a
'faithful subject' of the state, after which he was allowed to return to the
Shaker settlement.[83] Over the course of July more 'shaking Quakers' were
examined and an official policy crafted to deal with them. Events climaxed
on 24 July when a warrant was made to arrest 'John Partherton, William
Lees, Ann Standerren' who 'by their conduct and conversation disturb the
publick peace and are daily dissuading the friends of the American cause
from taking up arms in defense of their Liberties'. Two days later they
were brought to Albany, along with James Whittaker, Mary Partington
and American convert Calvin Harlow. All six affirmed that they refused
to take up arms and had preached the same to others, and all six joined
Hocknell, Darrow and Meacham in prison.[84] They were first confined in
the old City Hall, and later moved to a prison in an old fort specifically for
Tories (English loyalists).[85]

In late August, the Commission deemed the Shaker threat severe
enough that they sent Ann Lee south to Poughkeepsie, and directed she
be sent behind enemy lines towards New York City. Mary Partington,

---

[82] Victor Hugo Paltsits (ed.), *Minutes of the Commissioners for Detecting and Defeating
Conspiracies in the State of New York. Albany County Sessions, 1778–1781* (Albany: State of
New York, 1909–10), 2:453.

[83] Paltsits (ed.), *Minutes*, 2:456.

[84] Paltsits (ed.), *Minutes*, 2:469–70.

[85] Green and Wells, *Testimonies*, p. 72.

though not the object of the commissioners' ire, accompanied Mother Ann, having 'begged [her] persecutors to let me go with her—for I loved her so well that I could not bear to be separated from her, and I was willing to suffer with her—and so they let me go with her'.[86] When Ann Lee and Partington were incarcerated at Poughkeepsie, Mary Hocknell also travelled south to care for them.[87]

On 24 October 1780, the Commission examined an enslaved 'Negro Man' who had been captured on his way to the enemy. He claimed he was persuaded to go by a man named 'Shepherd who is one of the people called Shaking Quakers'.[88] This was almost certainly James Shepherd, and the first known instance of Shaker interaction with a black man. In light of their subsequent practice of racial equality one wonders if the Shakers opposed slavery on moral grounds at this early date. The Commission discharged the man.

Events took an unexpected turn in November 1780 when, without explanation, the Commission freed the Shakers imprisoned at Albany. William Lee was freed on 15 November 1780. His employer Jesse Fairchild put up £100 bail, and both are identified as blacksmiths in the record. James Whittaker, 'Labourer', was freed the same day, his £100 bail put up by William Lee. Both men were required to appear before the Commission whenever called, and to be of good behaviour during the continuance of the war. The next day, John Hocknell, 'farmer', was freed under the same requirement, his £100 bail put up by Peter Scharp, carpenter, of Albany.[89] Other Shakers who had been imprisoned throughout the year were freed over the following days, with the last released on 20 November. Altogether these Shakers spent nearly 5 months in jail. They returned to their respective farms, but Ann Lee remained captive in Poughkeepsie.

William Lee set out for Poughkeepsie armed with a letter from Lt General James Clinton to his brother Governor George Clinton dated 19 November. The letter introduced 'William Lees, of the Denomination of shaking Quakers', recording he had 'made application to me respecting his sister, Ann Standivin', and giving the General's opinion that 'if nothing material has been proven against her, I shou'd suppose she may

---

[86] *A Review of Mary Dyer's Publication*, pp. 65–8.
[87] Paltsits, *Minutes*, 2:507, 517–18; Green and Wells, *Testimonies*, p. 77.
[88] Paltsits (ed.), *Minutes*, 2:555.
[89] Paltsits (ed.), *Minutes*, 2:569–71.

[be] released agreeable to their requisition'. Further correspondence was exchanged between Poughkeepsie and Albany, with William Lee further petitioning the Albany Commission on 4 December to secure the release of Ann Lee (and presumably Mary Partington). Kept prisoners at the Baltus Van Kleek house in Poughkeepsie, they had not yet been sent behind enemy lines.[90] By late December, Lee and Whittaker were successful in securing Mother Ann's release, after putting up £100 as bond for her good behaviour. The Commission judged that the Shakers had been 'reformed and that no further Evil is to be apprehended from her influence'.[91]

FROM MISSIONS TO COMMUNITIES

Shakerism spread from New York far into New England through missionary tours led by English Shakers between 1781 and 1783. Ann Lee, William Lee, James Whittaker and Mary Partington were the leading missionaries, joined by two recent American converts, Samuel Fitch and Margaret Leland.[92] Large pockets of several hundred converts were gathered in Massachusetts and Connecticut in this period, as Shakers travelled back and forth between Niskeyuna, the New York–Massachusetts border region, and locations like Cheshire (then called New-Providence), Harvard, and Ashfield, Massachusetts. During this time, Mary Partington and Mary Hocknell remained close travelling companions within what scholar Marjorie-Procter Smith has called the 'court of Mother Ann'— though they were increasingly joined in this circle by American converts such as Leland, Hannah Kendall and Lucy Wright.[93]

The main source for Shaker activities during their missionary tour has commonly been the *Testimonies*, compiled from the memories 30 years after the event of Shakers active during the early 1780s. It is a valuable source, with many of its facts verifiable in outside sources, despite its bias towards depicting early Shaker leaders as heroic martyrs. *Testimonies*

---

[90] Filley, *Recapturing Wisdom's Valley*, pp. 22–3.

[91] James Clinton, *Public Papers of George Clinton, First Governor of New York, 1777–1795, 1801–1804* (New York and Albany: State of New York, 1899–1914), 6:420–1. For an image of this letter see Filley, *Recapturing Wisdom's Valley*, pp. 22–3. Paltsits (ed.), *Minutes*, 2:589, 592.

[92] Green and Wells, *Testimonies*, 83.

[93] Marjorie Procter-Smith, *Women in Shaker Community and Worship: A Feminist Analysis of the Uses of Religious Symbolism* (Lewiston, Maine: Edwin Mellen Press, 1985), p. 17.

emphasizes how, during their travels, the leading English Shakers bore the brunt of physical abuse from angry New Englanders who rejected the Shaker message of celibacy, pacifism and also their nationality. At Harvard, Massachusetts, in August 1782, James Shepherd was whipped by a mob armed with tree branches specifically because he was English.[94] At the same town a year later, a further mob tied James Whittaker to a tree and whipped him 'till his back was all in a gore of blood, and the flesh bruised to a jelly'. William Lee's turn was next and to the astonishment of the crowd he knelt and received the beating willingly.[95]

'Father William's sufferings' were especially glorified in Shaker sources, though they were perhaps as much linked to the illness that dogged him since he lived in England, as the violence and mockery of crowds. William's 'strength and gift' was reportedly 'almost continually spent in sufferings ... he discharged an abundance of blood, and died, seemingly, like a bleeding martyr'.[96] Apostate Daniel Rathbun recalled how William Lee had come from court at Great Barrington, Massachusetts, and 'fumbled in his speech and tumbled about, and spewed on the floor and was hurried away to bed under a pretence of great sufferings'.[97] Lee declined quickly following his return to Niskeyuna and died on 21 July 1784.[98]

A less familiar source from this period is the manuscript collection of letters written by New Lebanon Shaker apostate Angell Matthewson to his brother Jeffrey. Matthewson was present during the missionary period and offers virtually the only near-contemporary account of what Shakers actually did and said not written by a disgruntled apostate with an axe to grind. These letters offer new insight on John Partington in particular, about whom so little else is known, indicating his role supporting converts made during the Shaker mission in 1781–83. Partington's reported skill in preaching and directing a congregation lends some credence to apostate Amos Taylor's statement that he had been a Baptist preacher in England.

At Ashfield during the summer of 1784, Matthewson described Partington directing the dancing worship in the first purpose-built Shaker meetinghouse: 'a sanctuary of logs it was about 30 by 36 feet square all

[94] Green and Wells, *Testimonies*, p. 119.

[95] Green and Wells, *Testimonies*, p. 151.

[96] Green and Wells, *Testimonies*, pp. 341–2.

[97] Daniel Rathbun, *A Letter from Daniel Rathbun, of Richmond, in the County of Berkshire, to James Whittacor, chief elder of the church, called Shakers,*(Springfield, MA, 1785), p. 44.

[98] Green and Wells, *Testimonies*, pp. 341–2.

in one room with a chimney at one End built dutch fashin with a back & top'.[99] Under Partington's direction, the meeting house was 'acupied for worship continualey day & night the most of the time in the dance as that was the chief object of worship'. Following the dance and an exhortation, Partington introduced a key tenet of Shakerism: the concept of union. Union to one's lead is the affirmative endorsement that the work is one of God, and that the hierarchy of Ministry, Elders and so on was functioning as the restored Church of Christ on earth. Partington used the Believers at Ashfield to form a physical representation of this concept, by using

> ... his hand to take one man by the hand & leed him in to the middle of the room, then sined [i.e., signed] up annother & laid his rite hand on the others left sholder, then annother & laid his rite hand on the others left sholder, so on soon till the whole ware formed in a ring as here shone ... the Elder then said ... you must obsarv & do one thing you must alway keep up a chain of union from the greatist down to the lest you must alway be so nigh to each other in your simpathising feelings as to tuch & assist Each other in times of distress—this venerable old man on whos hoarey head the blossom of old age had far advanced proformed this Exhibition with great solemnity...[100]

The development of ideas of a 'chain of union' had clear relevance to a growing communal ethic, and a conscious discouragement of personal interests and valuing the individual self above the group. At Watervliet, Partington took umbrage at American convert Ebenezer Cooley's pride in his own preaching, by introducing the Shaker metaphor of 'great I'. Beginning with the peculiar Shaker custom of following his finger:

> ... his hand stretched forth he rose from his seat & folowed it. In this way he went round the room sevril times. His hand at last led him to the bible. He took it walked to Cooley, opned it to the first chapter of geneses. His hand drawed him to p[o]int at the first letter of the first virce. [He] asked cooley what letter is that[?] It is I sais Cooley. Parkinton sais, you say it is I. Yis Cooley sais it is great I. Yis partinton sais it is great I indeed. Great I has bin out & preeched & don great things & has convarted a great many & made them all crye & the lord has as it ware got in debt to great I. At the

---

[99] New York Public Library, Shaker Manuscript Collection, no. 119, Matthewson, 'Reminiscences in the form of a series of 39 letters to his brother Jeffrey', pp. 15–16.

[100] Matthewson, 'Reminiscences', pp. 58–9.

same time great I has not returned thanks to god who has made him an able minister of the gospil, but great I has don it all.[101]

Partington was here putting Cooley's individual achievements in their place—as no justification for thinking himself above others in the Shaker community. Apostate Daniel Rathbun's memories of Partington further reveal him to have been something of an enforcer for the nascent communal order. According to Rathbun, 'Elder John Partington' did not hesitate to 'chastise me openly and publickly for my coveteousness, in not giving up all I had to the church, and submitting, myself to their disposition'.[102]

The sole extant description of Niskeyuna in this period demonstrates that the first Shaker settlement was already administered as a cooperative enterprise, and presaging arrangements subsequently to be adopted in all Shaker communities—'Gospel Order':

> the Family that Resided hear ... held their property they had here, as a Joint Interest ... they gave that they had gained by their industry with the use and improvement of the Farm for the good and benifit of the Whole Society to be improved in the following manner, Viz. That there should be a free Table kept here and other necessaries for the Entertainment of those that came here to see them, that the poor might have an Equal priviledge of the Gospel with the Rich, and all those that came here, which were able had Liberty to contribute according to their own faith towards supporting table expences, and the poor that came here, and other necessary expences; None were compelled or ever desired to contribute but such as could do it freely believing it to be their duty, and were often cautioned and taught to deal justly with all men ... And none had any right of Possession to Houses or Land, on Account of his living, or Working here, any more than any of the rest of the Society, no Longer than he resided here.[103]

John Hocknell appears to have been the Elder who remained at Niskeyuna in the early 1780s, rarely visiting Shaker groups elsewhere, and largely ministering to this original settlement, managing the buildings, farm and communal arrangements.[104] Apostate Amos Taylor observed

---

[101] Matthewson, 'Reminiscences', pp. 57–8. Punctuation and capital letters added for clarity.

[102] Daniel Rathbun, *Letter*, pp. 118–19.

[103] 'A Representation of Wiliam Scales Living in the West District of Ranseler Wyck', OClWHi I:A-20.

[104] Youngs, *Testimony* (1808), p. 475.

Fig. 4.2   The early meetinghouse at Niskeyuna/Watervliet. Courtesy of Communal Societies Collection, Burke Library, Hamilton College, Clinton, New York

that at Niskeyuna 'Elder *Ocknell*, as he is called by that people, is chief.' Another Shaker recalled that Elder Hocknell took 'pleasure in subduing the bogs and digging out old stumps.'[105] Hocknell oversaw the construction of various buildings, including a 'Second House' in 1783, an addition to the 1778 Dwelling House in 1784, and a log Meeting House that same year (see Fig. 4.2).[106]

TRANSITIONS IN LEADERSHIP

It was to this nascent communal settlement at Niskeyuna that Mother Ann returned in 1784, every bit as battered as her brother. Following his death, she knew her days were numbered; she had herself fared badly at the hands of mobs at Ashfield and Petersham, Massachusetts, some of whom examined her physically to ascertain if she was biologically female.[107] Mother Ann was attended by Mary Hocknell on her death bed, and died on 8 September 1784.

---

[105] Taylor, *Narrative of the Strange Principles*, pp. 14–15. D.A. Buckingham, 'Epitome History of the Watervliet Shakers. No. 2', *Shaker*, 7:6 (June 1877), 41.

[106] OClWHi, I:A-20 'Buildings at Watervliet' [*c*.1825].

[107] Green and Wells, *Testimonies*, pp. 94, 142.

Lee's successor in Shaker leadership appears to have emerged quickly: James Whittaker, aged only 33. Whittaker was acknowledged publically at Mother Ann's funeral by Joseph Meacham, Calvin Harlow and John Hocknell, coming forward and praying that the 'gift of God rested upon him for their protection'.[108] Whittaker was reported to be 'chief speaker in the Assemblies' by one apostate, and was described by another as 'mild in his temper and soft in his manners', known for his preaching 'to the feelings and sentiments of his hearers'.[109] To Angell Matthewson, Whittaker was remembered as 'the greatist oritor':

> His address was smooth & flatring. He was cleenly in his parsonal habits. He had sharp black eyes & was much in the habit of looking people in the face. His mildness & polite address was such that he drawed the public attentuion what Ever the subject mite be.[110]

Not all Believers were thrilled with Whittaker's ascension to the lead. Around this time Richard Hocknell, John Hocknell's son from his first marriage, left the Shakers. To add insult to injury he left with Mother Ann's niece Nancy Lee. They were wed shortly thereafter.[111] Sometime before, John Hocknell had encouraged Richard to return to England to claim his share of the inheritance due upon his majority, but Richard refused. On Mother Ann's advice, John had transferred to Richard the 211-acre farm he had originally leased for the Shakers, and the 1790 United States census indicates that Richard Hocknell remained living on this Watervliet site, apparently having started a family with Nancy.[112] The Watervliet Shakers eventually repurchased Hocknell's farm at a court sale, though the fates of Richard and Nancy Hocknell beyond this are unknown.[113]

In August 1786, John Hocknell and John Partington took passage from New York back to England. The motivation for their journey remains unclear, though Thomas Brown alleged that Whittaker was

---

[108] Green and Wells, *Testimonies*, pp. 352, 356.

[109] Taylor, *Narrative of the Strange Principles*, pp. 14–15; Brown, *Account*, p. 323.

[110] Matthewson, 'Reminiscences', p. 25.

[111] Brown, *Account*, p. 326.

[112] Ancestry.com. 1790 United States Federal Census (database online). Watervliet, Albany, New York; Series: M637; Roll: 6; Page: 141; Image: 85; Family History Library Film: 0568146. Original Source: First Census of the United States, 1790. Records of the Bureau of the Census, Record Group 29. National Archives, Washington, D.C.

[113] Canterbury Shaker Village Archives, no. 244. 'Account of Elder Hocknell's family'.

strongly opposed to their plans, and raced to New York to stop them.[114] New Lebanon Shaker Rufus Bishop remembered the event differently, writing that Whittaker, who was at Tyringham when he heard of the trip, wanted to join them:

> Some who were left in England, when Mother and the Elders came from thence and retained a measure of faith, had strongly invited Father James [Whittaker] to visit them; and even offered to pay his passage. And as he felt that his work here was drawing to a close; he pretty much concluded to visit his native land, and see if he could be instrumental in saving some whom he had left behind. Elder John Hocknell and John Partington were going also; (as I think they had business there.) But when Father James reached New York, he found that the Ship, with the two brethren, had sailed; so he relinquished his design to the great joy of his children here in America.[115]

Historians of Shakerism continue to debate these conflicting accounts. Whittaker certainly wrote to Believers still in England, addressing some by name, and inviting them also to journey to America: 'And you, John Jackson & Betty Lee Widow to Charles Lee as I have a great love & respect for you so I greatly desire to see you in this land. God has begun his great & strange work in this land, & is carrying it on by swift degrees.'[116] And yet, even though both Hocknell and Partington did return shortly to America, Partington left the Shakers soon after.[117] No source gives a reason for this departure. Partington appears on the 1790 United States census as resident in Watervliet with one white male under 16 years of age and two white females.[118] From this, it appears possible that Partington brought more family members back with him in 1786. By early 1787, therefore, only four of the nine original Believers who came to America in 1774 remained Shakers: James Whittaker, John Hocknell, James Shepherd and Mary Partington, who did not follow her father in leaving the faith.

James Whittaker was the head of the Shakers for barely 3 years: he died on 20 July 1787, still in his mid-thirties, though he appears to have

---

[114] Brown, *Account*, pp. 326–7.

[115] OClWHi, VII:B-59, 'Note by Rufus Bishop regarding Father James Whittaker'.

[116] OClWHi, IV:A-77, James Whittaker to Jonathan and Ann Whittaker, Parts near Albany, 20 February 1784.

[117] Brown, *Account*, pp. 326–7.

[118] Ancestry.com. 1790 United States Federal Census (database online). Watervliet, Albany, New York; Series: M637; Roll: 6; Page: 139; Image: 83; Family History Library Film: 0568146.

known he was dying for some months, as he carried out a series of emotional final visits to Shaker congregations, and made out a will on 9 June 1787. In the will, Whittaker described himself as a weaver, and left all his worldly possessions to 'Help Support and furtherence of the Gospel and the Support of the Poor the Widows and the fatherless of the Church of my Communion' (see Fig. 4.3).[119] Although relatively brief, Whittaker's leadership, from 1784 to 1787, may be seen to have been instrumental in turning the Shaker 'Church', as he called it, towards a particular form of communal future requiring absolute commitment to the communal body. Whittaker taught that Believers must wean themselves from the bonds of natural and traditional familial relations, be it husband from wife, or father from son, or brother from sister. By doing so, he reportedly sought to 'prepare them for a spiritual relation in Church order, which he foretold was at hand, and often spoke of it'.[120]

Whittaker's letters to his parents reflect, often in the harshest of terms, this severance of earthly ties and affections from blood relations who did not embrace the gospel. In one letter to his parents back in England he refers to them as a 'stink in my nostrils'.[121] Such sentiments towards the natural family were apparently shared with Believers assembled at Watervliet. Father James warned those that were still attached to 'fleshly relations' that the 'treasure of a true and faithful Believer was in his brethren and sisters in Christ; and not in his earthly kindred'. 'I am willing', he continued, 'that all the interest I have in this world, should go to them that are faithful to serve God, here in America.'[122]

Several of Whittaker's prophecies and directions to Shaker congregations are taken to have signalled their gathering and submitting to communal regulations: 'I saw all the Believers travel, and then come to a stop, as up against a wall', Whittaker once revealed; 'and then they were brought into order'.[123] He went on to warn them: 'You need not be afraid of losing your lots, unless you lose them by transgression. Every one of you must labor in your own lots, lest by seeking to get another's lot, you lose your own.'[124] At New Lebanon, Believers built their first architecturally significant meetinghouse under Whittaker's ministration—a place of gathering

---

[119] OClWHi, I:A-20, James Whittaker, [Will], 9 June 1787.
[120] Green and Wells, *Testimonies*, p. 377.
[121] Meacham, *Concise Statement*, p. 22.
[122] Green and Wells, *Testimonies*, p. 357.
[123] Green and Wells, *Testimonies*, p. 367.
[124] Green and Wells, *Testimonies*, p. 371.

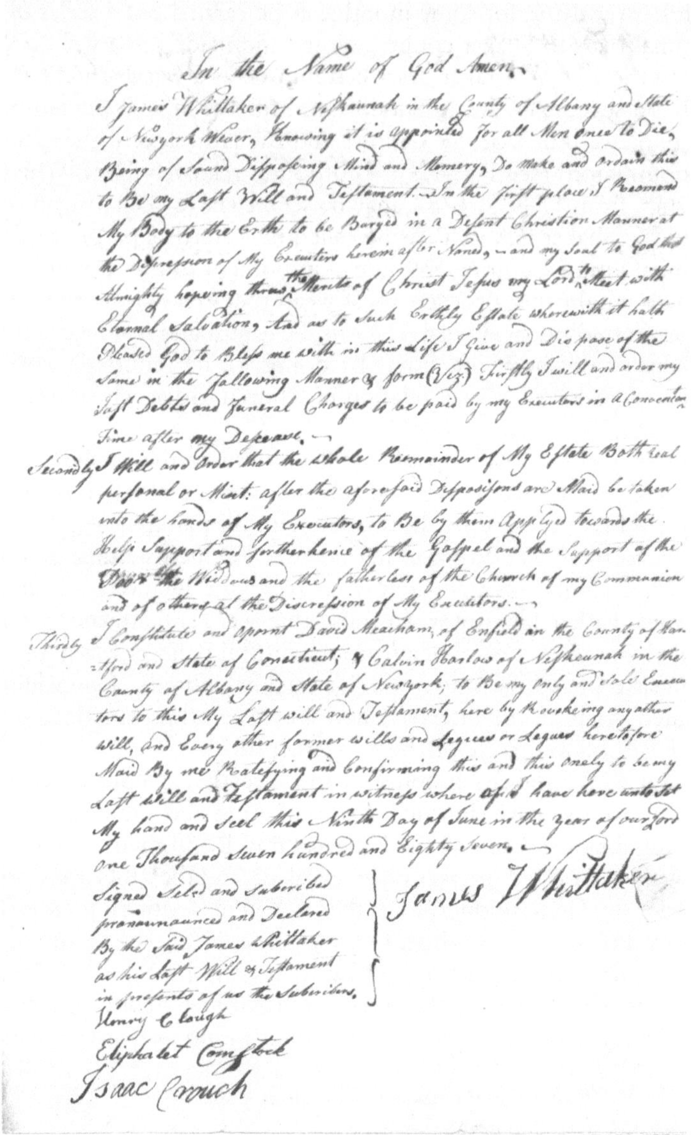
In the Name of God Amen,
I James Whittaker of Nishaunah in the County of Albany and State of Newyork Weaver, Knowing it is appointed for all Men once to Die, Being of Sound Dissposeing Mind and Memery, Do make and Ordain this to Be my Last Will and Testament. In the first place I Recomend My Body to the Erth to be Buryed in a Desent Christion Manner at the Dispression of My Executors herein after Named, — and my Soul to God that Almighty hopeing throu the Merits of Christ Jesus my Lord to Meet with Eternal Salvation, And as to Such Erthly Estate wherewith it hath Pleased God to Bless me with in this Life I Give and Dispose of the Same in the fallowing Manner & form (Viz) Firstly I will and order my Just Debts and funeral Charges to be paid by my Executors in a Conveenient Time after my Decease, —
Secondly I Will and Order that the whole Remainder of My Estate Both real personal or Mixt: after the aforesaid Dispositions are Maid be taken unto the hands of My Executors, to Be by them Applyed towards the Help Support and fortherance of the Gospel and the Support of the Poor the Widdows and the fatherless of the Church of my Communion and of others at the Discression of My Executors. —
Thirdly I Constitute and Apoint David Meacham, of Enfield in the County of Hartford and State of Conecticut; & Calvin Harlow of Nishaunah in the County of Albany and State of Newyork, to Be my Only and Sole Executors to this My Last will and Testament, here by Revokeing any other will, and Every other former wills and Legacies or Legues heretofore Maid By me Ratefying and Confirming this and this Onely to be my Last Will and Testament in witness where of I have here unto Set My hand and Seel this Ninth Day of June in the year of our Lord One Thousand Seven hundred and Eighty Seven, —

Signed Seled and Subcribed pronounanced and Declared By the Said James Whittaker as his Last Will & Testament in presents of us the Subcribers, — James Whittaker

Henry Clough
Eliphalet Comstock
Isaac Crouch

Fig. 4.3 The Last Will and Testament of James Whittaker, dated 9 June 1787. Made immediately prior to the formal implementation of communal property among the Shakers, Whittaker willed that his estate be left to support the 'Church of my Communion'. Courtesy of Western Reserve Historical Society, Cleveland, Ohio

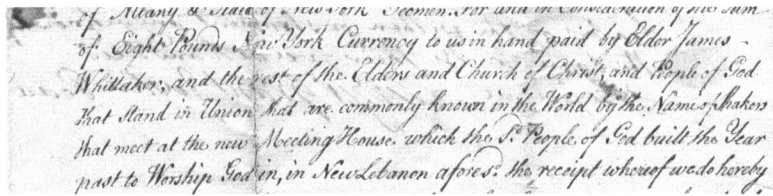

Fig. 4.4 Deed of the New Lebanon Meetinghouse naming James Whittaker 'and the rest of the Elders and Church of Christ, and the People of God that stand in Union that are commonly known in the World by the Name of Shakers'. Courtesy of Communal Societies Collection, Burke Library, Hamilton College, Clinton, New York

and communal worship. The deed to the property, consecrated by George and David Darrow on 3 May 1786, is made over to James Whittaker (see Fig. 4.4).[125]

With his strong instruction to foster union, especially to the lead, combined with the rejection of the world outside the community of Believers, Whittaker forged the linchpin of Church Order among the Shakers. Whittaker succeeded in inculcating these principles because, as one Believer wrote, 'his speech was such as inspired confidence and commanded respect'.[126] This respect facilitated his remarkable achievement of holding the Shakers together, and carrying them forward, after the death of Mother Ann Lee.

THE LAST OF THE ENGLISH BELIEVERS

James Whittaker's death in July 1787 led, directly or indirectly, to the departure of more of the English Believers. Within a month, Matthewson reported that James Shepherd 'was sencured for mis[c]onduct (altho 5 years before he was considred as a parfect man & had authority under god to forgiv sins) he resented it so much that he now abdicated the office & quit the comunity'.[127] Shepherd remains a mysterious figure in early Shakerism, and no reason for this censure is given in any source. Apostate Thomas Brown states that Shepherd had served as an 'inferior Elder'; yet clearly

---

[125] Hamilton College, Shaker Collection, II A, [Deed], George and David Darrow to James Whittaker, New Lebanon, New York, 3 May 1786.

[126] Green and Wells, *Testimonies*, p. 367.

[127] Matthewson, 'Reminiscences', p. 71.

Shepherd's censure by his new American brethren could not be borne.[128] Shepherd settled his accounts with the Shakers at Niskeyuna on 11 August 1787, and signed a document releasing 'John Hocknell or the estate of Elder James Whittaker Late Deceased or any of the Famely that Now reside at the house or Farm ... from any Demand'—evidence of the still informal nature of Shaker property sharing. Shepherd received a severance from John Hocknell, David Meacham and Calvin Harlow, who were part of the hierarchy emerging in the wake of Whittaker's death.[129] Shepherd made a further settlement with the Society accepting £15 from Joseph Bennet and Joseph Meacham for work 'on the farm and estates lying in the west district of Rensaelairwick', signed at New Lebanon on 18 February 1790.[130]

Another English Believer, Francis Hocknell, son of John, received his settlement and discharge of Timothy Hubbard at Niskeyuna on 13 January 1789 in the form of £5.16s, a shirt and a suit of clothes (see Fig. 4.5).[131] However, this discharge seems to have preceded his move to the New Lebanon community, where he was admitted the same year. It is impossible to tell whether Francis Hocknell officially left the Shakers and rejoined, or whether this was a method of reckoning accounts at the time, according to the strict financial record-keeping within, and separately among, Shaker families.

In the late 1780s, John Hocknell was the most prominent original English Shaker Elder, following the deaths of the Lee siblings and James Whittaker. After Whittaker, the leadership succession was more competitive: the leading candidates were Calvin Harlow, David Meacham and Joseph Meacham, all American-born. The controversy was resolved by the authoritative pronouncement of Job Bishop that Joseph Meacham 'was the anointed of God to lead his people', and his public endorsement by Hocknell. 'Immediately after this prophetic announcement' from Bishop, a Shaker chronicle records, 'Elder John Hocknell kneeled in prayer before the assembly, giving utterance to this expression only, "Blessed be God"'.[132] With this simple act Hocknell passed the torch of Shaker leadership from English to American Believers.

---

[128] Brown, *Account*, p. 327.

[129] James Shepherd, [release], 11 August 1787, DeWint, ASC 736. The document was witnessed by Henry Clough and Eleazar Rand; dated Nesqueanah [i.e. Niskeyuna]. Shepherd signed it, spelling his name as rendered here.

[130] James Shepherd, [release], 11 February 1790, DeWint, ASC 736.

[131] OClWHi, II:A-15, Frances Hocknell, [discharge], 13 January 1789.

[132] Henry C. Blinn, 'Father Job Bishop', *Shaker Manifesto*, 12:3 (1882), 53–5.

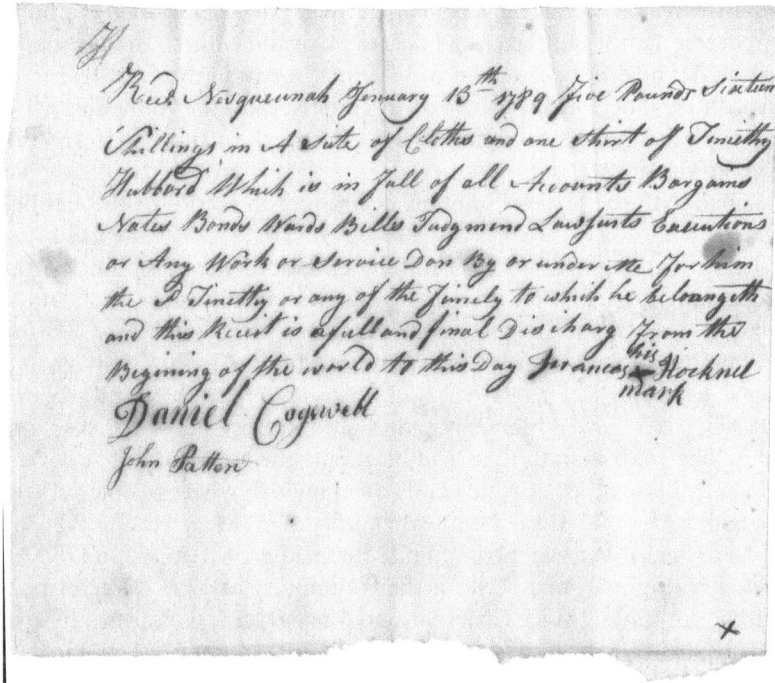

Fig. 4.5   Francis Hocknell's discharge papers from the Watervliet Shaker community, 13 January 1789. This demonstrates the careful accounting of community property by Shaker Trustees. Hocknell subsequently lived at the New Lebanon Shaker community. Courtesy of Western Reserve Historical Society, Cleveland, Ohio

Joseph Meacham oversaw the gathering of assembled pockets of Believers into Church Order after 1787. Hocknell was appointed Elder of the Church Family at Niskeyuna, which made eminent sense, as he was the original lessor of much of the land, and had continued to supervise the settlement since his return to America in 1785. The Niskeyuna land, soon renamed Watervliet, was eventually acquired by the Church in a formal arrangement. Elder John died at Watervliet on 27 February 1799, his beloved second wife Hannah having predeceased him on 18 October 1797.

Thomas Brown visited James Shepherd in 1807, finding him 'very low in circumstances and advanced in years; but an honest man'. Shepherd told Brown that he had given his best years in support of the Church. Supposedly James Whittaker had decreed that the Church should support Shepherd if he ever became infirm, whether he was in the faith or had left. Accordingly, Shepherd was invited to come and live at Watervliet, where he was placed in the backsliding order—reserved for those who had once accepted the gospel, but then turned away.[133] It is probable that Shepherd remained with the Shakers until his death, but no record of this has been located.[134]

The other English Shakers faithfully embraced the communal Gospel Order, and their place within it, living out their lives as rank-and-file Believers. Francis and Anne (or Anna) Hocknell lived at the New Lebanon community, on the New York–Massachusetts border, in the Church Family. Francis lived in the First Order, and was a hatter, cobbler and maker of pipe stems. He gave a humorous admonition to his fellow Believers on 9 September 1820, stating they 'had been taught not to spit out at the windows, nor blow noses & wipe hands on railings & where people pass, nor spit against the side of the house when in bed'.[135] Mary Hocknell lived at the Niskeyuna/Watervliet community that had grown up around the land her father originally provided for the community in 1775. When trouble with the apostates Eunice Chapman and Mary Dyer was at its height in the early 1820s, the Shaker leadership turned particularly to Mary Hocknell and Mary Partington for authoritative affidavits concerning the character and conduct of Mother Ann and Father William Lee.[136] Mary Hocknell died at Watervliet on 14 April 1825, aged 66; Mary Partington died on 10 September 1833, aged 78.

With Partington's death, the Shakers recognized the passing of 'the last of those who came with Mother Ann from England' aboard the *Mariah*.[137] Francis Hocknell, who had sailed on the second migration, lived as a faithful Believer until his death at New Lebanon on 4 May 1841. Six years later, Philemon Stewart recorded the passing of Francis's sister, the very

[133] Brown, *Account*, pp. 58, 327.

[134] William Haskett implies Shepherd seceded and returned several times, so it may be that Shepherd again departed the Shakers following his readmittance *c*.1807; *Shakerism Unmasked*, p. 94.

[135] LCW, Shaker Collection, ms. 42, Isaac Newton Youngs, 'Family and Meeting Journal: Including a Narrative of Various Events' (1815–23), [New Lebanon, NY].

[136] See Hocknell and Partington's affidavits in *A Review of Mary Dyer's Publication*.

[137] New York Public Library, Shaker Manuscript Collection, no. 1, Rufus Bishop, 'A Daily Journal of Passing Events'.

last of the English Shakers. His journal entry for 25 January 1847 noted that 'Anna Hocknell Departed this life between 4 and 5 o'clock this morning at the Second Order. Anna was the last that was left with us who came from England with our first Parents; she was about 85 years of age.'[138] Just 2 years prior to her death, Anna is recorded working at spinning and knitting.[139] With her died the last memories of Shaker origins in England. Although many others remained who knew 'Mother Ann' and the other Elders in America, none were left to recall the 'blessed fire' of the Shaker hymn, as it was originally kindled nearly 100 years earlier at Manchester in England.

The success of Shakerism in both England and America was a communal effort. The charisma of Mother Ann Lee was a powerful motivator, but the contributions of the faithful followers who emigrated with her should not be underestimated. The abuse and sufferings endured by the burly ex-soldier William Lee for the sake of the Shaker gospel set a powerful example for others to follow. The dedication and shrewd management of temporal assets by John Hocknell ensured that the Shakers not only reached America, but thrived there. John Partington's practical preaching taught new American converts the concepts of union and humility, and of consecrating all to the gospel. Finally, and perhaps most importantly, James Whittaker wove all of these principles together and presented his American successors with a body of Believers prepared to implement a restored Church centred on community of property.[140]

[138] Priscilla J. Brewer, *Shaker Communities, Shaker Lives* (Hanover: University Press of New England, 1986), p. 137.

[139] New York State Library, Albany, New York, Manuscripts and Special Collections, Shaker Collection, 1784–1992 (SC20330), box 19, folder 1, Isaac Newton Youngs, 'Domestic Journal of Daily Occurrences (1834–46)', [New Lebanon].

[140] The author would like to thank Jane Crosthwaite, David Newell and Philip Lockley for their generous help and advice during the writing of this essay.

CHAPTER 5

The Harmony Society in Württemberg, Pennsylvania and Indiana

Hermann Ehmer

The people who founded the Harmony Society on 15 February 1805 on a tract of land on the Connoquenessing River in Western Pennsylvania were Pietists from Württemberg in southwest Germany.[1] During the

[1] Karl J. R. Arndt, an American professor of German (and 1945–1950 member of the US Military Government in Württemberg-Baden), devoted much of his life to researching the Harmony Society. His key works, utilized for elements of this article, are: *George Rapp's Harmony Society 1785–1847*, second edn (Cranbury, NJ: Associated University Presses, 1972); *George Rapp's Successors and Material Heirs 1847–1916* (Cranbury, NJ: Associated University Presses, 1971). To this history Arndt added bilingual editions and translations into English of pertinent source material: Karl J.R. Arndt (ed.), *George Rapp's Separatists— Georg Rapps Separatisten 1700–1803. The German Prelude to Rapp's American Harmony Society. Die deutsche Vorgeschichte von Rapps amerikanischer Harmonie-Gesellschaft. A Documentary History* (Worcester, MA: Harmony Society Press, 1980); *Harmony on the Connoquenessing 1803–1815. George Rapp's First American Harmony. Harmonie am Connoquenessing. Georg Rapps erste amerikanische Harmonie* (Worcester, MA: Harmony Society Press, 1980); *A Documentary History of the Indiana Decade of the Harmony Society 1814–1824*, 2 vols (Indianapolis: Indiana Historical Society 1975–78); *Harmony on the Wabash in Transition to Rapp's Divine Economy on the Ohio and Owen's New Moral World at New Harmony on the Wabash 1824–1826* (Worcester, MA: Harmony Society Press, 1982); *Economy on the Ohio 1826–1834. The Harmony Society during the Period of Its Greatest Power and Influence and Its Messianic Crisis* (Worcester MA: Harmony Society Press, 1984); *George*

H. Ehmer
University of Tübingen, Tübingen, Germany

© The Editor(s) (if applicable) and The Author(s) 2016   105
P. Lockley (ed.), *Protestant Communalism in the Trans-Atlantic World, 1650–1850*, DOI 10.1057/978-1-137-48487-1_5

nineteenth century, the Harmony Society became one of the best-known and most successful communal societies in America. This chapter traces the social, political and religious context of their origins in eighteenth-century Germany, and relates this to their reasons for emigration across the Atlantic and their American experience. It demonstrates how the Harmony Society exemplified the trans-Atlantic transfer of European communal ideas on a religious basis, and the transfer of Pietist ideas into American communalism.

THE DUCHY AND CHURCH OF WÜRTTEMBERG

The Duchy of Württemberg was one of the smaller and less important States among the 360 principalities and Imperial cities then forming the Holy Roman Empire of the German Nation. Around 1800, Württemberg had a population of 650,000, living mostly in small towns and villages, the most important city being Stuttgart, the capital, with a population of only 18,000.

During the eighteenth century, Württemberg was ruled by more than one duke of extravagant habits and architectural ambition.[2] In 1704, Eberhard Ludwig (reigned 1667–1733) began building a palace and an entirely new city called Ludwigsburg north of Stuttgart to house his court and government offices. When Duke Charles (1744–93) was declared of age 30 years later, the representative assembly, the *Landtag*, consented to build another palace for the young duke back in Stuttgart, returning the court and the government offices to Stuttgart. During his reign Duke Charles had several smaller palaces built, both in the vicinity of Ludwigsburg and Stuttgart, and kept a magnificent court, founding a theatre and an opera house with hired singers, actors and dancers from Italy and France. The duke fostered education by founding a public library and a new university teaching modern subjects to compete with the historic university at Tübingen. Charles further enjoyed commanding an army of mercenaries and men press-ganged into the service.

Rapp's Years of Glory. Economy on the Ohio 1834–1847. Ökonomie am Ohio (New York: Peter Lang,1987); *George Rapp's Re-Established Harmony Society, Georg Rapps erneuerte Harmonie-Gesellschaft. Letters and Documents of the Baker–Henrici Trusteeship 1848–1868. Briefe und Dokumente zur Geschichte von Ökonomie am Ohio 1848–1868* (New York: Peter Lang, 1993).

[2] For this time period see Dieter Mertens, 'Württemberg', in *Handbuch der Baden-Württembergischen Geschichte* (Stuttgart: Klett-Cotta, 1995), 2:1–163, esp. pp. 137ff.

All this luxury cost more money than the small Duchy could provide in taxes, so Charles looked for ways and means to get more money. In time, every civil servant had to pay a sizable fee to obtain his position, and regiments of Württemberg soldiers were sold to other states, including to the Dutch to fight in their colonies in South Africa and Indonesia. Charles also received subsidies from the king of France, with the result that when war broke out between France and Prussia in 1756, the Duke's troops were ordered to march against Prussia. Many of the soldiers ran away before they saw action, so Charles did not gain fame as commander of his army. While Charles's public library still exists, his new university was closed at his death in 1793, because it proved to be too costly.

Every citizen in Württemberg was legally obliged to be a member of the Lutheran Church.[3] A few Roman Catholics here and there were allowed to live in the towns and villages, though without the full rights of citizenship. This confessional situation dated back to the Reformation when the then duke had sympathized with Martin Luther's church reforms. A law issued by the emperor and the Imperial Diet in 1555 stated that the citizens of a territory of the Empire ought to have the same religion as their ruler. This *Augsburger Religionsfrieden*, or Peace of Augsburg, was confirmed in 1648 by the Treaty of Westphalia, ending the 30 Years War, though from this date a ruler changing his faith was not to force his subjects to change theirs accordingly.

The Lutheran Church in Württemberg was well organized, and intimately connected to the state. The church was headed by a board of administrators called the Konsistorium, whose members were nominated by the duke. The country was divided up into districts for both secular administration and the administration of the church. A superintendent supervised all the churches in a district, visiting all the pastors and congregations in his district once a year. Each superintendent reported on their visits to one of four general superintendents in the country, who conferred with the duke's nominated *Konsistorium* regarding these reports

---

[3] See especially, Hermann Ehmer, *Kleine Geschichte der Evangelischen Kirche in Württemberg* (Leinfelden-Echterdingen: DRW Verlag, 2008). A short overview for the English reader is available in Hermann Ehmer, 'The History of Johannes Brenz's Territorial Church. An Overview of the Organization of the Württemberg Church', in Konrad Eisenbichler (ed.), *Collaboration, Conflict, and Continuity in the Reformation. Essays in Honour of James M. Estes on His Eightieth Birthday* (Toronto: Centre for Reformation and Renaissance Studies, 2014), pp. 175–93.

and issued general orders to the church as a whole, or special orders to individual ministers and congregations.

WÜRTTEMBERG PIETISM

The Harmony Society was a product of a broad religious movement for reform and the encouragement of a new piety within Protestantism in Germany and other parts of Europe towards the end of the seventeenth century: Pietism. Pietism is perhaps best understood not as a uniform movement but as a wide range of opinions.[4] Some leaders of Pietist opinion believed it necessary to study the Scriptures more closely and to follow their rules. Others thought it would not help to obey simply what was written in the Bible but instead directed individual believers to follow what the Holy Spirit had written in their heart.

Typical of Pietism was the forming of small groups—conventicles— for those who wanted to take being a Christian seriously. A question frequently arose over the relationship between these conventicles meeting in private houses or other places during the week, and the official church. Leaving the church was called separatism. Separatism was not only a religious matter but had implications for civil life because the church was so closely tied to the state. Not going to church or participating in communion, not having children baptized and not sending them to school, all caused a wide range of reactions on the part of the authorities, from admonitions to fines and even to sending offenders to jail. Such responses led easily to criticisms of the official church, though separatism as a religious protest could often reflect a political situation, and political protest itself could be disguised as religious protest in this way.

The Duchy of Württemberg was one of the centres of Pietism in Germany.[5] After initially opposing the early Pietist groups, the official Lutheran church came to terms with elements in the movement. A law issued in 1743 permitted the meetings of the Pietists, provided they followed a set of rules, for instance that their meetings did not take place

---

[4] On Pietism as a worldwide movement see now: Martin Brecht, Klaus Deppermannt, Ulrich Gäbler and Hartmut Lehmann (eds), *Geschichte des Pietismus*, 4 vols (Göttingen: Vandenhoek & Ruprecht, 1993–2004).

[5] See especially Martin Brecht, 'Der württembergische Pietismus', in *Geschichte des Pietismus*, 2:225–95.

at the time of church services.[6] Quite a number of the ministers of the State Church were Pietists themselves, inaugurating and leading Pietist groups in their congregations. This led to a great deal of consent between the institutional church and Pietism. However, towards the end of the eighteenth century, around the time of the French Revolution, separatism increased in popularity.

An important figure in Württemberg Pietism was Johann Albrecht Bengel (1687–1752), a prominent theologian still important today for his critical edition of the Greek New Testament of 1734.[7] Bengel published several works in biblical studies, including his *Gnomon*, a New Testament commentary. Bengel was convinced that the Bible revealed the stages of the history of the world, dealing not only with the salvation of the individual, but connecting history and revelation, the past and the future. For Bengel, the Bible told not only the sense of times past but also where humankind was going, according to God's economy or plan of salvation. Bengel tried himself to uncover this plan through ancient traditions, such as the Jewish Kabbala, and the symbolism of numbers in the Bible, notably in the Revelation of John. The key to Bengel's calculations was the number of the beast: 666 (Rev. 13:18). Assuming the total age of the world would be 7777 7/9 years, Bengel tried to find out where in this schedule he and his contemporaries were living. The central point of the time of the world had to be the second coming of Christ and the beginning of the Millennium, which Bengel by his calculations set on 18 June 1836. He envisaged the Millennium very clearly as a time when every person would live in obedience to God, enjoying healthy, fruitful, peaceful times, free of harm, with all spiritual and bodily welfare assured.

Friedrich Christoph Oetinger (1702–82), another Württemberg theologian, was also interested in the millennial age. Oetinger pondered the problems of the developing modern natural sciences against traditions of alchemy, and also the challenges to biblical philosophy from the philosophy of reason. Oetinger came to describe the Millennium as a

---

[6] Hartmut Lehmann, *Pietismus und weltliche Ordnung in Württemberg vom 17. bis zum 20. Jahrhundert* (Stuttgart: Kohlhammer, 1969), pp. 82–94.

[7] Gottfried Mälzer, *Johann Albrecht Bengel. Leben und Werk* (Stuttgart: Calwer Verlag, 1970). For Bengel's calculations, see *Geschichte des Pietismus*, 2:254–6. Hermann Ehmer, 'Johann Albrecht Bengel (1687–1752)', in Carter Lindberg (ed.), *The Pietist Theologians: An Introduction to Theology in the Seventeenth and Eighteenth Centuries* (Oxford: Blackwell, 2005), pp. 224–38.

reunification of sciences and philosophies into one philosophy. He was convinced that it was possible to prepare for the Millennium and published a book entitled *Die Güldene Zeit* (The Golden Age), a collection of contributions by various thinkers on the subject.

Oetinger's book was published in the vernacular German, as were several of Bengel's works. They received a wide readership, especially in Pietist circles. Speculation on an approaching millennial age spread widely in eighteenth-century Württemberg. The appeal of Bengel's speculations in particular remains visible in attempts to visualize his ideas in the form of clocks built at the time. Bengel's understanding of the stages of historical time was translated into a circular pattern—the end meeting the beginning like a clock face. Philipp Matthäus Hahn (1739–1790), a Württemberg pastor who had a mechanical workshop in his parsonage employing several workers building scales, clocks and watches, commissioned them to build four-sided clocks, with some faces showing the Bengel timetable of world history.[8]

IPTINGEN

George Rapp (1757–1847), the leader and founder of the Harmony Society, was born on 1 November 1757 in Iptingen, a sizable village not far from the former Cistercian monastery at Maulbronn, and 30 km northwest of Stuttgart (see Fig. 5.1). Like other villages in southwestern Germany, the population had doubled in the century since the end of the Thirty Years War (1618–48). This growth caused problems in a rural society because the land available to farm could not be increased, leading to severe food shortages whenever there were bad harvests in consecutive years, as there were around 1750, a few years before George Rapp was born. These critical years led to considerable emigration to North America from this region of Germany in the period.

Iptingen village society was a hierarchy, comprising a few well-to-do people, a more or less extended group in the middle and a few underdogs. George Rapp belonged to the lower end of the middle grouping of artisans and small farmers, but he was considered to have climbed a few steps up the social ladder by marrying a woman from an upper-class family in

---

[8] For a description and photographs of one of these clocks see *Philipp Matthäus Hahn 1739–1790. Quellen und Schriften zu Philipp Matthäus Hahn*, ed. Christian Väterlein (Stuttgart: Württembergisches Landesmuseum, 1989), pp. 396–7.

Fig. 5.1   George Rapp's house in Iptingen. Courtesy of the author

the nearby village of Friolzheim. While this shows that there was the possibility for social mobility, change might not be only for the better, and could more easily be for the worse. This was a society not of plenty but of scarcity. Thriftiness was an important virtue and marriage not so much a matter of love as an opportunity to improve the means of subsistence. The crucial reason for this was that in Württemberg every child in a family, male or female, had equal rights by law to inherit the property of their parents. Over time, the result of this was that family farmland was divided up into increasingly smaller portions—unlike in some other parts of Germany where the eldest son inherited everything, and younger brothers and sisters often ended up as servants.[9]

Village life in Württemberg in Rapp's time was of course not only determined by the economic situation of the villagers but also by institutional positions.[10] The two most important people wielding secular and spiritual authority were the *Schultheiss* (mayor) and the *Pfarrer* (pastor). They were by law obliged to support each other in fulfilling their duties; every year when the superintendent came for his inspection he would ask each one what he thought of the other. Aside from his ecclesiastical duties, the pastor had to supervise the local school because the school was supposed above all to transmit religious knowledge. In order to learn the catechism and hymns and to become familiar with the Bible, everyone had to learn to read and write. For this reason, the school system in Württemberg in the mid-eighteenth century was in relatively good condition and literacy was high compared with other parts of Europe.

The mayor presided over the village council as well as the village court. Every man in the village had the opportunity to be elected to these two bodies to take part in village affairs. The village court only had to deal with minor offences. More substantial crimes were reported to the bailiff. There was still another court in every village called the Kirchenkonvent.[11] Members of this court, installed in 1642 in every town and village in Württemberg to enforce the *Kirchenordnung* (church order) on a local basis, were the pastor, the mayor and a few other men whom the two considered fit for this task. The Kirchenkonvent supervised the morals of the villagers, for example ensuring that on Sundays no unnecessary work was undertaken, settling matrimonial quarrels and questioning any woman who got pregnant without being married, in order to report them to the bailiff. The Kirchenkonvent also had oversight of the local school and questioned and punished parents who failed to send their children to school.

[9] An in-depth study of family relations in a village in Southwestern Germany is David Warren Sabean, *Property, Production and Family in Neckarhausen, 1700–1870* (Cambridge: Cambridge University Press, 1990), and idem, *Kinship in Neckarhausen* (Cambridge: Cambridge University Press, 1998).

[10] For the following see Eberhard Fritz, 'Die Kirche im Dorf: Studien und Beobachtungen zur kirchlichen Situation in der ländlichen Gemeinde des Herzogtums Württemberg', *Zeitschrift für württembergische Landesgeschichte*, 52 (1993), 155–78.

[11] Hermann Ehmer and Sabine Holtz (eds), *Der Kirchenkonvent in Württemberg* (Epfendorf and Neckar: Bibliotheca Academica, 2009).

In the village church every person had a designated pew according to their station in the village society. When a pew stayed empty everybody of course asked why. In order to receive communion, people had to register with the pastor. Records were kept, meaning if anyone stayed away for an unacceptable time, their case would be passed to the Kirchenkonvent. In this way, significant control was exercised by the church on each individual within a village such as Iptingen.

Even so, for the village community to function, a relatively high degree of communal self-government and individual responsibility was expected of village people. Individual self-control and cooperation was demanded by facets of village life, and not just enforced by the institutions already discussed. For instance, woodland and some pastures often belonged to the entire community.

Woods were essential for fuel and building materials, so were supervised by the forester, an official appointed by the Duke, and responsible for preventing their destruction. Every citizen of the village had the right to receive their share of fuel every year plus building materials when needed. Arable land was divided up in three sections in order to secure crop rotation. Every farmer normally had pieces of land in all three sections and had to plant whatever crop had been assigned to be grown there that year. Self-discipline and a communal ethic was therefore necessary to be a good member of this society.

GEORGE RAPP: FROM PIETIST TO SEPARATIST

As a young man in his early twenties, George Rapp travelled for a couple of years, probably working as a linen weaver, a trade which he had adopted like so many others to supplement his income from farming. Unfortunately, we do not know where Rapp went on his travels or whom he met, but it is very likely that he adopted some of the new religious ideas of radical separatist Pietism at this time.[12] Later, Rapp revealed an intimate knowledge of the writings of Jakob Böhme (1575–1624), the mystic

---

[12] Hermann Ehmer, 'Der ausgewanderte Pietismus. Pietistische Gemeinschaftsprojekte in Nordamerika', in Rainer Lächele (ed.), *Das Echo Halles: Kulturelle Wirkungen des Pietismus* (Tübingen: Bibliotheca Academica, 2001), pp. 315–57, esp. pp. 326–44; Eberhard Fritz, *Radikaler Pietismus in Württemberg. Religiöse Ideale im Konflikt mit gesellschaftlichen Realitäten* (Quellen und Forschungen zur württembergischen Kirchengeschichte 18; Epfendorf am Neckar: Bibliotheca Academica, 2002), pp. 122–63.

shoemaker from Silesia in eastern Germany.[13] Böhme had combined interests in philosophy, alchemy, mysticism and the Jewish kabbala, and must
have read widely in these fields. His thought covered theology, cosmology
and anthropology. In his own letters, Rapp would handle Böhme's mystic
and alchemistic terminology without difficulty.

When Rapp returned home from his travels and settled back in his
native village he married Christine Benzinger, and the couple had two
children. Rapp did not develop his new religious ideas right away, but after
some years he started staying away from church services and especially
from communion. When Rapp was questioned in 1785 by the Iptingen
Kirchenkonvent, the local body of elders, as to why he did not attend
church, he said that Christ had revealed himself to him in his heart so
he did not have to come to church any longer. On further questioning
he answered that as Jesus was enshrined in his heart he did not believe he
needed the external means of salvation like sermons and sacraments.

Rapp's opinions were typical of separatist Pietism in his period, and
were not an unusual form of religious protest. Yet Rapp clearly gained
notoriety and a position of leadership, as his example was soon followed
by many others, who came to him from all over the surrounding region.
Rapp began to hold religious gatherings outside of official church services,
even though people knew they should not travel across country to such
meetings. One protest quickly led to another. Rapp's followers refused to
bring their children to be baptized, did not send their children to school
and did not have them confirmed. Most disturbingly for the Württemberg
authorities, they refused to give the oath of allegiance owed to the prince
at every man's coming of age. All these protests amounted to a radical
withdrawal from the accepted standards of established society.

First local then government authorities realized they would have to deal
with Rapp's case, though for some time government officials, influenced
by the principles of tolerance and freedom of conscience encouraged by
the Enlightenment, had become quite lenient in religious affairs.[14] Rapp's
case was not settled for two years, as officials hoped simply to keep peace
and order. This situation changed drastically, however, after the French
Revolution. At this time, the authorities in Württemberg, like many other

---

[13] For a comprehensive presentation of Böhme and his followers see, Martin Brecht, 'Die
deutschen Spiritualisten des 17. Jahrhunderts', in *Geschichte des Pietismus*, 1:205–40, esp.
pp. 205–14.

[14] Hartmut Lehmann, *Pietismus und weltliche Ordnung*, pp. 117–34.

parts of Europe, suddenly became wary of any civil disobedience in their own country. By 1791, Rapp and his followers were threatened with expulsion from the country if they would not stop disdaining the church and its rites. In the bailiff's office in Maulbronn, Rapp spoke up against the bailiff, who remarked that he was not a prophet. Rapp boldly answered, 'I am a prophet and called to be one.' Rapp and his followers continued to stay away from churches, declaring the State Church to be the great whore depicted in Revelation 17.

For the Württemberg authorities, the most serious problem with Rapp was that he had many followers, not only in his own and neighbouring villages, but from places some distance away. Rapp's following in the 1790s has been estimated at between ten and twelve thousand, but this is likely an exaggeration. Even so, there were evidently many hundreds willing to travel hours and days to meet with Rapp in Iptingen. In the following years, however, attention was drawn away from Rapp and his people, when far more serious problems faced the whole country, as the armies of revolutionary France threatened Württemberg. In 1796 the country became a battlefield for the war between France and Austria. Both armies, especially the French, exacted contributions in money, food and other supplies.

Rapp's career as a Pietist leader in Württemberg may be usefully compared with that of Michael Hahn (1758–1819), who was only one year younger.[15] Hahn came from the same social background as Rapp, from a small farming family which had a trade on the side. While Rapp was away from home as a journeyman, Hahn started a butcher's apprenticeship, but soon dropped out to help on the family farm. Hahn had his spiritual awakening in 1775–1776 and read Jakob Böhme. He had visio-auditions in 1778 and 1783, and, like Böhme, Hahn experienced a *Zentralschau*, or key vision, which gave him fundamental insights concerning God, people and the world. The influence of Böhme may be seen in Hahn's theology, anthropology and cosmology, which he expressed in Böhme's own terminology. Hahn was also influenced by mysticism and alchemy. He started to hold his own meetings and was criticized by the Lutheran ministry for expounding his own ideas, which did not accord with the Bible. Hahn continued his meetings regardless.

---

[15] Joachim Trautwein, *Die Theosophie Michael Hahns und ihre Quellen. Quellen und Forschungen zur württembergischen Kirchengeschichte* (Stuttgart: Calwer Verlag, 1969), pp. 73–4.

Hahn and Rapp met at least once to exchange ideas. Hahn counselled Rapp that the way to spiritual purification had to be gradual. Both believed that the second coming of Christ was imminent. As an ardent reader of Böhme, Hahn linked celibacy to the nature of human relations in the millennial age, and adopted the discipline himself. Many of Hahn's followers also practised celibacy, though he stated that this was not for everybody. Rapp would only adopt celibacy for his Society once in America. Rapp and Hahn probably also exchanged opinions about their attitudes towards the established church, as Rapp advocated separation, while Hahn wanted to remain within the church. One consequence of this was that Hahn was not in favour of emigration from Germany, unlike Rapp.

Emigration for Salvation

The French Revolution and the ensuing turmoil in Europe had a deeper meaning for Rapp, his followers and a variety of other separatist Pietists. In the book of Revelation they believed they had found their explanation. The Revolution and more than two decades of endless wars were 'the three woes' of the Apocalypse (Rev. 9:12). Before their very eyes, Rapp believed the events predicted in the book of Revelation were happening. 'The cities of the nations' mentioned in Revelation 16:9 were about to fall. This meant that Europe was doomed. Whoever wanted to escape this disaster had to do as the mysterious 'Woman clothed with the Sun' described in Revelation 12:6, who 'fled into the wilderness, where she hath a place prepared of God'. The Millennium—a period mentioned in Revelation 20—was therefore not only a change for the better but also believed to be a time of judgement, where only a few would be saved. Salvation from judgement could, Rapp, his followers and some other Pietists believed, be found in the wilderness. But the question remained, where was this wilderness?

Pietists across Württemberg discussed whether this wilderness was to be found to the East or West. Johann Heinrich Jung-Stilling (1740–1817), a well-known religious writer of the time, published a book, *Das Heimweh* (Homesickness), between 1794 and 1796, describing the travels of the soul to the heavenly home, much like John Bunyan's *Pilgrim's Progress*. Jung-Stilling supposed that the haven, the safe place, would be somewhere in the East and so he supplied the idea for an extensive emigration to southern Russia. In 1817, more than ten thousand people from Württemberg emigrated to Transcaucasia.[16]

It has sometimes been assumed that Rapp and his followers decided to emigrate because of pressure from the Württemberg church and state authorities, but it is clear that it was not so much the problem of persecution but a result of their beliefs that they opted to leave. For Rapp and his people, there was no doubt where this wilderness could be found: it was across the ocean in the new world called America. Emigration from southwestern Germany to North America had been taking place for almost a century, ever since the Palatines—refugees from the Palatinate and neighbouring regions—were given passage to the New York colony in 1709. Communication between German settlers in America and their states of origin meant the Württemberg population knew fairly well what to expect on the other side of the Atlantic.[17] In September 1803, George Rapp set out to prepare for his people and himself the place of God suggested by their reading of Revelation 12:14, which in the King James English translation reads, 'And to the woman were given two wings of a great eagle, that she might fly into the wilderness, into her place, where she is nourished for a time, and times, and half a time, from the face of the serpent.'

Martin Luther's German Bible, which Rapp's followers knew, translates this passage slightly differently, talking of one time and two times and half a time. These dark hints in Revelation provoked speculation not only among Separatists but also among respected Lutheran churchmen like Johann Albrecht Bengel. Rapp clearly knew about Bengel's calculations regarding world history, but did his own mathematical calculations. Rapp believed his followers were the elect flock on their way to salvation. On this path they stayed—according to Rapp's own interpretation of the numbers in the biblical passage—one 'time' in Germany, then two 'times' and half a 'time' in the American wilderness. The first 'time' spent back in Germany must have begun in 1794–1795 when Rapp's group was organized. Although there is no documentary evidence to fix a certain date for the founding of his group, the first pastoral letter of Rapp issued to

---

[16] Hermann Ehmer, 'Die pietistische Rußlandwanderung und der fromme Zar Alexander I', in *Zar Alexander I. von Russland und das Königreich Württemberg. Familienbande, Staatspolitik und Auswanderung vor 200 Jahren* (Stuttgart: Haus der Heimat des Landes Baden-Württemberg, 2006), pp. 64–74.

[17] On discussion of emigration in Württemberg in this time, see Eberhard Fritz, *Radikaler Pietismus*, pp. 203–8.

his followers dates from 1794. By this time, his group must have been formalized to a certain extent. The two 'times' spent in America started with the arrival of Rapp's followers there and were marked by the founding of the Harmony Society on 15 February 1805. The future history of the Harmony Society shows that, according to Rapp, one biblical 'time' in Revelation amounted to 10 years. So the beginning of the Millennium would be in 1829, when the two and a half times would be up.

But just who were the people who followed Rapp to America? The best and earliest source for the names of the members of the Harmony Society is the so-called Jefferson Petition addressed in 1804 to President Thomas Jefferson by the newly arrived followers of Rapp asking for a grant of land to establish a settlement. This petition was signed by 202 men. These men were heads of families and therefore the Jefferson Petition is one of the few clues to the approximate number of persons belonging to what soon became the Harmony Society. This number would be around 800 if a family had an average of four members. Indeed, one of the early visitors to the first Harmony settlement in Western Pennsylvania, John Melish, counted about 800 inhabitants in 1811.[18]

The Jefferson Petition consists only of signed names without giving the places where these people came from. But by comparing these names with a list of Württemberg Separatists it is possible to identify almost three quarters, namely 145 of 202, of the people represented by the signatures.[19] These 145 people and their families came from 42 different villages in Württemberg. This proves that George Rapp had connections across the country, not only in and around Iptingen but also in villages far away. Looking at the villages with three or more followers of Rapp, a picture becomes quite clear. There were three different centres of Rapp's influence: Iptingen and its vicinity; the Remstal, a valley east of Stuttgart, and lastly the border of the Swabian Jura facing the Neckar River. Undoubtedly, Rapp was known across an extensive region, and the people who followed him to America lived within a journey of up to two days' distance. They sold all their possessions and moved to America with Rapp, believing that they were evading the divine judgement about to fall on Europe.

---

[18] Melish's description has been reprinted as John Melish, *Harmony in 1811 from Travels in the United States of America* (Harmony, PA: Historic Harmony, 2003).

[19] Eberhard Fritz, *Separatistinnen und Separatisten in Württemberg und in angrenzenden Territorien. Ein biographisches Verzeichnis* (Stuttgart: Verein für Familienkunde und Wappenkunde in Württemberg und Baden, 2005).

HARMONY IN PENNSYLVANIA

The new village founded in Pennsylvania on 15 February 1805 was called Harmonie—Harmony in English—and its inhabitants called themselves the Harmoniegesellschaft (the Harmony Society).[20] The name Harmony refers to the communal ownership of all goods in primitive Christianity as described in Acts 4:32. The groups of Württembergers who set out for Transcaucasia in 1816 and 1817 would similarly call themselves 'Harmonies' and pooled their money in order to cover the expenses for the journey.

The geographic situation of Harmony in a loop of the Connoquenessing River where a road crossed the river on a ford resembled very much the landscape back home. There were even hills where vineyards could be planted in terraces just like in Württemberg (see Fig. 5.2). Three hamlets surrounding Harmony today reveal the place names the settlers brought with them. One is Oilbraun (*Ölbronn*) east of Harmony on the Little Connoquenessing, the name of the village north of Pforzheim where the largest group of the signers of the Jefferson Petition came from. The second hamlet is Ramsthal (*Remstal*), north of Harmony across the Connoquenessing, named after the valley east of Stuttgart where further settlers came from. A third German placename southeast of Harmony at the Connoquenessing is Eidenau, which may be a corruption of *Ödenau*, but otherwise does not seem to refer to a specific place in Württemberg.

It has sometimes been asked why Rapp and his people did not just sit down and wait for whatever was to come? Some simply suggest that the Harmonists were not the kind of people to sit down, but had to stay busy. This is to forget, however, that the Harmonists believed that the second coming of Christ meant the beginning of the Millennium. Likely influenced by Johann Friedrich Oetinger's work, especially his *The Golden Age*, Rapp linked the Millennium to complete transformation of the whole world, and yet recognized the possibility of preparing now for the perfection to come in the Millennium.

It was widely believed that there would be no private property in the Millennium. Introducing the general ownership of all goods in the present would prepare for this state of things. This is exactly what the Harmony

---

[20] A recent overview of the Harmonist settlements in America is given in Eberhard Fritz, *Radikaler Pietismus*, pp. 208–30.

Fig. 5.2 One of the original houses at Harmony, built in 1809. Once a store, now a museum. Courtesy of the author

Society did on their founding day in 1805. They wrote down everything that each person had given to the common funds in a book (later burned controversially in 1818). It was also believed that there would be no marriage in the Millennium, so why not now 'live as the angels of God in heaven' (Matt. 22:30)? Rapp had advocated abstention from sex even within marriage since 1785. Full celibacy was eventually recommended for his Harmony Society in 1808, and from then on celibacy was a common feature of the Society until its very end.

It is worth acknowledging that general ownership of goods was not unfamiliar to these people, given the Württemberg traditions of communal grazing grounds for cattle and communal woods from where every household received its yearly share of fuel. A communal baking oven or communal kitchen was not unknown to a German villager, and for a feast such as a wedding the whole village would gather. With this background it would arguably not have been difficult to convince every member of the Harmony Society to extend communal ownership to other worldly possessions. It may also be speculated that a group of people transported to a new and unfamiliar environment would tend to close ranks even more.

Celibacy was notably not Rapp's own idea, but reflected a long tradition in elements of Pietism, starting with Jakob Böhme, who taught that the existence of the two sexes was a result of Adam's Fall. Böhme's belief in an original androgynous Adam, who carried both the masculine and the feminine principle, is touched on in several chapters of the present volume.[21] By forming Eve out of Adam's rib, Böhme believed the masculine and the feminine had been separated, and the salvation or restoration of man would involve the reunification of the two principles in humanity.

Böhme ascribed an androgynous character not only to Adam, the original man, but also to God. Böhme's theology remained trinitarian, holding that God was one in the Father, the Son and the Holy Spirit. But for Böhme this was not a static situation but a dynamic process. God the Father is forever giving birth to the Son, which means that the fiery wrath of God is converted into the warmth of love. The third principle in God, according to Böhme, is God revealed. Influentially for a variety of mystical traditions in Pietism, Böhme's teachings also referred to the heavenly Sophia. Sophia did not belong to the Trinity, but she is the power that goes out of God, the personification of God's wisdom. Böhme's speculation about Sophia or Wisdom was drawn from specific references in Scripture, for example in Ecclesiastes, but was also imagined to be the feminine principle in God. This meant that God was also androgynous like the original Adam. The virgin Sophia became the bride of the man that aspires to mystical unification with God. Böhme thus created a mystical veneration of a heavenly virgin Sophia.

Some of Böhme's followers thought that having or hoping to have Sophia as a bride excluded marriage. Böhme himself did not think so, as he was married and had children. Another later Pietist follower of Böhme, Gottfried Arnold (1666–1714), published in 1700 a book entitled *Das Geheimnis der göttlichen Sophia oder Weisheit* (The Mystery of the Divine Sophia or Wisdom). Arnold was an ardent worshipper of the heavenly Sophia. In his book, he maintained that nothing was comparable to the love of Sophia, not even carnal love. Yet Arnold was married, much to the disappointment of his contemporary Johann Georg Gichtel (1638–1710), another follower of Böhme, who influenced the founder the Ephrata community, Conrad Beissel. Gichtel himself tried to live up to Böhme's ideas

[21] See pp. 22 and 47.

by rejecting marriage. A real Christian, Gichtel said, would not live as a sexual being, but imitate Adam before his fall, and prepare for their restored life and body in the future millennial age. In the Millennium, the real Christian would experience a spiritual marriage with the heavenly virgin Sophia. Like Beissel and the Ephrata community, we know that Rapp and his followers read the works of Böhme and Gichtel, with the additional influence of Arnold.

Efforts to improve all aspects of human life in preparation for the Millennium also shaped economic activities. There are quite a few reports from contemporaries about the Society's economic progress and achievements. The most widely read was by John Melish, who visited Harmony in 1811 and printed his report in his *Travels in the United States* in Philadelphia in 1812.[22] Melish found Harmony a self-sustaining community of some 800 people, which did not rely only on agriculture but had taken to cloth-making as well. In 1811 the Harmonists were on the verge of becoming an industrial community.

About a thousand sheep grazed on the pastures of Harmony and the wool from these sheep was transformed into cloth by the community. Flax grown by the Harmonists was similarly turned into linen. As members of the Harmony Society possessed everything in common, and possessed the skills among themselves both to grow and work these materials, they naturally took responsibility for every step of the manufacturing of both woollen and linen cloth within their community. This way the added value of each step of the manufacturing process stayed inside the community. By a stroke of good fortune, the Harmony Society hit upon precisely the right moment to undertake cloth production in the United States, because imports from England—the main source of manufactured cloth for Americans—were hindered by the Napoleonic wars in Europe and later by the War of 1812. The restrictions on free commerce across the ocean before 1815 served the early prosperity of the Harmony Society.

According to John Melish there were a variety of other tradesmen practising in the community such as shoemakers, tailors, saddlers, smiths, cabinet-makers, carpenters and soap- and candle-makers. These artisans made the community self-sustaining. The Society even had their own doctor, who tended a herbal garden for medicinal purposes. Although everybody called him Doctor Christoph Müller, he was not a university-trained

---

[22] John Melish, *Harmony in 1811*.

physician, but had acquired his medical knowledge as an apprentice much like other tradesmen.

The traced list of Württemberg Separatists yields the professions of at least 66 people who came to Harmony. Fourteen of them were farmers, ten vinedressers, eleven weavers, seven shoemakers, while others had professions to be found in any Württemberg village at that time: blacksmith, cooper, cartwright, tailor, baker and barber. The type of small-scale farming which had developed because of land-holding patterns in Württemberg forced people to have a trade as a sideline, or the other way round: a man working at a profession would have to do some farming to be able to sustain a family when business was slow. It was just this combination of people of all trades which led to the economic success of Harmony, aided significantly by the contemporary political situation which shut off the United States from the English cloth supply, so boosting the domestic market for Harmony cloth.

In 1815, Eusebius Böhm drew a map of Harmony naming the head of household in each house—a total of 97 names (see Fig. 5.3).[23] This was 11 years after the signing of the Jefferson Petition, and only 50 of those 97 names were on the original petition. This reveals that there was some turnover in the Harmony population over these 11 years, for the inscription on the entrance of the Harmony cemetery refers to about a hundred people being buried there. Of the 97 heads of household, it is possible to identify the home towns of just over half. They came from 21 different places in Württemberg. Evidently, some new persons had come from the old country and joined the Society, while others had passed away or left the Society. These few newcomers made it to Harmony even in a time when Napoleon's closing of the continent made trans-Atlantic emigration from Europe to America almost impossible.

The Harmony Society was self-sustaining in its religious life. Its undisputed spiritual leader was George Rapp. John Melish reported attending a church service directed by Rapp. Melish's description makes clear it resembled the Lutheran church services back home in Rapp's native Württemberg.

Most members of the Harmony Society had little connection with the outside world, probably only meeting strangers occasionally—those who happened on the community's land by chance, or visited on purpose such as John Melish and a few others interested in reporting their impressions of Harmony. Friedrich Reichert, the adopted son of George Rapp (and

---

[23] This 1815 map survives in the Old Economy Archives, Ambridge, Pennsylvania.

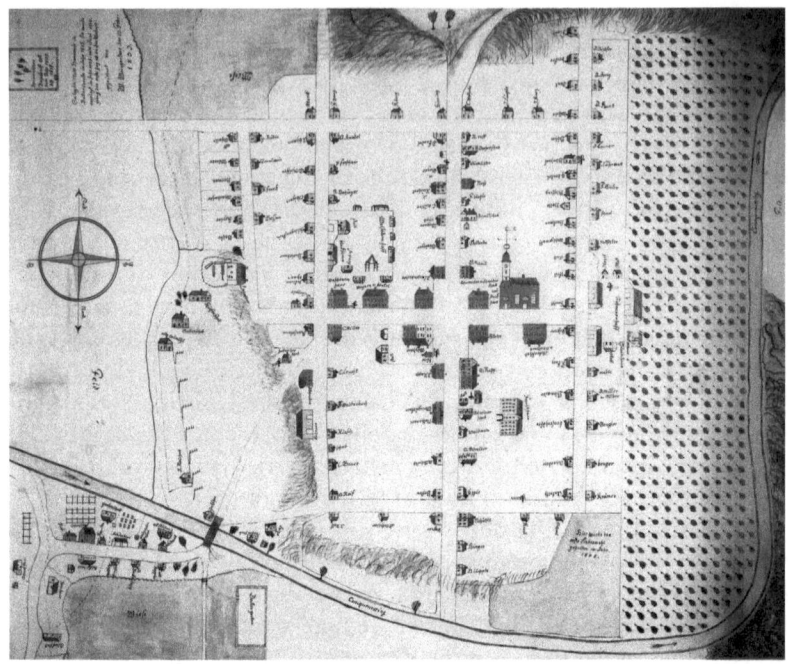

Fig. 5.3 Map of Harmony, Pennsylvania (*c*.1815). Courtesy of Old Economy Archives, Ambridge, PA

commonly known as Frederick Rapp), was the person who handled the relations of the Society with the outside world.

Within a couple of years, the Harmonists had built their first village and after ten years left it. They sold Harmony, Pennsylvania, to a Mennonite. One of the stipulations of the sale was that the buyer had to keep the cemetery. This remains an area outside the village with a stone wall around it, and a peculiar revolving door made of a slab of stone. Of the one hundred people buried here, the grave of Rapp's only son is the only one marked.

New Harmony in Indiana

The Harmony Society moved from Pennsylvania to Indiana. On the Wabash River, they founded another village also called Harmonie, today New Harmony. The only advantage to the new place was that it could be reached quite comfortably by boat. Otherwise the place offered great hardships, the swampy land breeding disease, which caused many deaths. In spite of these problems the Society succeeded in building an improved Harmony and making it a quite comfortable place. The first church they built replicated the one back in the first Harmony. In 1822 they commenced a new, grander church shaped like a cross with a cupola on it.

There exists a map of New Harmony drawn by Walrat Weingärtner in 1832, seven years after the Harmonists had left the town.[24] Weingärtner's map gives the names of 131 heads of household, among them some women, though half a dozen of the names can not be read due to damage. The plan shows that in New Harmony only about 50 family names are consistent with the Böhm map of the first Harmony. This is significant proof that new people had joined the Society in the meantime, but it is impossible to give an estimate of the turnover that took place in the Harmonist group across this period. A further difference is demonstrated in the new map: the plan of Harmony in Pennsylvania shows only individual homes, while the plan of New Harmony has four community houses, which were meant to house single people. This signifies the disintegration of family structure, probably due to the adoption of celibacy in 1808. The later plan also shows an expansion of manufacturing in Indiana, though the community's principal economy was still based on farming.

PIETIST SETTLEMENTS IN WÜRTTEMBERG: KORNTAL AND WILHELMSDORF

Back in Württemberg things had changed drastically with the rise of Napoleon.[25] Duke Frederick of Württemberg, who came to reign in 1797, was forced to ally with Napoleon in 1805 and became a member of the Rheinbund—the Federation of the Rhine—in 1806. Frederick was compensated with Imperial cities and several monasteries for his territorial losses on the left bank of the Rhine. He then absorbed the lands of some less powerful princes. In this way, Württemberg doubled in size and Napoleon promoted Duke Frederick to King Frederick. As an ally, Frederick had to raise troops for the French Emperor and remained loyal even after the great retreat from Russia in 1812. In order to raise troops

---

[24] This 1832 map is also stored in the Old Economy Archives, Ambridge, Pennsylvania.
[25] Bernhard Mann, 'Württemberg 1800 bis 1866', in *Handbuch der Baden-Württembergischen Geschichte*, 3:235–331, esp. pp. 235–62.

for Napoleon, King Frederick introduced conscription in 1806. To keep the conscripts in the country, emigration was forbidden. Rapp and his followers had therefore left just in time. They saw their beliefs confirmed by these turbulent events in Europe, and were probably glad that they had left the old country.

In Württemberg, it is clear that Rapp and his departing followers were not forgotten, but many were kept informed about Rapp's settlements in America. It was well known that Rapp exerted an absolute rule over his followers. Yet, there were still people who emigrated to join the Harmonists, especially when emigration became possible again after 1816. In 1817, an alternative Pietist tradition, the Separatists of Rottenacker in southern Württemberg, also crossed the Atlantic to found a communal society at Zoar in Ohio.[26] Similar reasons appear to have lain behind this emigration: the destabilizing effects of the wars with Napoleon meant their separatist civil disobedience remained a serious offence in Württemberg. Such offences included using the common 'Du' as an address for superiors and not lifting one's hat for persons of authority. Those who tried to evade conscription in order not to fight Napoleon's wars also suffered years in jail and forced labour. When the ban on emigration from Württemberg was lifted, the Rottenacker Separatists left—the same year as the extensive migration east to Transcaucasia.

It was the larger emigration to Russia in particular which bred the idea of erecting an independent community for Pietists in Württemberg. This was Korntal, a few kilometres outside Stuttgart, founded in 1819. By the privileges granted by King Wilhelm I (1816–1864) this community was independent from the state church. Michael Hahn was supposed to move there as a spiritual leader, but he died the same year Korntal started. Gottlieb Wilhelm Hoffmann (1771–1846) who had suggested the idea of Korntal then became the secular head of the village. Württemberg law did not permit the same realization of communal ownership of all goods that was possible in America, so a Society for buying land (Güterkaufsgesellschaft) was founded, which allotted shares to the members of the community. It was soon clear that living on an agricultural basis was unsustainable for the size of community, so very soon institutions were founded for orphans and disabled people as well as boarding schools. These institutions created income and jobs for the new community.

---

[26] Eberhard Fritz, *Radikaler Pietismus*, pp. 164–86, 233–8.

When requests were made to the King and Württemberg government for more settlements like Korntal, they hesitated, and eventually consented only if a new settlement would improve the country. Wilhelmsdorf in southern Württemberg was founded in 1824, where a swampy area was drained for arable land. The settlement at Wilhelmsdorf is laid out in a cruciform shape. In the middle there is the four-sided meeting hall (*Betsaal*) with a cupola. This building looks strikingly like the second church in New Harmony. While the Betsaal in Wilhelmsdorf still exists, the church in New Harmony was later torn down and the bricks used to build a wall around the Harmonist cemetery. The resemblance between the second church in New Harmony and the Betsaal in Wilhelmsdorf suggests some contact between the two settlements of Württemberg Pietism. However, the cultivated land did not yield much and Wilhelmsdorf lived through years of difficulty before institutions and schools like those in Korntal could be founded.[27]

ECONOMY IN PENNSYLVANIA

The new church with the cupola in New Harmony, Indiana, was not quite finished when in 1824 the Harmony Society packed up again. They sold their second settlement to Robert Owen, who was planning to set up a community there according to his own vision. The people of the Harmony Society moved back to Pennsylvania. Here they founded Ökonomie (Economy) just north of Pittsburgh on the Ohio, their third and last home. The name Economy meant God's economy, or the divine way of salvation, which was supposed to come true in this location with the people of Harmony Society. Here they waited for the consummation of all things around the middle of September 1829. While they were waiting they set up yet another flourishing community (see Fig. 5.4).

September 1829 arrived, and at first nothing spectacular happened. Then on 24 September a letter came from one mysterious Count Leon, who called himself the Lion of Judah and the Anointed of God, announcing he would visit Economy. The identity of this self-appointed Count

---

[27] For more on these German communities, see Johannes Hesse, *Korntal einst und jetzt* (Stuttgart: Gundert, 1910); Andreas Bühler (ed.), *175 Jahre Wilhelmsdorf. Festschrift. Beiträge zur Geschichte und Gegenwart* (Wilhelmsdorf: Gemeinde Wilhelmsdorf, 1999); Eberhard Fritz, *Radikaler Pietismus*, pp. 247–54.

Fig. 5.4 George Rapp's house at Economy, where he died in 1847. Courtesy of the author

Leon, who came from Frankfurt-am-Main in Germany, is still disputed.[28] At any rate he let the Harmony Society wait for him quite a while. In 1831 he duly arrived and began to contest Father Rapp's authority. This caused a split in the Society. One third of the membership went over to Count Leon and left Economy with him to settle across the Ohio to found a new settlement called Phillipsburgh, renamed Lionsburgh (today called Monaca). The secessionists, adopting the name of the New Philadelphia Society, wanted their share of the Harmony Society's wealth and succeeded in obtaining some after this case was settled in court.

George Rapp overcame this crisis—the most significant of his career. After this, his authority remained uncontested up to his death on 7 August 1847. Rapp continued to claim he was setting up God's own people to be ready for the Millennium to come. But Christ did not come in 1829, or after. How did Rapp explain this to his followers? They had trusted in Rapp's calculations back in Europe and given up almost everything to follow them. And now their expectations proved to be wrong.

---

[28] The most recent study on this topic is Eileen Aiken English, 'The Life and Legacy of Count Leon—the Man who Cleft the Harmonie', *Communal Societies: The Journal of the Communal Studies Association*, 34 (2013), 45–82.

Rapp had little difficulty in explaining what had happened. It could be found in the Scriptures, yet again in Revelation 12, verse 3, where a red dragon appeared 'having seven heads and ten horns and seven crowns on his head'. Rapp pointed out that this clearly referred to Count Leon, a man with many names and titles. And this dragon's tail—so the passage in Revelation continues—'drew the third part of the stars of heaven and did cast them to the earth'. This third of the stars was nothing else but the third of the Harmonists who had gone with Count Leon across the Ohio waiting for their share of the Society's wealth. As long as the Harmony Society was threatened by Count Leon and his New Philadelphia Society from across the Ohio it was relatively easy for Rapp to keep his flock together.

However, the New Philadelphia Society dissolved in August 1833, and most of Count Leon's seceders moved away to Louisiana. With this challenge resolved, the question as to why Rapp's calculation proved to be wrong reappeared. Rapp clearly overcame this situation, but we do not yet know how. Rapp's sermons from the time, which remain unstudied in the Harmony Society's archives in Economy, may still offer a solution to this question.

From the late 1820s and long after, thriving Economy was a point of interest for travellers from Europe, including Paul, Duke of Württemberg, the economist Friedrich List and the poet Nikolaus Lenau, who spent two months in Economy. Frederick Rapp—Rapp's adopted son who managed the Society's relations to the outside world—died in 1838. Two trustees took Frederick's place. The prosperity of the Harmony Society grew even more during the industrialization of the Ohio Valley, with the growth of the steel industry, the building of railroads and the discovery of oil.[29] The Society spent some of its riches on similar communities. They helped the Hutterites with their emigration from Russia to North America, they supported the Shakers and Community of True Inspiration at Amana and they also aided the Temple Society of Württemberg with their emigration to Palestine and settlement building there.

The Society slowly died out, despite accepting some newcomers and adopting orphans over the years.[30] The race for the inheritance of the

---

[29] The classic description of Economy in its later years was by Charles Nordhoff, first published in 1875, reprinted as Charles Nordhoff, *The Communistic Societies of the United States from Personal Visit and Observation* (New York: Dover, 1966), pp. 63–95.

[30] A meritorious magnum opus is Eileen Aiken English, *Demographic Directory of the Harmony Society* (American Communal Societies Series 4; Clinton, NY: Richard W. Couper Press, 2011).

Harmony Society was won by the musician John Duss, who entered the Society together with his wife. The Society was legally disbanded in 1905. A lawsuit between Duss and the Commonwealth of Pennsylvania ended in 1916 with an agreement that the state receive the centre of the town, whereas Duss receive the considerable rest. It was not until the 1950s that Economy became a tourist attraction. Today visitors are principally drawn to experience how people lived two centuries ago without the amenities of present-day life.

CONCLUSION

The Harmony Society was a genuine offspring of Württemberg's separatist Pietism. George Rapp and his followers made the apocalyptic theology of Bengel and Oetinger their own: they believed that the beginning of the Millennium would bring the day of judgement, and so, according to Scripture, it was necessary to find a safe haven. Emigration was therefore for the members of the Harmony Society a necessary part of the apocalyptic drama which had begun with the turmoil in Europe triggered by the French Revolution. For this reason, it was not religious persecution which caused these Pietists to leave their country and find a new home in America, as some have assumed. The few fines and a single night of arrest in the village prison which Rapp personally endured occasionally, together with some of his followers, was notably not for their religion but for their civil disobedience. It was religious ideas which principally influenced this Protestant trans-Atlantic migration. It was the same ideas, including beliefs about life in the coming Millennium, which combined with their experience of German collectivist village life to produce their communal ownership of goods.

Others who believed in Bengel's millennial calculations for 1836 stayed in their native Württemberg. They experienced the calming down of the situation in Europe after Napoleon's final defeat in 1815. For them the safe haven was Korntal beginning in 1819 and Wilhelmsdorf beginning in 1824. Of course, these Pietists also had finally to overcome the fact that Christ did not come for a second time in 1836. The explanation given at this point was, in broad terms, that it was not time yet, but time to try to make the world a better place by all kinds of activities. This is how Korntal and Wilhelmsdorf have survived to the present as living communities, whereas the settlements of the Harmony Society have been turned into open-air museums.

In Harmony, New Harmony and Economy, the history of the Harmony Society is just one period of the overall history of the towns. It is somewhat similar to ancient Troy where one stratum is covered by others. This is most obvious in New Harmony where the ten years of the Harmony Society are covered up by the Owen tradition. The Owen family, which still owns parts of the town, was, and still is, successful in making New Harmony a centre for numerous cultural activities. At the local museum called the Atheneum, built by the architect Richard Meier, the period of the Harmony Society is visualized by a model of the town according to the plan of 1824. In Harmony, Pennsylvania, a private association, 'Historic Harmony', cares for local history by maintaining a museum in the Society's old store building, organizes activities throughout the year and tries to convince the private owners of historical buildings to preserve them as monuments. Economy is now part of Ambridge, named after the American Bridge Company. This company and the other steel producers in the town brought immigrants from southern and eastern Europe into the area in the twentieth century. Of course these people and their descendants have no ties to the history of the Harmony Society, a situation intensified by the rapid decrease of the steel industry in the Ohio Valley. Yet state-operated Old Economy was able to build a tourist centre with staff and volunteers to care for the grounds, a museum and the archives. The records and papers of the Harmony Society have been moved from the Harrisburg State Archives back to Old Economy and remain there at the disposal of any researcher interested in the history of this example of trans-Atlantic Protestant communalism—so long as they can overcome the trans-Atlantic language barrier.

CHAPTER 6

The Trans-Atlantic Odyssey of the Community of True Inspiration, 1714–1850

Peter Hoehnle

The Community of True Inspiration, whose adherents are known as 'Inspirationists', was founded in 1714 by radical Pietists in the Wetterau region of Hessen in central Germany. The Inspirationists grounded their belief structure in the Pietist tradition while, significantly, embracing the concept of modern-day inspiration through chosen instruments, or *Werkzeuge*. Their prophetic beliefs were linked to developments among the French Camisards as early as 1688, the so-called 'French Prophets' in London, and related missionary activity in the German states in the early 1710s.

The tradition declined for an extended period following the death of its final eighteenth-century *Werkzeug*, Johann Friedrich Rock; yet it experienced an unexpected revival in Germany after 1817, largely directed by a new *Werkzeug*, Christian Metz. Seeking to overcome the increasingly difficult political and economic situation of the scattered Inspirationist communities in the 1820s, Metz assembled the faithful on leased estates in the relatively liberal province of Hessen. On these estates, the Inspirationists

P. Hoehnle
Amana Church Society, Amana, Iowa, USA

© The Editor(s) (if applicable) and The Author(s) 2016   133
P. Lockley (ed.), *Protestant Communalism in the Trans-Atlantic World, 1650–1850*, DOI 10.1057/978-1-137-48487-1_6

developed common industries, a unified system of governance, a limited common purse and a shared sense of living within a *Gemeinde* (community) separated from the world.

In 1842, Metz led the Inspirationists to the United States, where around one thousand of them established the Eben-Ezer Society on a communally owned tract of land near Buffalo, New York. The encroachment of external 'worldly' influences on this community soon led Metz to direct a complete relocation to a 26,000-acre tract in east central Iowa. Here the Inspirationists established seven villages with farms, craft shops and industries which maintained the economic, social and religious vitality of the Society until 1932, when the membership elected to cease communal life. Since this date, a joint stock corporation has continued to maintain the economic interests of the group, and the separate Amana Church Society has directed religious affairs. Together, this American corporation and religious society maintain an unbroken thread back to the European origins of the Inspirationists and their shared, yet still evolving, bond of community.

The religious origins, doctrines and practices of the Inspirationists, including communal living, were all established prior to the sect's migration across the Atlantic to the New World. The common narrative of Inspirationist history suggests that communal living was initially adopted as an economic expedient, possibly influenced by contact with the Society of Separatists of Zoar, Ohio. In reality, the Inspirationists moved along an axis of communalism extending from their leased estates in Hessen to Eben-Ezer, New York and, finally, to Iowa. At each stage of this migration westward, the Inspirationists adapted their communal arrangement, steadily tightening the bonds of communal life and maintaining those bonds until 1932, when they were relaxed—a change which for the first time represented a direct influence of American culture and practice upon the social relations of the sect. Theologically, the influence of American culture was much later, not making its full appearance until the 1960s. Thus, the Inspirationists' communal tradition was German and European in its origin and practice.

BEGINNINGS

The Inspirationist movement essentially began with the rise of the French Huguenot mystic Camisards in 1688. In that year, dozens of individuals, primarily children, began to deliver prophetic utterances within the beleaguered Protestant communities of the Cevennes Mountains in France. The prophetic, millennial and even militant proclamations of these prophets ultimately inspired the armed revolt of the Camisards from 1702 to 1710. Following the rebellion, three of the more notable Camisard prophets, Elie Marion, Durand Fage and Jean Cavalier, migrated to London where they again proclaimed their prophetic messages.[1]

Although attracting a following in England, the prophets attempted to return their message to the continental milieu from which it had initially sprung. A missionary journey by prophets Elie Marion and Jean Allut to Holland, Germany and Austria was followed by a second in 1712 that took the prophets through Sweden and into Poland, where they were imprisoned for several months under suspicion of being spies. After this, they travelled back into the German states. During this second journey, the prophets spent 4 weeks in Halle, the centre of the German Pietist movement, and home to its leading spokesman, August Hermann Francke. Here, the prophets were observed by the brothers Johann Tobias, August Friedrich and Johann Heinrich Pott.

Soon after the prophets departed Halle, the three Potts began to deliver testimonies of their own, typically accompanied by a period of glossolalia-like 'trumpeting', trembling and shaking, followed by the testimony, often delivered while the speaker was exhibiting wild physical movements and speaking in a thunderous voice. The Potts made a missionary expedition to Berlin and, in late 1714, began a tour of the Wetterau region of Hessen, an area that had become a refuge for Separatists—those Protestant groups that believed in independent gathered worship, frequently founded on a claimed experience of the Holy Spirit, and not a state-directed church assembly. Hessen's liberality in religious matters was largely due to the personal or pragmatic views of its governing nobles: they were either sympathetic to the teachings and plight of Separatists, or they saw a policy of religious toleration as a practical means of repopulating a region still reeling from the severe trauma of the Thirty Years War. One of these princes, Count Ernest Casimir of Ysenburg-Büdingen, issued a proclamation of tolerance in 1711. The four small states north and west of Frankfurt, including that controlled by Ysenburg-Büdingen, were collectively known

---

[1] The principal source on the French Prophets is Hillel Schwartz, *The French Prophets* (Berkeley: University of California Press, 1980). The connection between the French Prophets and the Inspirationists is most thoroughly explored in Clarke Garrett, *Origins of the Shakers* (Baltimore: Johns Hopkins University Press, 1998; first published 1987).

as 'the Wetterau', and enjoyed complete religious toleration to a degree unknown in the other German states. Clarke Garrett notes that the influx of Anabaptists, Waldensians, Philadelphians, Huguenots and others created a diversity of religious practice and belief in the Wetterau that rivalled that of the English Puritan Commonwealth.[2]

Among the Separatists attracted to the Count's region as a result of this proclamation were Eberhard Ludwig Gruber and Johann Friedrich Rock. Gruber received a theological education at the University of Tübingen and served as a Lutheran clergyman until his radical Pietist leanings led to his dismissal. Rock, the son of a Lutheran clergyman, was a spiritually inclined saddle-maker who, with his mentor Gruber, settled in the tiny village of Himbach.

The arrival of the Inspired Pott brothers and their associate Johanna Margaretha Melchoir in the region created great excitement. Gruber initially opposed this ecstatic religious movement, but a visit by the Inspirationists to Gruber's home on 15 November 1714 convinced him that the word as proclaimed by these *Werkzeuge* was genuine. Accordingly, Gruber organized a small meeting of his separatists neighbours on 16 November, the date commonly accepted as the founding of what came to be called 'the Community of True Inspiration'. Once converted, Gruber became the main apologist for the Inspirationist movement, which grew rapidly. Within a short time, several new *Werkzeuge*, including Gruber's own son Johann Adam, and Johann Friedrich Rock, began to deliver testimonies of their own.

The sudden religious activity in Himbach—specifically the missionary activity in violation of an Edict of Tolerance granted in Ysenburg in 1712—led to the expulsion of Gruber and his flock from the area in March 1715. Gruber settled in Schwarzenau, a community which, just a few years previous, had witnessed the formation of the Church of the Brethren by Alexander Mack. During the following decades, Inspirationist *Werkzeuge* engaged in repeated and far-ranging missionary journeys. After 1719, Rock emerged as the sole remaining prophet of the movement and, in this capacity, undertook 94 visitational journeys throughout southern Germany, Saxony, Alsace Lorraine and Switzerland, typically travelling on foot for months at a time. His constant mobility led Rock to sometimes refer to himself as 'Im Fort-während Reisen'—'always on the road'.[3]

---

[2] Garrett, *Origins of the Shakers*, p. 67.

[3] Douglas H. Shantz, *An Introduction to German Pietism: Protestant Renewal at the Dawn of Modern Europe* (Baltimore: Johns Hopkins University Press, 2013), p. 167.

The Inspirationists of this period conceived of themselves as associated conventicles, groups of believers emphasizing fellowship and the priesthood of all believers. Johann Heinrich Reitz, a fellow radical Pietist and proponent of the conventicle model, suggested that such groups permitted the faithful to teach, instruct, train, admonish, discipline and comfort one another in love, humility and submission.[4] Gruber, in particular, wrote against the establishment of formalized sects. During his lifetime and for nearly a century following his death, the Inspirationists remained a peripatetic, loosely organized series of widely separated conventicles, united both through shared belief and by the regular visits conducted by Johann Friedrich Rock and his associates. The Inspirationist conventicles represented a reimagined form of religious community, one that existed without the formality and strictures of the established church or of a formalized sect.

Under Rock's direction, the movement expanded, and several scattered centres of Inspirationism emerged. The principle centre of the movement returned to the Wetterau and more specifically to the Castle Ronneburg, a dilapidated mediaeval fortress owned by Count Ysenburg-Büdingen and rented as a refuge to a diverse assemblage of separatists, gypsies and Jews. In 1737, Count Nikolaus von Zinzendorf temporarily occupied the Ronneburg with his Moravian followers (the *Unitas Fratrum*) before relocating, first to the leased estate of Marienborn and then to their Herrnhaag, a complex constructed by the Moravians to represent the New Jerusalem and to serve as a centre for education and missionary activity.[5] Ultimately, the Moravians in this region were forced to leave, and many migrated to their settlements in the American colonies. A brief period of friendly relations with the neighbouring Inspirationists led to serious discussion of a merging of the two sects, the mirror to Zinzendorf's attempts to unite the Ephrata community and other traditions in Pennsylvania in this period.[6] However, the discussion in Europe ended acrimoniously (like in Pennsylvania), with Rock denouncing Zinzendorf, and Zinzendorf remaining unreconciled to the validity of Rock's prophetic utterances.

After 1742, Rock retired from his missionary expeditions and received the faithful at his home within the ruins of the Barbarossa castle in the middle of the Kinzig River at Gelnhausen. Here, Rock died in 1749, after which a series of strong elders, most notably his scribe Paul G. Nagel and

---

[4] Shantz, *Introduction to German Pietism*, p. 155.
[5] Moravian communalism was discussed further in Chap. 2, pp. 18–20.
[6] See Chap. 3, pp. 59–60

Jonas Wickmark, maintained the movement. With the eventual death of these and other leaders, the Inspirationist movement began to decline rapidly towards extinction.

REVIVAL AND COMMUNITY CONSOLIDATION

In 1817 a journeyman tailor, Michael Kraussert, professed the gift of Inspiration and, after meeting Inspirationist elder Wilhelm Nordmann, presented himself to the remaining Inspirationists as a new *Werkzeug*. While some Inspirationist congregations accepted Kraussert, others refused to acknowledge him. Barbara Heinemann, an illiterate maid, likewise divided opinion at this point, when her inspiration was recognized by some in the movement. Christian Metz, a young carpenter who had lived with his family within the Inspirationist stronghold of the Ronneburg Castle, was among those who accepted Kraussert. With the cooperation of his close friend Wilhelm Mörschel and others, Metz held Inspirationist services centred on the youth living at the Ronneburg. Soon, Metz himself began to speak 'in Inspiration'. When Kraussert fell from grace and left, Heinemann was initially the primary leader. Yet her decision to marry and subsequent apparent loss of the gift of Inspiration meant it was Metz who emerged as the leading *Werkzeug* after 1823.[7]

In the early years of his leadership, Metz continued the pattern of visitational journeys to the Inspirationist communities in the Wetterau and Alsace, delivering, on average, 39 testimonies per year, with a pastoral message focused on conversion, humility and repentance.[8] As in the eighteenth century, the Inspirationist message appealed mostly to members of the labouring and artisan classes, typically living in townships or small urban settings.[9] These artisans were confronted with the dislocation of the German economy and its social system wrought by the tumultuous Napoleonic invasions, then developing industrialization, both of which

---

[7]The backgrounds of the later generation of *Werkzeuge* are discussed in Jonathan G. Andelson, 'Communalism and Change in the Amana Society, 1855–1932' (PhD thesis, University of Michigan, 1974).

[8]This average is of the testimonies delivered between 1823 and 1830. For the 4 years beginning in 1826, Metz delivered a remarkably consistent number of messages, ranging from 47 to 53 per year.

[9]Andelson, 'Communalism and Change', p. 23.

destroyed much of the guild and village system that had shaped German life since the medieval period.

The Inspirationist congregations were groups of closely bound individuals, united by religious faith and the relentless opposition to their beliefs and practices faced from neighbours and officials. On 6 August 1821, the Edenkoben congregation agreed to a set of 20 rules governing the care of the sick and dying, funerals and burials. The rules indicated that an elder would appoint individuals to care for the sick, and otherwise codified a hierarchical relationship in which the individual was secondary to the community.[10] This relationship, in turn, replaced those of the village and church institutions and society from which the Inspirationists were now separated.

By the mid-1820s the political and economic circumstances confronted by the Inspirationists shifted further. Tighter restrictions from local governmental authorities placed heavy burdens on individual Inspirationist congregations. Finally, in early March 1826, the Inspirationists of Schwarzenau learned that they could either associate with the state church or emigrate from the region within six months, leading to months of uncertainty and turmoil.

On 20 May, while visiting the congregation of Edenkoben, Metz delivered a communication indicating relocation, not only for the Schwarzenau congregation but for other Inspirationist communities as well. Metz, writing in inspiration, proclaimed,

> Be comforted, My people, for I the Lord, the Almighty God, am with you and I have My work among you. My power and honour are wondrous. That which I begin, I shall bring to a glorious conclusion.
>
> Before this can occur, human wisdom and self-reliance must be overcome. The work shall then be recognized as being done by the wise and wondrous hand of God alone which is far beyond human comprehension. Then no mortal may proudly say; It is I who brought this or that about. For such would certainly devalue the power, wisdom and honour of your God ...
>
> Therefore, I proceed in wondrous ways, speaks your God. My ways are seldom openly seen. I shall establish My dwelling place in the depths and shall direct My path across great waters. I will prepare a place in the

[10] 'The 20 Rules and Laws, given as an appendix to the 24 rules', Translated by Magdalena Schuerer. Amana Heritage Society, Amana, Iowa, Nineteenth Century Manuscripts Collection, Folder 24.

wilderness and, where there was none, I will establish My dwelling place. I will alter My customs and My habitation. I shall bring all things to a wondrous conclusion, for I am a wondrous and all-wise God ...

I have yet other sheep, unknown to you, which I shall bring to be united with you, to become one in My Spirit. Consider this and take it to heart.[11]

The testimony further urged the faithful to submit to divine authority in humility and obedience.

Attempts by Metz to have other Inspirationist congregations absorb members from Schwarzenau failed. At this juncture, Metz learned that it would be possible to lease a portion of a Marienborn Estate in Ysenburg as a refuge. The Inspirationists were aided in the leasing of property belonging to the Meerholz jurisdiction due to the intercession of a sympathetic district magistrate in Büdingen. This complex of buildings represented the remains of a medieval cloister that had later been converted into a residence by an earlier Count of Ysenburg-Büdingen. In the 1730s, Marienborn had served as a locus for Zinzendorf and his followers before the building of nearby Herrnhaag, and was, in fact, where Zinzendorf was visited by a young John Wesley in 1738. The Schwarzenau congregations relocated to Marienborn by the Fall of 1826 and were soon joined by individual Inspirationists and families from other German states.

Although the Inspirationists had always conceived of themselves as a *Gemeinde*, or 'community' called from the world, and had lived in close relation to one another as at the Ronneburg Castle, the rental of Marienborn represented the first time in which members of the sect systematically relocated to form a community which, of necessity, required some sharing of resources.

As early as 1825, the congregation of Inspirationists at Bischweiler (Bischwiller in Alcase) had grown fearful of the loss of religious tolerance in their region. The congregation was investigated for conducting their own, uncertified schools and for assembling illegally. Authorities fined and jailed members, and otherwise ordered them to desist from continuing their prayer meetings and educational activities. A court decision decreed

---

[11] Christian Metz, 'Testimony No. 23, 20 May 1826', in *J.J.J.*[,] *Jahrbücher Der Wahren Inspirations Gemeinden ... Erste Sammlung* (Amana, IA: Amana Society, 1871), pp. 68–71. Translated by Janet W. Zuber.

that the Inspirationists could not assemble in groups larger than 20. As a result, the Bischweiler congregation appealed to the king of France:

> Our plea is that we, as faithful and willing servants of our beloved Fatherland, be allowed to earn our necessary daily bread in peace and safety. Additionally, though we are more than twenty persons, we ask to be allowed to assemble undisturbed while we strengthen one another in all that is good as we attempt to secure our salvation ...[12]

By May of 1828 conditions for the Bischweiler Inspirationists had deteriorated and Metz delivered a testimony declaring,

> The time will come, and it is not far distant, when I will remove My luminaries from there and put them in a different place. Eventually, I will gather all those who follow and remain true to Me. I will assemble them into one nation and into one flock. It is My desire to cast and spread My banner of Love over you as one nation and one flock belonging to the Lord ...[13]

During 1827, Inspirationists in Edenkoben, east of Heidelberg, found their freedom of religion curtailed and their ability to conduct their own school denied. The Inspirationists were fined for their refusal to send their children to public schools. Eventually, some families were unable to continue payment of these fines, and as a result surrendered possessions to government authorities. According to the Inspirationists' own chronicle, authorities entered homes to confiscate these items, principally wine, which were then auctioned, with the proceeds accepted in lieu of payment of the fine.

By March of 1828 the congregation at Edenkoben faced a similar ultimatum and was forced to relocate. Metz identified the remnants of the Herrnhaag complex as a new haven for the faithful. Leased from the Count of Ysenburg-Büdingen, whose family had taken possession of the settlement when the Moravians left in the 1750s, this estate was less than six km from the Ronneburg Castle. Only three of the large structures built by the Moravians remained by this time, the rest having fallen into ruin and utilized as a quarry by locals in the years since. In occupying Herrnhaag, the Inspirationists

---

[12] Quoted in Gottlieb Scheuner, *Inspirations Historie, 1817–1850: Or Historical Account of the New Awakening, Assembly and Establishment of the Community of True Inspiration in Germany through the Year 1850 Including the Emigration to America*, Trans. by Janet W. Zuber (Amana: Amana Church Society, 1987), p. 49.

[13] Metz, 'Testimony No. 181 Bischweiler, 10 May 1828', in *J.J.J.*, p. 313.

were, for the first time, moving into structures that had been planned and constructed for the very type of theocratic community life that they were now formulating. It seems likely that the carefully ordered structures of the Moravians had an impact on the development of Inspirationist communalism. The Inspirationists repaired and restored facilities at Herrnhaag prior to their occupation under the direction of Andreas Rockenbach, a trained mason.[14]

Herrnhaag experienced rapid growth, and was filled with Inspirationists by 1829. Among the residents of this estate (known among the Inspirationists simply as 'the Haag') were refugees from Edenkoben and Bergzabern and surrounding villages in the Palatinate (*Pfalz*) region (over 80 people) as well as individuals from Bischweiler and villages in Lorraine.[15]

Although the Inspirationists now ensconced at Marienborn and Herrnhaag were from particular congregations and had, in some cases, been neighbours and co-religionists for some time, the pressures of living within the confines of the estates proved difficult. These tensions were especially apparent at Marienborn where, the Inspirationist chronicle notes, '[t]he membership did not want to become submissive to the spiritual or Brotherly restraints and so they were often severely reprimanded through the Word [testimonies]'.[16]

The community of Herrnhaag, having experienced rapid growth, was not without its own concerns. Now living in the close confines of the stone dormitories at Herrnhaag, individuals also had to adjust to the trauma of relocation, abandoning property and being in regular and very close contact with others. Additionally, these members lived within property leased by the Inspirationist leaders and, as a result, were called upon to submit to their authority. As each estate filled to capacity with new arrivals, Inspirationists who had in some cases left behind comfortable homes now found themselves in cramped, less than adequate conditions. Writing of his family's early months at Herrnhaag, farmer Theobald Heimburger observed,

> We had … a good [experience] especially for the inner [spiritual], even if we did not have it quite so comfortable, outwardly, as at our home. We had to live on the third floor of a large house, and this was combined with burdens and troubles, but we never looked back.[17]

---

[14] Rockenbach was not only the first Inspirationist to occupy Herrnhaag, but also the first to die there, on 19 February 1830; Scheuner, *Inspirations Historie, 1817–1850*, p. 61.

[15] Scheuner, *Inspirations Historie, 1817–1850*, p. 59.

[16] Scheuner, *Inspirations Historie, 1817–1850*, p. 56.

[17] Theobald Heimburger, 'A short account by Theobald Heimburger at the time of the awakening concerning Godly leading and how he was drawn closer to God', trans. by

Problems with youth who were 'often thoughtless and disobedient' were frequently reported at Herrnhaag.[18] Perhaps unsurprisingly, concerns over the conduct of youth would remain a concern for Inspirationists throughout their time on the estates and, later, as a communal organization in the United States.

Repeated reprimands in the form of inspired testimonies spoken by Metz served to control dissention and mediate internal disputes, but did not end the struggles. In 1835, Metz proclaimed, in a testimony, that because of 'the wretched state' of the Marienborn congregation, a special covenanting service would be postponed. This proclamation stirred the congregation and after discussion the service was reinstated.[19]

Although from the beginning the estates were individually governed by elders appointed by Metz, it was not until early 1829 that Metz issued a testimony instructing these elders to meet with regularity to discuss 'various inner and outer concerns'.[20] Part of this governance involved conducting regular *Unterredungen* (confessional or spiritual examination services) in the various communities.

As the communities at Herrnhaag and Marienborn continued to fill with new arrivals, the Inspirationist hierarchy began to develop a small textile industry in order to provide poorer members with a form of livelihood. To this end, Elder Friedrich Heinemann was dispatched from Marienborn to Herrnhaag in order to begin a mechanized spinning operation there.

Expanding and Moving Communities

As the congregations scattered across German lands began to migrate to the new estates, Metz's attention was turned towards the remaining Inspirationists in Switzerland and in Saxony. In late August 1830, Metz and a travelling companion made an initial missionary journey to Switzerland. Although Johann Friedrich Rock had established several congregations in Switzerland in the early eighteenth century, contact between these Inspirationists and their counterparts in Hessen was non-existent. Metz travelled to Switzerland with no contacts and seemingly without a plan beyond visiting the descendants of the earlier Inspirationists. Metz and his

Magdalena Schuerer. Amana Heritage Society, Amana, Iowa, Nineteenth Century Manuscripts Collection. Heimburger's memoir was written shortly before his death in 1866.

[18] Scheuner, *Inspirations Historie, 1817–1850*, p. 90.

[19] Scheuner, *Inspirations Historie, 1817–1850*, p. 119.

[20] Scheuner, *Inspirations Historie, 1817–1850*, p. 57.

scribe, Martin Bender, first stopped at Thäingen and asked an innkeeper if there were individuals in that area who assembled for prayer meetings. The innkeeper directed them to a man named Ock who, fortunately, had been a member of the Inspirationists. During the Inspirationist reawakening of 1817–1818, opponents of Michael Kraussert had sent unfavourable reports to Switzerland which had deterred the Swiss Inspirationists from associating with the reawakened group led by Metz.

Metz made a positive impression on the Inspirationists in Ock's village and, from them, learned of Inspirationist contacts elsewhere in Switzerland, particularly at Gächlingen, which had the largest concentration of Swiss Inspirationists. Metz made eight return visits to Switzerland and summoned the faithful to relocate to the estates in Hessen. Entire congregations heeded the call and relocated. The message that Metz proclaimed, as summarized in the Inspirationist chronicle, was that it was now God's

> Holy will and decision to summon believing souls from various places and lead them to a common place. Such a unified people … [God] Himself through His Spirit would guide, direct and rule. Through them and with them, He would advance accomplishing greatly and mightily.[21]

The call to join the Community in Hessen, then, was not only an invitation to associate with like-minded believers in a liberal state with greater religious freedom, but to live in a community, often referenced by Metz as a 'flock', that was God-directed and God-centred.

In 1832, the Inspirationists found the terms by which they were offered continued lease of the Ronneburg Castle unacceptable. Requiring a new location to which they could transfer the members from Ronneburg, Metz and other elders learned of a third vacant property, the Cistercian monastery of Arnsburg near Lich, less than 50 km north. Visiting this location, they found this third estate included a flour mill, commodious workshop and dormitory areas, and land for gardens. Founded in 1174, Arnsburg was abandoned as a monastery in 1803, and the property belonged to the Count of Solms-Laubach. The Inspirationists leased Arnsburg beginning in March 1832 and renamed it Armenburg, meaning refuge of the poor. Armenburg received the Inspirationists from Ronneburg, including Metz, thereby becoming the centre of the Inspirationist movement.

---

[21] Scheuner, *Inspirations Historie, 1817–1850*, p. 68.

The Armenburg community soon increased, as Inspirationists from Schwarzenau moved there. By October 1833 a further 60 members of the Gächlingen, Switzerland, congregation and further families from Saxony had arrived.

The continuing influx of new arrivals led to the lease of the former Cloister Engelthal, located 17 km from Ronneburg Castle in the autumn of 1834. A convent abandoned in 1803, Engelthal was a further property of the Count of Solms-Laubach. The facility included a large dormitory, agricultural outbuildings as well as the abbey church, all surrounded by a stone wall. Engelthal was about halfway between the other estates and as such served as a place of rest for Inspirationists travelling between communities. An Inspirationist chronicle noted Armenburg and Herrnhaag were 'nine hours' apart, with Engelthal located conveniently in-between, and only one and a half hours from Marienborn.[22] Once Engelthal was secured, a further influx of Swiss Inspirationists, this time from the Canton of Bern, arrived in April 1835.

In Count Otto von Solms-Laubach and his counterpart, the Count of Ysenburg-Büdingen, the Inspirationists found tolerant and accommodating landlords willing to extend protection to the sect in the interests of leasing their large, otherwise unoccupied, estates. All four estates had stood vacant for some time and were in disrepair. The almost constant need to renovate and repair aging stone structures added greatly to the financial worries of Metz and the Inspirationist leadership. Among other needs, the spaces within the former convents and monasteries had to be altered in order to house families and community needs. The rent and the cost of wood needed for repairs were high.

When writing of the settlement of Engelthal (the estate where he himself was born in 1837), the nineteenth-century Inspirationist chronicler and elder Gottlieb Scheuner noted the difficulty in establishing a new Inspirationist community. He suggested that

> were it not for the fact that the direct Word evidenced Itself so extraordinarily, powerfully and mightily in the regulation and direction as well as in the persuasion, restraining and to the comfort of these people, it would have been entirely impossible to begin nor to carry forth such a Work.[23]

---

[22] Engelthal is approximately 38 km from Arnsburg, 19 km from Herrnhaag and 11 km from Marienborn.

[23] Scheuner, *Inspirations Historie, 1817–1850*, p. 114.

Thus, Metz's role as an Inspired instrument was central to maintaining the fabric of community life. As Scheuner further acknowledged, after this period Metz travelled on an almost daily basis between the communities, 'for the work was now plentiful and urgent'.[24] In late 1835 complaints about conditions voiced by members of the congregation at Engelthal were met by an inspired utterance: 'How am I to continue My Work among you? You have scarcely begun and already you grow weary of meeting the cost, both materially and spiritually, required.'[25]

Metz's testimonies or inspired communications increased significantly during this period. During the 1820s, he presented as few as seven in one year, and averaged 39 per year across the decade. By the mid-1830s Metz was delivering 113 testimonies per year. In 1833, Metz delivered 164 testimonies or, a testimony almost every other day. In total, between 1823 and his death in July 1867, Metz delivered 3598 testimonies, or an average of 82 per year. Metz's testimonies often contained words of admonition directed towards individual members as well as to an entire Inspirationist community. During 1834, continued troubles within the Marienborn community led to a complete lack of testimonies directed to its members due to 'the Lord regarding this congregation disdainfully and as unworthy of receiving His Word'.[26] In 1837 at the Herrnhaag, 'where matters concerning certain families were especially bad', Metz directed the community to hold an atonement service.[27]

During the period of his missionary activity in Switzerland and Saxony, Metz continued to visit Inspirationists in Strasburg and Alsace, in the Pfalz, in the Duchy of Baden and as far away as Prussia and Munich, converting new members and persuading those who had been members of Inspirationist congregations for years to relocate to the estates. Particularly vexing for Metz was the continued intransigence of the congregations in Neuwied—his own birthplace—and in Liebloos, a village near Ronneburg that had long sheltered a wealthy and influential Inspirationist enclave.

Some Inspirationists found life within 'the community' too confining, or rejected Metz's leadership, and left. These departures were likely mutually beneficial, as they diminished internal opposition—a 'winnow-

---

[24] Scheuner, *Inspirations Historie, 1817–1850*, p. 115.

[25] Metz, 'Testimony No. 141, Armenburg, December 14, 1835', in *J.J.J.[,] Jahrbücher Der Wahren Inspirations Gemeinden ... Zehnte Sammlung* (Eben-Ezer, NY: Eben-Ezer Society, 1856), p. 666. Translation by Janet W. Zuber.

[26] Scheuner, *Inspirations Historie, 1817–1850*, p. 109.

[27] Scheuner, *Inspirations Historie, 1817–1850*, p. 127.

ing' effect that arguably benefitted the stability of the Inspirationist communities long after their migration to the United States. Some detractors shared negative assessments of the Inspirationist community with others in their home community who had not yet decided to migrate. These accounts were particularly effective in dissuading several Swiss families from relocating.

THE NATURE OF ESTATES COMMUNALISM

Records of the day-to-day life on the estates are somewhat obscure. What is of note, however, is that by 1828 the Inspirationists began to maintain a record of deaths within 'the community' and the elders of the various communities began to hold periodic 'elder conferences' in order to consider issues of mutual interest. Apparently, any Inspirationist with agricultural experience had individual fields assigned to them.[28] Jakob Ruff, whose family was the first to move to Armenburg, wrote of separate garden plots assigned to each family and, once additional lands around the Armenburg buildings were leased, he wrote of assigned crop land. Theobald Heimburger, writing of his life at Engelthal, recorded losing his own cattle to anthrax, indicating that he retained personal ownership of the animals that he had purchased and brought into the community. Jakob Ruff's father, who had operated a combination store and inn in their native Alsace, operated a store at Armenburg, apparently as an independent business. While Ruff's account references individual family-maintained fields, most descriptions of the community at this time suggest that the estates were farmed cooperatively, although this may not have been the case on all the estates or in every department of agricultural production, as the memoirs cited here suggest. What is clear is that on all the estates the members educated their children, worshipped and prepared and ate their meals together. Living in cramped common dormitory-type dwellings, collective activity likely occurred on many levels, if not from religious or economic motivation then from sheer necessity.

While not sharing full community of goods yet, the residents of the Inspirationist estates and, to a lesser extent, members living in the remaining congregations, lived under the direction of Metz and the other leading elders. All, of course, were expected to heed the various admonitions and warnings delivered by Metz through Inspiration and all were expected

---

[28] Scheuner, *Inspirations Historie, 1817–1850*, p. 59.

to conform to the various rules and guidelines established within the community. The first and foremost of these were the Twenty Four Rules of True Godliness presented as a testimony by Johann Adam Gruber in 1716. The influence of Metz and the estates on the lives of the non-estate living members was strengthened and maintained by Metz's frequent missionary visits.

A surviving *Tagbuch für Engelthal* provides a record of life at the former cloister during the years 1839–1843. Essentially a record marking the visits of residents to other communities and the visits of others to Engelthal, the *Tagbuch* also demonstrates the strong ties of communication that existed between the estates. Letters and messengers appear to have been dispatched between communities with regularity, as were shipments of supplies, such as raw wool.[29]

The population of Inspirationists on the various estates is difficult to determine. In 1838, Scheuner noted that 91 individuals (probably meaning adults) lived at Armenburg and participated in the Love Feast (communion service) held that year.[30] Andelson estimated the combined population living on the estates was between 350 and 400 persons. Immigration records from the 2 years in which the estates were liquidated support this estimate, as does a recent effort to formulate a database of Inspirationists known to have lived at one or more of the estates during this period.[31] Those individuals who moved to the estates did so in the face of abandoning homes and family and, in many cases, relocating long distances to live on crowded facilities among German and Swiss Inspirationists who often not only spoke different dialects but lived by different cultural norms.

A circumstance that concerned the leaders was the fact that many of the members were unable to pursue profitably their livelihoods in the relative isolation of the estates. In late 1840, the Inspirationists began to consider some sort of shared industry. Because several leading elders had prior experience in the developing textile industry, the leaders determined

[29] Amana Heritage Society Library, Amana, Iowa, 'Tagbuch für Engelthal, 1839, 1840, 1841, 1842, 1843', A transcription of this important manuscript account has recently been completed.

[30] Scheuner, *Inspirations Historie, 1817–1850*, p. 144.

[31] Andelson, 'Communalism and Change', p. 38. The immigration numbers cited here are based on the carefully constructed database of Inspirationist families and their arrivals in the United States compiled by Anne DuVal Rehfuss. The author is presently engaged in creating the database of known estate residents mentioned here.

to establish textile production facilities at Herrnhaag and Armenburg, and glove and stocking manufacturing at Engelthal. Five elders pledged varying sums of southern German Gulden towards the endeavour which was formally named Mörschel, Winzenried and Company after its largest contributors, the elders Wilhelm Mörschel and Karl Winzenried. In the articles of incorporation, the shareholders stated that the new firm was not developed for personal profit, but for the benefit of the Inspirationist members on the estates, and that these individuals would constitute its preferred workforce.

A portion of the textile operation was located at Hammermühle, a fifth Inspirationist settlement located near Herrnhaag. At this site, the Inspirationists constructed a factory building and house with living quarters for workers. Some Inspirationist families moved to this location, constituting a small congregation. Although clearly regarded as a separate community at the time, mention of this fifth settlement is almost completely absent from secondary accounts, in large part because it was small, and apparently closely associated with Herrnhaag. Despite its manufacturing establishment, it is also not mentioned often in surviving primary sources.

Beyond the collective pooling of assets represented by Mörschel, Winzenried and Company, the Inspirationists had always paid their large estate rents from a common fund. Some sources indicate that an additional fund 'made up of voluntary contributions and of legacies left by deceased members' also existed for the benefit of needy Inspirationists whom the elders, if they deemed it necessity, could allow to borrow without interest. This fund apparently predated the rental of the estates.[32]

During the brief period 1835–1840, while faced with some irritation from state authorities, the Inspirationists appear to have believed that they were able to develop a peaceful, ordered life on the estates that would endure for some time. Despite persistent complaints about the exorbitant rents required by their landlords, the Inspirationists were apparently always able to meet financial obligations, suggesting that, from an economic standpoint, life on the estates was relatively secure, if not verging on prosperous.[33]

---

[32] Charles F. Noé, 'A Brief History of the Amana Society, 1714–1900', *The Iowa Journal of History and Politics*, 2 (April 1904), 169.

[33] This view is shared by Andelson in 'Communalism and Change', p. 39.

Local government authorities continued to antagonize the Inspirationists on such issues as swearing oaths and on maintaining certified school facilities. In addition, neighbours cast aspersions on the Inspirationists, suggesting, among other things, that the large influx of labour from other areas was detrimental to local employment. Government agencies pondered the issue of granting permission for Inspirationists from other German states and Switzerland to reside within their jurisdiction. Official actions also threatened the Inspirationist freedom to affirm, rather than swear, oaths. One apostate, Alan Amman, who left the community after 6 months, reported to the authorities that the Inspirationists had mistreated a mentally deranged woman, leading to an investigation which found no wrongdoing.[34] At least one wild rumour regarding Inspirationist religious practices was started following the deaths of two young women shortly after their families had moved to Armenburg. The rumour suggested that they had been killed as part of a human sacrifice ritual by the Inspirationists—an allegation commonly thrown at minority religious groups, including early Christians in the Roman Empire and Jews in medieval and early modern Europe.[35]

THE MOVE TO AMERICA

By late 1840 as many as 500 adult Inspirationists were living on the five estates in Hessen. Among Inspirationists living outside the estates, most remained independent of the organized community, though some joined after emigration to the United States. A testimony by Metz on 8 November 1840 signalled the end of this 'gathering period': 'Darkness is now gathering everywhere. The time of assembly is drawing to an end ... Watch, assemble and be prepared, for another time and hour approacheth.'[36]

[34] Scheuner, *Inspirations Historie, 1817–1850*, pp. 159–69.

[35] In his memoir, Wilhelm Mörschel wrote, 'In this year the daughter of Br. Fried[rich] Weinhold by the name of Louischen and also a young girl named Caroline, daughter of Br. Feye [died]. The first one died suddenly and the world spread the bad and wicked rumor that we had sacrificed this girl, that it was in our ground rules that in certain years we would sacrifice a human being from our neighborhood. Some people from around us came to watch a legal search warrant which they said would happen [etc.] this was a devilish defamation [and] just and upright people did not believe these black lies' (Amana Heritage Society, Amana, Iowa, Nineteenth Century Manuscripts Collection, Wilhelm Mörschel, Tagbuch and Memoir, Trans. by Magdalena Schuerer).

[36] Metz, 'Testimony No. 101, Armenburg, November 8, 1840', in *J.J.J.*[,] *Jahrbücher Der Wahren Inspirations Gemeinden ... Fünfzehnte Sammlung* (Eben-Ezer, NY: Eben-Ezer

On 21 July 1842 Metz issued a testimony proclaiming that it was God's Will that the now assembled community emigrate:

> I have spoken in the darkness and am now coming closer into the light, gradually and step by step. This might still be all too sudden for you until you come to the realization and understanding of what is to be. Hear and see with open ears and eyes! Comprehend the situation as it actually is! This land will not support you nor will they who rule therein. You are contrary to them and they shall not allow you to flourish ... You cannot stay here any longer—You are to migrate a great distance to a destination I will disclose. Look to where the land is open and to where, through the Spirit, My Hand shall direct. There you shall seek and prepare a place where you may live. Obtain a space for you and for your children ... Then I shall erect My dwelling place of rest and peace among them...[37]

To the faithful, this proclamation was as lightning from a clear sky. Inspirationist chronicles suggest that the possibility of a mass emigration had not been discussed previously, and that Metz's proclamation, supported by additional testimonies, came as a shock. Within weeks, at a series of meetings on the estates, the community elders pledged their support for emigration. Metz delivered testimonies appointing himself and three other men to a committee to travel to the United States, and the party departed in September 1842.

After a 6-week crossing, Metz and his associates arrived in New York City. Here, they consulted with the agent of a German emigration society who advised them that land suitable for a settlement was to be found in Chautauqua County in far western New York. Accordingly, the Inspirationist agents travelled to Buffalo via the Erie Canal. Once in Buffalo, they learned that the Buffalo Creek Indian Reservation, located approximately seven miles from the city centre, was for sale. After visiting the site, the party began the process of negotiating the purchase of a 5000-acre tract.

The Inspirationist chronicle notes that the faithful in Hessen expected that once Metz and company had made their selection they would return to Europe and then the emigration would begin. The move, however, happened much more quickly than anticipated. The leading elder of the

---

Society, 1858), p. 475. Translated by Janet W. Zuber.

[37] Metz, 'Testimony No. 88, Armenburg, July 21, 1842', in *J.J.J.*[,] *Jahrbücher Der Wahren Inspirations Gemeinden ... Siebzehnte Sammlung* (Eben-Ezer, NY: Eben-Ezer Society, 1859), pp. 432–3. Translated by Janet W. Zuber.

Inspirationists in Germany, Peter Mook, opposed the relocation and attempted, by various means, to prevent its occurrence. Since the Hessen estate leases were held in Mook's name, the elders charged with liquidating the German communities were faced with an additional challenge. Working around Mook, they were able to dissolve the contracts for the various rentals, estate by estate. As each property was liquidated, the Inspirationists living there formed travelling parties to the United States. While many of the faithful paid their own travelling expenses, the relative poverty of others created the possibility that they would not be able to remain with the sect.

An agreement by various elders created a common fund, evidently managed through the accounts of Mörschel, Winzenried and Company, to pay expenses in receipt of promissory notes from those receiving funds, in the expectation that these funds would be repaid within a stated period. The first large immigrant party arrived at Buffalo in 1843. This group was augmented by large groups over the next 2 years. By 1846, the major portion of the Inspirationists had arrived in New York and settled on the land purchased by Metz and his associates and named Eben-Ezer—a biblical term found in 1 Samuel 7:12, meaning 'thus far the Lord has helped us'. Within a few years, the Inspirationists had constructed four villages—Middle, Upper, Lower and New Eben-Ezer on the tract. Later, two small outposts on land the Inspirationists acquired in Canada, named Kenneburg and Canada Eben-Ezer, brought the number of settlements to six.

Most accounts of Inspirationist history state that the original contingent that arrived to settle Eben-Ezer was approximately 800 people. Careful analysis of Inspirationist records compared with ship's manifests demonstrates that, while the population that had lived on the estates may have been in the United States by the end of 1845, large numbers of Inspirationists continued to arrive each year up until 1855 when the Society began its relocation to Iowa. Close to 700 Inspirationists had arrived at Eben-Ezer by 1 January 1846, a number that increased to as many as 1183 individuals by 1850. During the years 1843–1850 an average of 147 Inspirationists left Europe to join their co-religionists in the United States each year, with the largest number of arrivals occurring in 1843 (246) and 1844 (271). By the time that the relocation to Iowa was underway, between 1492 and 1507 Inspirationists had arrived in the United States.[38]

---

[38] The immigration numbers cited here are based on the research of Anne DuVal Rehfuss, an independent scholar and Inspirationist descendant. Over several years, Rehfuss has examined ship records and through careful work has managed to trace nearly 80 percent of

Writing in later life, Jakob Ruff recalled his own family's departure from Armenburg. Their party left at 1 a.m. in order to pass through neighbouring villages without attracting undue attention. As the leaders were able to find individuals to whom the leases could be transferred, the Inspirationist communities departed, first the members at Engelthal, then Marienborn and, finally, at Herrnhaag, Hammermühle and Armenburg.[39]

In a letter written to Metz from Armenburg in 1844, Wilhelm Mörschel commented, 'what an upheaval this is and what work it has been up to now! I could write an entire book about it!' 'And yet, for the most part', Mörschel reflected, 'hearts have remained undeterred. The grapevine, which for some time has lacked the necessary pruning, has become quite wild and ignoble. For many, the severe pruning which must of necessity take place will be very painful.'[40] By the early 1850s the majority of Inspirationists had emigrated to the New World. Remnants of the sect persisted in Germany, though most of these had joined their co-religionists in America by the early 1880s.

COMMUNAL ARRANGEMENTS IN AMERICA

Before the emigration commenced, Metz had already sketched a preliminary plan for a temporary communal organization at Eben-Ezer that would represent a tighter economic and social bonding than had existed in Europe. Metz outlined his proposal in a letter to his lifelong friend, Wilhelm Mörschel:

> I have already mentioned this in one of my letters: the well-to-do, advance their money and receive interest on it and have land as security, they all help working, each one according to their profession, as well as in the businesses and agriculture. The poorer families get some wages (certain amount). Each family lives alone. Each family gets a piece of land for their own use near them, for a garden. The large field is communal, also a large garden. The things raised there can be sold well in the city. The main cattle herd is [to be] communal and is kept separate, each family has one or two cows for itself.

communal era residents of Eben-Ezer and Amana back to the ship on which they or their family arrived. Rehfuss's numbers make clear that the 800-member figure so often cited in the existing literature on the Inspirationists is an estimate without basis in actual data. I am grateful to Rehfuss for sharing her data with me for this study.

[39] Scheuner, *Inspirations Historie, 1817–1850*, p. 206.
[40] Scheuner, *Inspirations Historie, 1817–1850*, p. 221.

Everything is under supervision. This is our plan so far, there is much more going on, that I cannot write about, but I think that the Lord will reveal all of that later on, but all the Elders will have to agree on that otherwise it [will] not work out.[41]

Metz drafted a provisional constitution, revised by Wilhelm Noé, which embodied the principles he had written to Mörshel. The preliminary constitution, also called a charter, contained 35 separate clauses. Essentially the plan called for the land and property to be held in common with each member's financial contribution secured by a proportionate share of the community real estate. These contributions were to accrue interest, payable at the conclusion of a proposed 2 years.[42] Among the document's other provisions, members were to receive wages and buy food, although there is no evidence that this provision was ever carried out.

Historians of the Inspirationists have long puzzled over where Christian Metz's communal ideas originated. As none of Metz's known personal writings, including his journal or his letters, has been found to indicate precisely when the idea of a communal arrangement took hold, the question has tended to provoke unsatisfying and oversimplified answers. That the idea did indeed have its origins with Metz, possibly through discussion with his three companions in New York, is suggested by a letter in which Metz explained the plan for the new settlement to his close associate Wilhelm Mörschel. Metz's presentation in this letter suggests that this arrangement had not been discussed prior to his departure, and that it had not been discussed in the outline that he now envisioned.

Metz's twentieth-century biographer, F. Alan DuVal, suggested that Metz's brief visit to the Zoar Community in Ohio was a key influence on Metz in supporting the efficacy of communal life.[43] Yet Metz's visit to Zoar was brief and by his own account he found little that impressed him during his stay. Significantly, Metz had already drafted the preliminary constitution or charter before his Ohio visit, so the acquaintance with

---

[41] Amana Heritage Society, Amana, Iowa, Nineteenth Century Manuscripts Collection, Christian Metz to Wilhelm Mörschel, February 5, 1843. Translated by Magdalena Schuerer, Folder 24.

[42] Noè, 'A Brief History', p. 176. A single copy of the preliminary constitution, in both Metz and Noé's hands, exists in a private collection.

[43] DuVal's original 1948 University of Iowa dissertation was published as F. Alan DuVal, *Christian Metz: German-American Religious Leader and Pioneer*, ed. Peter Hoehnle (Iowa City: Penfield, 2005).

Zoar and its arrangements may have done little more than strengthen his resolve to institute communal property.[44] In the later 1840s, Metz further referenced the Harmony Society of George Rapp, suggesting at least a passing familiarity with that organization, but even then no direct linkage between the two organizations before an 1860 visit has been found. An early account of the Inspirationists alternatively suggested that leaders of the Society were inspired by French journalist and social theorist Etienne Cabet's utopian work *Voyage en Icarie*, published in 1840.[45] Given that a German translation of the novel, completed by August Herrmann Ewerbeck, was not published until 1847, and there is no evidence that Metz read French, this seems unlikely, even if Metz could have known of the theorist's work through reports in German, or from associates familiar with it. Some within Metz's circle were proficient in French, including Wilhelm Noé, one of the three agents who accompanied Metz, and the individual noted for composing the original preliminary constitution. A native of Neuwied and a trained businessman, Noé may have been familiar with Cabet's writings, but there remains no evidence that he or any other French-speaking Inspirationist circulated Cabet's ideas.

The simplest answer to the question of where Metz's communal ideas came from is that Metz was adapting communal arrangements already experienced by the Inspirationists on the German estates and extending them in a new world setting. Metz likely tightened the pre-existing communal bonds on arrival in America in the belief that the communal order would be a temporary expedient for settlement and then the Society would revert to a looser form of theocratic community as had existed

[44] Andelson, 'Communalism and Change', p. 52. During that brief visit to Zoar, Metz nevertheless met with the Society's hired business agent, Charles Mayer. Following the visit, Metz and Mayer corresponded, and he later came to join the Eben-Ezer Society in 1843. Mayer spoke fluent English, and served as an invaluable emissary between the Inspirationists and outside government and business leaders. Mayer also assisted in the drafting of the Eben-Ezer Constitution, though the Eben-Ezer Constitution does not resemble the Constitution governing Zoar. Mayer's entire role in its drafting may have only been to translate the drafts by Mörschel and Winzenried into English and to ensure that its provisions were within the constraints of New York State law.

[45] William Rufus Perkins and Barthinius L. Wick, *History of the Amana Society of Community of True Inspiration* (Iowa City: State University of Iowa, 1891), pp. 43–4. Perkins and Wick are known to have worked closely with Metz's scribe and later Inspirationist historian, Gottlieb Scheuner. Presumably, Scheuner reviewed the completed manuscript as well. While the assertion may have no basis in fact, Scheuner's seeming acquiescence may suggest some truth to this statement, though this is speculation until corroborating evidence is found.

in Europe. In the event, the Eben-Ezer Constitution of 1846 essentially made the communal arrangements permanent. But the most likely sources for Metz's communalism were biblical—especially the precedent of the earliest Christians depicted in Acts 2 and 4—and European, rather than rooted in the United States.

The new Constitution decreed that instead of the wages provided for in the preliminary charter (but perhaps never actually paid), members were to receive a yearly allowance determined by the elders. There would be no interest paid on the funds withdrawn by departing members, as in the original agreement. Whether or not the tightened communal arrangement met with much opposition is unrecorded in the Inspirationist chronicle, beyond continued references to Peter Mook who purchased a farm near the Inspirationists but refused to live within the community. When Mook was later cheated of his property by a son-in-law and was forced to return to the Society destitute, his tale of woe was interpreted as just punishment for his intransigence.[46]

The initial temporary nature of the communal fund seemingly helped to reconcile opponents to accept it. The decision to make it permanent was fraught with dissention; even the ever faithful Mörschel recorded his unease with Metz and his associates' late 1845 proposal in his memoir. Mörschel, Winzenried and Carl Mayer drafted the Eben-Ezer Constitution, which they sent to a prominent Buffalo attorney for review prior to submission to the New York General Assembly for approval. On 1 January 1846, Metz presented a testimony declaring that those individuals who did not have sufficient faith to commit their means to the community, permanently, should leave. Scheuner reports that several families, in fact, did depart at this time.[47] Once approved, the members of the Society ratified the document by their signatures during the latter part of January 1846.

The new constitution authorized the Society to elect a 13-member governing board of trustees in whose individual names the land and improvements were assigned. This board met monthly to discuss major purchases and construction projects, as well as to establish the times and order of particular special worship services.

---

[46] In an addendum to his father's uncompleted memoir, Johann Georg Heimburger noted, 'even Br. Peter Mook was so against it [communalism] that he had left the community and bought a place for himself, but the Lord did not help him so that he lost everything and later came back to the community'. Heimburger, 'A short account', p. 27.

[47] This was Metz, 'Testimony No. 1, January 1, 1846', in J.J.J.[,] *Jahrbücher Der Wahren Inspirations=Gemeinden … Ein und zwanzigste Sammlung* (Eben-Ezer, NY: Eben-Ezer Society, 1863), pp. 3–11; Scheuner, *Inspirations Historie, 1817–1850*, pp. 236–7.

In an 1843 letter to his father, Joseph Prestele provided his view of communal living at that early period in Eben-Ezer, and the benefits that he believed it provided for a family of modest means, such as his own:'

> Our communal way of life is different and peculiar, but very good, especially for the poor, who are thereby relieved of all worry about food and nourishment. We all live and work for the community and, in return, are supplied with food and clothing. When all the communities from Germany are over here, then another rule or arrangement might be made. We are, thank God, in good health, and we live together in love and peace as if we had been here for ten years already.[48]

The practical aspects of communal life, building homes and barns, clearing and tending fields, establishing shops and factories, organizing schools and creating a system of communal kitchens for the preparation and serving of food, required time and patience, as well as the continued guidance received from Metz's testimonies. Each of the first three villages had its own store, farm, bakery, blacksmith, tailor and cobbler, as well as numerous communal kitchens (see Fig. 6.1). Other community industries include watchmakers, a soap works, a calico printing operation, an oil mill and saw and grist mills. Each village was semi-independent, with barns on their periphery that housed the stock and equipment utilized by the farm labourers who went to farm the fields surrounding the village each day.

Among the more unusual income-generating operations of the Eben-Ezer Society was the production of botanical illustrations. Joseph Prestele, a trained artist specializing in lithography, was a late convert to the Inspirationists whose religious enthusiasm soon brought him into a leadership role as an elder. Upon arriving in the United States, Prestele had initially been involved in developing the community orchards and gardens. Soon, however, Metz and the other lead elders allowed him to resume his work as an artist, although the visual arts were, as a rule, frowned upon by the Inspirationists. Prestele quickly established contacts with leading American botanists, such as Asa Gray, and, over the next two decades completed a number of notable illustrations for government publications and for nurseries.[49]

---

[48] Amana Heritage Society, Amana, Iowa, Nineteenth Century Manuscripts Collection, Joseph Prestele to Martin Prestele, 15 October 1843. Translation by Magdalena Schuerer, Folder 24.

[49] Prestele's reputation as a botanical artist was rekindled through the publication of Charles van Ravenswaay's monograph *Drawn from Nature: The Botanical Art of Joseph*

Fig. 6.1 Lithograph of Middle Eben-Ezer by Joseph Prestele (*c*.1850). The building in the foreground is the Middle Eben-Ezer meeting house. The central house in the row to the left was occupied by Christian Metz and family. Courtesy of Amana Heritage Society

In around 1850 Joseph Prestele produced a second series of drawings of scenes in Eben-Ezer and used these and his earlier depictions of the German estates to create a large composite lithograph—the cover illustration of this book. This represented the European origins of the Inspirationist community, their migration to the United States and, finally, the Eben-Ezer villages.[50] A ship, specifically the *Florida* on which Prestele's family had emigrated, was at the centre of the image, with some scenes of New York Harbour below, representative of the new and different world to which he and his co-religionists had come. The Eben-Ezer villages as depicted by Prestele were tidy collections of frame structures, surrounded by well-tended fields. Prestele's drawings included the board fences that completely surrounded each village. Although Union Road passed through the village of Lower and Middle Eben-Ezer, a gate could

Prestele and His Sons (Washington, D.C.: Smithsonian Institution Press, 1984).

[50] Because of the difficulty in producing good impressions of such a large and detailed image, Prestele's lithograph was produced in only a limited quantity. Currently, only six examples of this print are known to survive: one in the collection of the Amana Heritage Society; the other five in private Amana family collections. A reproduction of the composite lithograph appears in van Ravenswaay, *Drawn from Nature*, p. 36.

close this stretch of the road to traffic, which was then diverted around the village. The gate, a practice that was not repeated a decade later when the Inspirationists moved to Iowa, represented an interesting dichotomy in Inspirationist life. Visitors and the world beyond the villages were made unwelcome by the gate as well as other cultural barriers, most particularly their language, so keeping out intrusive elements. In terms of social and theological life, the Inspirationists remained Germans, strangers, as it were, in a strange land (see Fig. 6.2).

Economically, the little villages were as independent as possible from the world beyond. The large tract of farm and timber land surrounding the settlements, and later, additional villages established in Canada, provided for basic subsistence. Within the villages, blacksmiths, carpenters, masons, watchmakers, basket weavers, school teachers and even the society's own physicians provided for as many needs as they were capable of fulfilling. The major interaction between the world and the Society was its textile industry. As the Society moved to the United States, its finances were channelled through Mörschel, Winzenried and Company, the textile firm established at Herrnhaag and Armenburg in 1840. Once the Society adopted formal communalism, Mörschel, Winzenried and Company

Fig. 6.2   Lithograph of Lower Eben-Ezer by Joseph Prestele (*c.*1850). The main portion of the village is visible in the distance. The structural features, including the design of sash window, grape trellis fastened to buildings, board fences and pitched roofs, are characteristic of Inspirationist architecture at both Eben-Ezer and Amana. Courtesy of Amana Heritage Society

was absorbed within a new entity known as the Eben-Ezer Society. The constitution creating the Society was, in large part, the work of Wilhelm Mörschel and carl Winzenried. Once the Society was in place, both men assumed high leadership roles, effectively replacing Peter Mook and the vestiges of his financial leadership of the communities in Germany. When the Inspirationist leadership determined to move to Iowa in 1855, it was Winzeried who was dispatched, along with his half-brother, Johann Beyer, and two other elders, to begin making the land purchases, and it was Winzenried who remained the effective leader of the Society until his death in 1886. Later, Winzenried's half-brother, nephew and grandson followed him as president. Mörschel's son managed woollen operations, in concert with Winzenried's nephew, until his death in 1903, at which time he was succeeded by Winzenried's grandson. In this way, the major economic power, if not the spiritual power, within the community remained firmly entrenched in the hands of Mörschel and Winzenried and their heirs.[51]

The woollen mill and, to a lesser extent, a calico printing operation provided textiles for sale beyond the confines of the Society and the income necessary to purchase those goods and services which the Society membership could not provide internally. Thus, the Society was tied to the wider American economy even while it struggled to remain distinct from that same economy, attempting still to maintain strict borders between American society and the tiny world of the Eben-Ezer community. This dichotomy was not unique to the Inspirationists, and was shared by many other communal ventures in the United States in the period.

After decades of dealing with religious and government authorities in Europe, Metz wrote that the situation of the Eben-Ezer community provided a nice respite, in that it afforded the Inspirationists the opportunity to function largely without the interference or intervention of the outside world. Writing to Count Otto von Solms-Laubach, from whom the Inspirationists had leased Armenburg, Metz reflected, 'We live quietly … free from all religious pressure because everybody [in America] is interested in riches and trading and not to what religion one belongs.'[52]

---

[51] The continuance of authority within the families of the woollen mill incorporators is traced in Peter Hoehnle, 'Machine in the Garden: The Woolen Textile Industry of the Amana Society, 1785–1942', *The Annals of Iowa*, 61 (Winter 2002), 24–67.

[52] Amana Heritage Society, Amana, Iowa, Nineteenth Century Manuscripts Collection, Christian Metz to Otto von Solms-Laubach, n.d. Translation by Magdalena Schuerer. Folder 24.

From Ebenezer to Amana

By 1850, the year in which Prestele's composite lithograph was likely completed, the Eben-Ezer Society numbered approximately 1200 members. The journalist, reformer and utopian enthusiast Parke Godwin had visited the Society in 1848, providing a vivid description of the Inspirationist settlements within 5 years of settlement:

> Since purchasing their estate, these enterprising Germans have cleared completely and put in the best order, nearly five thousand acres of land, erected a great many miles of durable fences, planted twenty-five thousand fruit-trees of various sorts, settled three compact villages, about one mile apart; each containing one hundred [sic] large and commodious dwelling-houses, some thirty or forty barns, of the largest size and most substantial structure, four saw-mills, which are kept constantly running, one flour-mill, one oil-mill, one large woollen factory, calico-print works, a tannery, a variety of workshops for mechanics, public halls, and several school-houses. Besides these, they possess extensive herds of cattle and swine, their sheep alone numbering above two thousand heads ... Such are some of the internal advantages of unitary labour.[53]

By this date, the Eben-Ezer Society was the second largest communal organization in the United States after the Shaker villages. Within a few short years, however, the entire Inspirationist society would face yet another, final, relocation. The rapid growth of the Eben-Ezer Society meant that the original tract of land purchased by Metz and his associates was inadequate to meet its needs. Additionally, the rapid growth of the nearby city of Buffalo exerted pressure on the Inspirationists in other ways. While Buffalo provided a ready market for its products, the growing city, particularly its large population of German emigrants, presented tempting alternatives to the more Spartan life of the communal Inspirationists. Buffalo's growth also encouraged the development of a rail line that threated to split the Inspirationist fields, as well as a hydraulic dam that severely compromised the workings of the Society's own mills. In the face of these pressures, and in response to a general desire for greater isolation, Metz delivered a testimony calling upon the faithful to move farther into the American wilderness. After an abortive attempt to purchase land in Kansas, the Inspirationists located, purchased and began to settle a 26,000-acre tract

---

[53] Parke Godwin, 'Letters from America', *The People's Journal*, 4 (1848), 219.

of land in Iowa County, Iowa. Over the course of ten years, the entire Eben-Ezer Society transferred to Iowa. For many Inspirationists, this relocation was their third, having moved first from their original German village to one of the estates, then to Eben-Ezer and, finally, to the new villages in Iowa, collectively known as the Amana Society. No longer isolated conventicles scattered across the German states and Switzerland, the Inspirationists were now a monolithic theocratic community.

In 1881 the population of the Amana villages reached its highest number of 1813 members in seven villages, surrounded by 26,000 acres of farm and timber land, with two woollen mills, a calico mill and hundreds of homes, craft shops and enormous barns to house livestock.[54] For a period between the decline of the Shaker communities and a tremendous growth in population in Hutterite colonies in the twentieth century, the Amana Inspirationists became the largest communal society in the United States. By the late 1920s, however, economic pressures, aggravated by a severe fire at the Amana Woollen Mill, and the Great Depression, coupled with growing dissatisfaction with the restrictions of communal life, led the Inspirationists to undertake a reorganization by which the commercial interests of the old Society were absorbed into a new joint stock corporation known as the 'Amana Society' and the religious aspects of Inspirationism became the basis for a separate 'Amana Church Society'. These two entities and the seven villages created by the Inspirationists continue to this day—American heirs to a Protestant communalism forged in a trans-Atlantic odyssey.

---

[54] The Inspirationists conducted a census of membership as of the end of each calendar year between 1855 and 1932. The numbers reported at the close of 1881 were 1273 adults and 540 children, representing the total membership of 1813 reported here. The increase over 1880 was 92 individuals, including many new converts from Germany. By 1882, the population had declined to 1765, and would thereafter decline to the 1381 members present at the end of 1931, shortly before the Inspirationists abandoned communalism. Gottlieb Scheuner, *Inspirations-Historie oder Beschreibung des Gnadenwerks des Herrn in den Gemeinden Der Wahren Inspiration [1877–1883]* (Amana, Iowa: Amana Society, 1916), pp. 323, 390; August Koch, 'Inspirations-Historie oder Beschreibung des Gnadenwerks des Herrn in den Gemeinden der Wahren Inspiration ... Das Jahr 1931' (unpublished manuscript, Amana Heritage Society Library, Amana, Iowa), p. 35.

CHAPTER 7

Mormon Communalism and Millennialism in Trans-Atlantic Context

Matthew J. Grow and Bradley Kime

The Church of Jesus Christ of Latter-day Saints—whose members are known as Latter-day Saints or Mormons—is often seen as the quintessentially American religion. The historiography of the movement, including its communal aspects, has traditionally integrated the Mormon story within themes in American history, such as the Second Great Awakening or the westward movement. In recent decades, the religion's international aspect has attracted increasing scholarly attention as the Church has spread rapidly in the global south. Nevertheless, Mormonism was surprisingly trans-Atlantic from its early days. Mormon missionaries first reached England in 1837, seven years after the founding of the Church. By the 1840s there were thousands of converts in Britain and for the rest of the century this proved fertile missionary ground. Areas of the European continent—particularly Scandinavia—also yielded a steady stream of converts, many of whom 'gathered' with the Latter-day Saints in the western United States.

The Latter-day Saints' deep roots in communalism and millennialism unsurprisingly developed in a trans-Atlantic context. Indeed, the worlds

M.J. Grow (✉)
Church History Department of the Church of Jesus Christ of Latter-day Saints, Salt Lake City, Utah, USA

B. Kime
University of Virginia, Charlottesville, Virginia, USA

     163
P. Lockley (ed.), *Protestant Communalism in the Trans-Atlantic World, 1650–1850*, DOI 10.1057/978-1-137-48487-1_7

of trans-Atlantic Protestant communalism and trans-denominational millennialism flowed in and out of Mormon attempts at communal life and economics, but not in a continuous stream. Disparate communalists from the United States and Europe influenced Mormon communalism while others drew significantly from the Latter-day Saints for their own communal projects. Still others left behind Protestant communal traditions and converted to Mormonism because they believed that it fulfilled millennial prophecy. As a result, many Latter-day Saints saw themselves not as an American utopian community but as the millennial fulfilment of a recognizably trans-Atlantic communal quest.

MORMON COMMUNALISM IN OVERVIEW

Latter-day Saint communal efforts drew not only on New Testament precedents, like most other religiously inspired communalisms in the trans-Atlantic world, but also on their own scriptures. Joseph Smith published the Book of Mormon, which he stated that he translated from records left by inhabitants of ancient America, in March 1830, the month before he founded his Church. It denounced selfishness and individualism and expressed a vision of a godly society in which people had 'all things common among them' and thus 'there were not rich and poor, bond and free, but they were all made free, and partakers of the heavenly gift'.[1] In the early 1830s, Smith reported frequently receiving divine revelations, many of which mandated that God's saints be unified socially, religiously and economically. 'If ye are not equal in earthly things', one revelation declared, 'ye cannot be equal in obtaining heavenly thing[s].'[2] Another revelation expanded upon the biblical narrative of the prophet Enoch to describe how Enoch's people 'built a city that was called the City of Holiness, even Zion'. The inhabitants of Zion, rather like early Christians in the New Testament book of Acts, 'were of one heart and one mind, and dwelt in righteousness; and there was no poor among them'.[3]

---

[1] The Book of Mormon, 4 Nephi 1:3.

[2] Robin Scott Jensen, Robert J. Woodford and Steven C. Harper (eds), *Revelations and Translations, Volume 1: Manuscript Revelation Books*, vol. 1 of the Revelations and Translations series of *The Joseph Smith Papers*, ed. Dean C. Jessee, Ronald K. Esplin and Richard Lyman Bushman (Salt Lake City: Church Historian's Press, 2011), p. 207 (also known as D&C 78).

[3] The Pearl of Great Price, Moses 7:18–19.

Smith's visions proved persuasive to many of his contemporaries, who, like him, had suffered from the economic instability brought on by ante-bellum America's accelerating participation in a market economy and from the religious confusion of the Second Great Awakening. The creation of an ideal society, which Mormons named Zion after the city built by Enoch, promised to rescue converts from the rampant individualism of Jacksonian America. Like other communal groups, nineteenth-century Mormons not only challenged ideas of individualism and private property, but also tradi-tional notions of family—not with celibacy, like the Shakers or Harmonists—but by embracing plural marriage, beginning in the early 1840s.

While communalism runs deeply throughout Mormon history, Mormons made two specific large-scale attempts at communal economics during the nineteenth century. In the early 1830s in Missouri, Mormons initially practised what they called the 'Law of Consecration and Stewardship'. Mormons would deed all of their property to the Church and would then receive management back of specific properties proportionate to their particular needs. This attempt at communal living suffered from inter-nal discord and external pressure, as local settlers forced the Mormons on three separate occasions to abandon their Missouri settlements in the 1830s. The memory of this attempt to establish Zion left an indelible impression on nineteenth-century Latter-day Saints, including Smith's successor Brigham Young, who led most Mormons to Utah. In Utah, Mormons engaged in a variety of cooperative economic projects under Young's direction, including the establishment of a cooperative economic system in Brigham City in 1864, and the founding of Zion's Cooperative Mercantile Institution (ZCMI) in Salt Lake City in 1868.

In the late 1860s and early 1870s, partly as a result of the completion of the transcontinental railroad which threatened to end Utah's isolation, Young encouraged the establishment of communal societies, known collec-tively as the United Order of Enoch, in many Mormon communities.[4] The United Orders were generally producer cooperatives in which local Saints, after pooling their property and labour, received profits and income in pro-portion to what they had contributed. In a few communities more concerted United Orders prevailed, in which the Saints donated all of their resources, aimed for self-sufficiency and shared equally in the products of their labour.

---

[4] For an overview of Mormon communalism, see Dean L. May, 'One Heart and Mind: Communal Life and Values among the Mormons', in Donald E. Pitzer (ed.), *America's Communal Utopias* (Chapel Hill: University of North Carolina Press, 1997), pp. 135–58.

EARLY MORMONISM AND
THE FIRST COMMUNAL CONVERTS

The trans-Atlantic context of early Mormon communal efforts can be traced through converts who came from other communal groups. Initially, these converts came from groups in the United States, including the Shakers and Harmonists, which had emerged from trans-Atlantic communal milieus.[5] Later converts with roots in trans-Atlantic communalism also came from abroad. Some converts found Mormon communalism compelling because they compared it to other communal groups or because they believed it augured the Millennium. Some of these converts brought communal convictions with them that influenced Mormons' own communal efforts. And many of them tried to convince other communalists on both sides of the Atlantic to join the Mormon effort before the imminent Millennium overtook them.

The earliest introduction of communal economics among the Mormons displayed traces of trans-Atlantic communalism from the frontier of the United States. Joseph Smith's revelation establishing the 'Law of Consecration and Stewardship' occurred a few months after members of a communal society converted virtually 'wholesale' to Mormonism in late 1830.[6] This was Sidney Rigdon's common-stock community which he called 'The Family'. Rigdon had been a prominent preacher closely connected to Alexander Campbell, leader of the Disciples of Christ, but his determination to replicate the Christian communism described in the book of Acts forced his split with Campbell. In Kirtland, Ohio, Rigdon gathered one of his congregations onto the farm of Isaac Morley to attempt living with 'all things in common'.[7] Though Rigdon's immediate inspiration was the New Testament account, he also admired several modern models of communalism. He was most familiar with the Shakers, but also knew well the experiments of Robert Owen, the Harmony Society, and the German Pietist Separatists at Zoar, Ohio. Rigdon's attempt never cohered because it lacked clear organization and structure to channel the chaos of common ownership. After Rigdon's congregation converted to

---

[5] For a brief overview of this type of convert in early Mormonism, see Val Dean Rust, *Radical Origins: Early Mormon Converts and Their Colonial Ancestors* (Urbana: University of Illinois Press, 2004), pp. 13–16.

[6] Mark Lyman Staker, *Hearken, O Ye People: The Historical Setting of Joseph Smith's Ohio Revelations* (Salt lake City: Greg Kofford Books, 2009), p. 56.

[7] Acts 2:44.

Mormonism, Joseph Smith moved with other Church members from New York to Kirtland to build around this new nucleus, and requested that they abandon their common-stock principle in favour of something better. 'The Law of Consecration and Stewardship' subsequently replaced common ownership with individual stewardships within the context of communal consecration.[8]

Like Rigdon's congregation, a small number of Shakers also converted to the Mormon movement.[9] Leman Copley, a former Shaker and large landowner, joined the Church by early 1831 in northern Ohio and sparked an interest in missionary work among the Shakers. John Whitmer, one of the Church's earliest historians, recorded that Copley was 'anxious that some of the elders should go to his former brethren and preach the gospel'.[10] On 7 May 1831, Smith dictated a revelation that directed Copley, along with Parley P. Pratt and Rigdon, to visit the Shaker community of North Union, Ohio, and call it to repentance. Shakers shared with Mormons a relatively recent origin, belief in modern prophecy and ardent millennialism. But the revelation criticized the Shakers' neglect of baptism and laying on of hands for the Holy Spirit, and it condemned many of their doctrines, including celibacy, vegetarianism and the divine role of founder Mother Ann Lee.[11] While Rigdon had admired Shaker communalism from afar, Pratt had familial ties to Shakers and had grown up in the shadow of their New Lebanon community in New York, which he had proselytized the previous year. Furthermore, Pratt had visited the North Union Shakers and left several copies of the Book of Mormon with them the previous fall.

[8] Leonard J. Arrington, Feramorz Y. Fox and Dean L. May, *Building the City of God: Community & Co-operation among the Mormons* (Salt Lake City: Deseret Book Company, 1976), p. 19; Mario S. De Pillis, 'The Development of Mormon Communitarianism, 1826–1846' (PhD thesis, Yale University, 1960), pp. 39–81.

[9] For a comparison of Mormon and Shaker forms of communalism, see J. Spencer Fluhman, 'Early Mormon and Shaker Visions of Sanctified Community', *BYU Studies*, 44:1 (2005), 79–110.

[10] Karen Lynn Davidson, Richard L. Jensen and David J. Whittaker (eds), *Histories, Volume 2: Assigned Histories, 1831–1847*, vol. 2 of the Histories Series of *The Joseph Smith Papers*, ed. Dean C. Jessee, Ronald K. Esplin, and Richard Lyman Bushman (Salt Lake City: Church Historian's Press, 2012), p. 37.

[11] Terryl L. Givens and Matthew J. Grow, *Parley P. Pratt: The Apostle Paul of Mormonism* (New York: Oxford University Press, 2011), pp. 48–9; Michael Hubbard MacKay et al. (eds), *Documents, Volume 1: July 1828–June 1831*, vol. 1 of the Documents Series of *The Joseph Smith Papers*, ed. Dean C. Jessee et al. (Salt Lake City: Church Historian's Press, 2013), pp. 297–303.

Rigdon and Copley arrived at North Union, some 15 miles from Kirtland, on the evening of 7 May, and Pratt arrived the following day. The Shakers allowed the Mormon elders to read Smith's revelation, which Ashbell Kitchell, the community's presiding elder, quickly dismissed. Pratt then enraged Kitchell by dramatically shaking his coat-tail as a testimony against the Shakers for rejecting the revelation. Kitchell was also furious at Copley for deserting 'the living word of God'.[12] Whitmer recorded the end of the mission: 'the shakers hearkened not to their words, and received not the gospel at that time; for they were bound up in tradition and priestcraft'.[13] Copley, who had allowed dozens of Mormons from New York to settle temporarily on his land, soon returned to the Shakers following this failed mission. Ironically, his re-conversion to the Shakers propelled forward Mormons' own communal impulses. Joseph Smith soon dictated a revelation instructing these New York Mormons to migrate to Missouri, where they would be instrumental in founding 'Zion', or the Mormon conception of an ideal community.

Nevertheless, the Mormon connection with North Union was not finished. Five months after the May mission, Jesse Gause, who became the most influential communal convert to early Mormonism, arrived at North Union. Gause had been a Quaker before becoming a Shaker in 1829 and moving to the community of Shakers in Hancock, Massachusetts. Two years later, Gause moved with his wife and their young child (born before they became Shakers) to the Shaker village at North Union, arriving in October 1831.[14] By February 1832, Gause had left the Shakers for the Mormons and was apparently living in Kirtland. He quickly became one of the Mormons' most prominent leaders. On 8 March, he and Rigdon were ordained by Smith as his counsellors in the presidency of the high priesthood—the initial organization of the Church's presiding leaders that would become known as the First Presidency. Learning of his appointment,

---

[12] Ashbell Kitchell 'A Mormon Interview', in Lawrence R. Flake (ed.), 'A Shaker View of a Mormon Mission', *BYU Studies*, 20 (Fall 1979), 95–9; Givens and Grow, *Parley P. Pratt*, pp. 49–50.

[13] Whitmer, *History*, 26, in *Joseph Smith Papers. Histories* 2:38.

[14] On Gause, see De Pillis, 'Development of Mormon Communitarianism', 170–89, 325–7; D. Michael Quinn, 'Jesse Gause: Joseph Smith's Little-Known Counselor', *BYU Studies*, 23 (Fall 1983), 487–93; Erin B. Jennings, 'The Consequential Counselor: Restoring the Root(s) of Jesse Gause', *Journal of Mormon History*, 34 (Spring 2008), 182–227.

Shaker Matthew Houston wrote to a fellow Shaker that Gause was 'second to the Prophet or Seer—Joseph Smith'.[15] Smith soon dictated a revelation that instructed Gause to preach 'among thy Brethren'—likely a reference to Quakers and Shakers.[16]

Gause's sojourn with the Mormons was brief. Yet, he likely influenced the trajectory of the Latter-day Saints' communal experimentation, as a month after he became Smith's counsellor, he travelled with Smith to Independence, Missouri. Here, Gause not only visited Mormons expelled from Copley's land, but also participated with Smith and other leaders in organizing the United Firm, which would oversee some aspects of Mormon economic practices, as well as the Literary Firm that would supervise Church publications. Historian Mario De Pillis has suggested that Gause acted as Smith's 'adviser in all communitarian matters during their visit to Zion'. In particular, De Pillis has pointed persuasively to the appointment of a 'double bishopric' (meaning Mormon bishops stationed in Ohio and in Missouri, charged with overseeing the implementation of communalism in their jurisdictions) as a Shaker influence that 'doubtless came from Gause', as Shakers likewise had an eastern and a western bishop.[17]

In August 1832, Gause went on a mission with Zebedee Coltrin during which they visited many of Gause's earlier Quaker associates and relatives. Coltrin recorded the end of their mission on 20 August: 'Brother Jesse & I After praying with & for each other parted in the fellowship of the Gospel of our Lord & Saviour Jesus Christ.'[18] Gause then disappears from Mormon records, being excommunicated from the Church on 3 December 1832, in absentia.[19] Nevertheless, his experience demonstrates that converts from communal groups with trans-Atlantic roots occasionally had direct influences on organizational aspects of Mormon communal efforts.

---

[15] Quinn, 'Jesse Gause', 489–90.

[16] Matthew C. Godfrey et al. (eds), *Documents, Volume 2: July 1831–January 1833*, vol. 2 of the Documents Series of *The Joseph Smith Papers*, ed. Dean C. Jessee et al. (Salt Lake City: Church Historian's Press, 2013), p. 208 (D&C 81).

[17] De Pillis, 'Development of Mormon Communitarianism', 171–85.

[18] [Latter-day Saints] Church History Library, Salt Lake City (CHL) Zebedee Coltrin diaries, 20 August 1832, 2:35, MS 1443.

[19] Jennings, 'Consequential Counselor', 214–15.

JACOB ZUNDEL AND THE HARMONISTS

During Gause's August 1832 mission, he and Coltrin visited the Harmonist village of Economy, Pennsylvania, though the sources do not mention their activities there. About this time, John Zundel joined the Latter-day Saints. Zundel's father was John Eberhard Zundel, an associate of George Rapp in Württemberg, Germany, who brought his family into the Harmony Society and emigrated with them to the United States. Following John Zundel's conversion, his older brother Jacob Zundel was baptized a Mormon in 1836, and Jacob remained a devout Mormon until his death in 1880. He maintained contact with the Harmonists for the next several decades.[20]

In April 1846, two months after the exodus of Mormons from their city of Nauvoo, Illinois, had begun, Jacob Zundel wrote to the Harmonists in Economy, apparently responding to a request made two years earlier for information. As he would throughout his correspondence with the Harmonists, Zundel urged his former co-religionists to become Latter-day Saints by drawing on their shared belief in an oncoming Millennium.[21] To Zundel, Mormonism was the fulfilment of the millennial expectations which had led the Harmonists to cross the Atlantic.

Zundel reminded his friends, 'your father [George Rapp] taught much which is now being fulfilled and some which will yet be fulfilled in regards to the coming of Christ and the Millennium'. The Mormons, Zundel continued, were laying 'the foundation to the Kingdom of God on earth' in preparation for Christ's return. As in biblical times when 'something important was to take place', God had, in this millennial time of 'greatest happenings', appeared in person, sent angels, called a prophet and gathered his people—all among the Mormons.[22] A year later Zundel wrote directly to Rapp, who had, unknown to Zundel, died the previous month:

> I could remind you of a great many things which you spoke of and which are now being fulfilled. I no longer need to study the cloud over the sanctuary and other things in the books, but here, dear father, if you will believe me, in our Temple the angels of the Lord teach us.

---

[20] Karl J. Arndt, 'The Harmonists and the Mormons', *American-German Review*, 10 (June 1944), 6–9; De Pillis, 'Development of Mormon Communitarianism', 324–32.

[21] Unfortunately, only Zundel's side of the correspondence appears to have survived.

[22] CHL, Jacob Zundel to Friends, 3 April 1846, typescript translation, MS 9095.

Zundel pleaded with Rapp to prepare for the imminent Millennium by heeding the Mormon message. Likewise, he assured his friends that all the things they, their fathers and the prophets had prophesied and taken comfort in regarding 'these our latter days ... are now being fulfilled before your eyes'. 'Is it possible that you will let them pass?'[23]

Long after Rapp's death, in letters written in 1865 and 1870, Zundel's millennial zeal was unabated, proclaiming to the remaining Harmonists the

> ... spread of the Kingdom of God and ... the gathering of the people and the judgments which surely will come, according to the word of God which we received so definitely and truly through messengers of the Lord, the same as Noah, Abraham, or Moses ... [in these] the latter days, when the greatest things shall take place which ever have occurred.[24]

Of the Harmonist Society, he asked, 'What have you done or how far have you gone with the Kingdom of God during nearly 70 years?' Of the Mormons, he stated, 'we are sent to make known the will of God ... out of love for our fellow men, to warn them and to save them from destruction which will overcome them'. Zundel closed his final letter as he had begun his first, by reminding his friends of Rapp's prophecies and proclaiming their millennial fulfilment in the Mormon community.[25] Zundel's letters highlight the millennial meaning Mormonism held for some of its converts who had joined from other communal groups. For Zundel, the Latter-day Saints' special relationship to the second coming of Christ trumped the Harmonists' cooperative economics and answered the Harmonists' millennial yearnings, leading him to trade one communal society for another.

LOUIS BERTRAND AND THE ICARIANS

Few early Mormon converts illustrate the trans-Atlantic context of Mormon communalism better than Louis A. Bertrand.[26] Bertrand also illustrates a persisting relationship between religious communalism and

[23] CHL, Zundel to Friends, 28 September 1847, typescript translation, MS 9095.
[24] CHL, Zundel to Friends, 26 November 1865, typescript translation, MS 9095.
[25] CHL, Zundel to Mr Hinrizi, 1870, typescript translation, MS 9095.
[26] On Bertrand, see Christian Euvrard, *Louis Auguste Bertrand (1808–1875): Journaliste Socialiste et Pionnier Mormon* (Tournan-en-Brie: Author, 2005); Richard D. McClellan, 'Not Your Average French Communist Mormon: A Short History of Louis A. Bertrand', *Mormon Historical Studies*, 1:2 (2000), 3–24; Erik Freeman, 'Louis A. Bertrand's Voyage from Icarianism to Mormonism: French Romantic Socialism and Mormon Communalism in the Nineteenth Century' (Master's thesis, Brandeis University, 2013).

trans-Atlantic socialism discussed further in Philip Lockley's following chapter. Prior to the 1848 revolutions, Bertrand became a follower of the French utopian Etienne Cabet and joined his society of Icarian communalists.[27] In early 1848, at the recommendation of the secular British utopian Robert Owen, Cabet directed his followers in a communal colonization effort in Texas.[28] After the poorly planned effort ended in disaster, the Icarians looked north to Nauvoo, Illinois. The Mormon city modelled the possibilities of communal living for the frustrated French socialists, just as Mormon Utah would later draw the attention of their fellow countryman, Victor Considerant. As leader of the French Fourierist socialist movement, Considerant, like Cabet, looked to the American west for a place to plant a new utopia, and was 'struck' by the 'remarkable and rapid development of the Mormons'. 'Thanks to ... a truly socialist solidarity', Considerant wrote, 'the Mormons have realized incredible prosperity in a few short years', despite their 'baggage of retrograde doctrines'.[29] Similarly aware of the successes of Mormons in Nauvoo, the Icarians bought up the abandoned city after the Mormons went west.[30] The purchase brought the religion to the attention of Bertrand, who was editing Cabet's socialist newspaper, Le Populaire, in Paris.

Bertrand researched the Mormons after Cabet purchased Nauvoo and analysed them in several articles for Le Populaire in early 1849. 'Mormons put all in common and are united by the bonds of brotherhood and socialism', Bertrand wrote. While Cabet was in Nauvoo, Bertrand expressed hope that the Icarian leader would learn from the Mormons' example and that 'our Icarian brothers will fraternize with these American Communists'. Bertrand recognized that 'the Mormon's religious and social system ... is based on the principles of the *community*', and that they drew their strength 'principally through the brotherly

---

[27] The standard study of the Icarians is Robert P. Sutton, *Les Icariens: The Utopian Dream in Europe and America* (Urbana: University of Illinois Press, 1994).

[28] Jonathan Beecher, 'Building Utopia in the Promised Land: Icarians and Fourierists in Texas', in François Lagarde (ed.), *The French in Texas: History, Migration, Culture* (Austin: University of Texas Press, 2003), pp. 197–225.

[29] Victor Prosper Considerant, *Au Texas* (Paris: La Librairie phalanstérienne, 1854), p. 17. Translation mine. See also, Jonathan Beecher, *Victor Considerant and the Rise and Fall of French Romantic Socialism* (Berkeley: University of California Press, 2001), pp. 301–2.

[30] For a comparison of Mormon Nauvoo and Icarian Nauvoo, see Sarah Jaggi Lee, 'Utopian Spaces: Mormons and Icarians in Nauvoo, Illinois' (PhD thesis, College of William and Mary, 2009).

devotion and love of their numerous members, and ... legitimize their existence on the texts of gospel scriptures and precepts'. He concluded, 'We see by this how many similarities there are with the Icarian doctrine.' Though aware of myriad utopian societies on both sides of the Atlantic, Bertrand believed 'there is not one more interesting than that of the Mormons.'[31]

Mormon missionaries led by John Taylor arrived in France that same year and made contact with Bertrand and other Icarians. In their efforts to convert the Icarians, the missionaries utilized the Church's communal appeal but insisted that true religion was the root of the religion's compelling communal aspects.[32] Bertrand accepted the missionaries' invitations to hear the message and study their literature. 'My knowledge of English permitted me to familiarize myself with the doctrines of this new Church', he recalled later; 'I found in their writings ... the complete demonstration of the divinity of this work'. Bertrand's conversion was more rational than ecstatic. 'All the questions, all the objections that I asked them were cleared or refuted to my entire satisfaction. After three months of study and serious reflection, I accepted baptism [in December 1850].'[33] It was another year before he left the Icarians behind, and even when he did, he brought his communal impulse with him. Ultimately, he viewed his conversion as the culmination of his own trans-Atlantic communal quest and as a mandate to convert others to the Mormons' communal efforts. For the next 25 years, until his death in 1875, Bertrand split his time between Mormon missionary service in France and cooperative efforts in Utah, all the while writing prodigiously on Mormon millennialism and communalism in hopes of convincing his countrymen.

After his conversion, Bertrand cast Mormonism as the communal society that trans-Atlantic socialists had all hoped for. Jules Remy's widely read 1860 travelogue, *Voyage au Pays des Mormons*, defended Mormonism as being something more than mere socialism—an indication that in

---

[31] Louis A. Bertrand, *Le Populaire*, 20 May 1849 and 18 February 1849. Quotes and translation from, Freeman, 'Louis A. Bertrand's Voyage from Icarianism to Mormonism', 1, 31–2.

[32] Freeman, 'Louis A. Bertrand's Voyage from Icarianism to Mormonism', 33–4.

[33] Louis A. Bertrand, *Les Mémoires d'un Mormon* (Paris: Collection Hetzel E. Dentu, 1862), pp. 7, 8.

France the two were sometimes equated.[34] In his 1862 *Les Mémoires d'un Mormon*, Bertrand went a step further. For him, Mormon communalism was unparalleled:

> Who will now tell us why this perfect social harmony, this communion of thought, of feeling and will, exists only among Mormons? How can you explain this miracle of a people gathered from among all others and animated by the same religious, social and political sentiment?

Bertrand believed Mormon communalism achieved a unity and prosperity unequalled by any other utopian society. Noting the failures of Owen, Cabet and Fourier to put communal theory into successful practice, Bertrand asked that the Mormons 'be permitted to smile a bit about the impotency of contemporary utopias'. 'Compare, if you will', he wrote, 'the astounding progress of the one to the fruitless efforts of socialists of both hemispheres. Was there ever a contrast so striking?' While Bertrand recognized that Mormons had not fully succeeded in their own communal efforts, his intensely millennial treatise traced a future timeline for the 'complete fusion of collective wealth' among Utah Mormons. 'Sooner or later the reign of "mine" and "thine" will cease in the Great basin', Bertrand declared. 'The neediest of emigrants, shipwrecked from the old societies, arriving in Zion tired, naked, hungry and penniless, will be clothed and sheltered immediately with the same comfort enjoyed by any other of his brethren.'[35] Bertrand never lived to see that day, but over the course of two and a half decades, he encountered, lived and promoted Mormonism as a trans-Atlantic communal society, oriented towards an imminent Millennium.

BRITISH AND SCANDINAVIAN CONVERTS

Most of the needy emigrants from the old societies, to whom Bertrand referred, came to Zion (whether in Nauvoo or Utah) from Britain. Like Bertrand, they were drawn to Mormon community and dedicated to the building up of Zion. But unlike Bertrand, radical Protestantism more than trans-Atlantic communalism shaped their perceptions of the religion's

[34] Jules Remy, *Voyage au Pays des Mormons* (Paris: E. Dentu, Libraire-éditeur, 1860), esp. p. 187.

[35] CHL, Louis Alphonse Bertrand, *Memoirs of a Mormon*, trans. Gaston Chappuls (n.p., 196?), pp. 168–9, M273 B549m.

communal elements and their expectations of Zion.[36] British converts were more like Zundel than Bertrand: although community and the Millennium remained inseparable, millennialism appears to have pulled them into Mormon communalism more than communalism pointed them towards the Mormon Millennium.[37] Daniel Holding of Shropshire, England, for example, recorded a 'Gloreas Vision' that caused his conversion to Mormonism in 1842: 'I had the End of this present World shoead [showed] before me and the Mileniel Reaighen [millennial reign] of Peace.' Holding saw a community of saints sitting with their 'Saviaur ... in joing [enjoying] peace and harmony' and, in contrast, 'The Wicked ... running tuea and fraue [to and fro].' Then 'The Voice sead [said] if thoue wilt join that happey People thou must join the Later day Saints.'[38] Holding was baptized and, within a few years, gathered to Zion in Utah, believing it was the community where the Millennium would commence.

The journals of British converts describe their departures for Utah in similarly millennial, more often than communal, terms; they often rolled the restoration of primitive Christianity, the renewal of spiritual gifts and the imminent Millennium into the same momentous present.[39] Henry Emery and Elizabeth Brewerton's patriarchal blessings (ritual pronouncements regarding an individual's spiritual life by a designated Mormon patriarch) offer an illustration of this. Both were converts from Yorkshire, and they each received patriarchal blessings independently in 1845 before their emigrations and marriage en route to Utah. Henry was promised the power of God in gathering converts to Zion, where, the patriarch pronounced,

> ... thou shalt share in a blessed inheritance in lands that shall yield their abundant increase[;] flocks and continued herds shall be added unto thee and thou shall have thy vine and olive yards and eat the fruit of them ... and behold the glorious coming of the blessed Redeemer and his holy Angels ... and live in the great melienuin [sic] with thye blessed redeemer.

[36] Stephen J. Fleming, 'The Religious Heritage of the British Northwest and the Rise of Mormonism', *Church History*, 77:1 (March 2008), 73–104.

[37] Grant Underwood, *The Millenarian World of Early Mormonism* (Urbana: University of Illinois Press, 1993), pp. 127–38; W.H. Oliver, *Prophets and Millennialists: The Uses of Biblical Prophecy in England from the 1790s to the 1840s* (Oxford: Oxford University Press, 1978), pp. 218–38; Malcom R. Thorp, 'The Religious Backgrounds of Mormon Converts in Britain, 1837–52', *Journal of Mormon History*, 4 (1977), 63.

[38] CHL, Daniel Holding journal, 4–5, MS 20914.

[39] Thorp, 'Religious Backgrounds', 63; Underwood, *Millenarian World*, pp. 127–38; Oliver, *Prophets and Millennialists*, pp. 218–38; Fleming, 'Religious Heritage', 73–104.

Elizabeth, likewise, was promised that she

> ... shall have thy blessed inheritance among the faithful saints in lands and corn and wine and oil and flocks and herds added unto thee and eat the fruit of thy vine and olive yards ... with the admiring saints in sweet communion ... and live in the reign of righteousness with [thy] blessed Redeemer and in the Great melleniun [sic].[40]

An envisioned economic inheritance in Zion emerged primarily out of British converts' eschatological expectations. Nevertheless, Mormon millennialism and communalism remained inseparable and pulled in the same direction—across the Atlantic to the gathering in the West.

Some of the earliest Latter-day Saint Scandinavian converts, in contrast, came from communal backgrounds. In 1825, a Norwegian adventurer named Kleng Peerson convinced a group of 52 Quakers and radical Pietist *Haugianere* (followers of the itinerant preacher, Hans Nielsen Hauge) to purchase a tiny sloop—named the 'Restoration' and later referred to as the 'Norwegian Mayflower'—and sail for New York. After a first failed attempt at communal living, Peerson and five of the 'slooper' families established the Fox River Settlement in La Salle County, Illinois in 1834, to be joined three years later by 215 more Norwegians, many of them *Haugianere*. The first Norwegian-speaking Mormon missionary, George Dykes, reached the settlement in 1842, and within two years had a thriving congregation of over one hundred converts, at least six of them from the original 'sloopers'. Several of these later lent their efforts to United Orders in Utah. Canute Peterson, for example, helped direct the Leeds, Utah United Order as bishop, and Christian Hyer became president of the Richmond, Utah Co-operative Mercantile Institution.[41] These United Orders during the Utah period also attracted some converts with communalist backgrounds still living in Scandinavia, like Johan Henrik Bergstedt, a socialist member of the Norwegian Labour Party. Helge Seljaas has argued that such Scandinavians ensured that 'the most successful united orders tended to be districts with heavy Scandinavian settlement'.[42]

---

[40] CHL, Henry Emery, reminiscences, 4–5, 16–17, MS 7498.

[41] Gerald Myron Haslam, *Clash of Cultures: The Norwegian Experience with Mormonism, 1842–1920* (New York: Peter Lang, 1984), pp. 1–6; CHL, Goudy Hogan to Brigham Young, 12 April 1877, CR 1234 1.

[42] Helge Seljaas, 'Scandinavian Mormons and Their "Zion"', *Scandinavian Studies*, 60 (Autumn 1988), 445–6.

THE UNITED ORDERS IN TRANS-ATLANTIC CONTEXT

During the late 1860s, as Mormon leaders considered establishing cooperative economics in Utah, Latter-day Saints studied cooperatives in England, including the consumer cooperative famously founded at Rochdale by Lancashire textile workers in 1844. In 1865, an article in the Church-owned *Deseret News* praised cooperatives in England and the eastern United States, describing how 'working men and others of limited means unite, put their pittances together, stock and store, and while that store undersells the regular retail dealers, receive a fair percentage of interest on their invested capital, however little that may be'. The article asked: 'why should we not have such co-operative action here? ... As a community we are better organized for accomplishing a thing of this kind than any other.'[43]

In 1868, the *Deseret News* lamented the strife between capital and labour throughout the world, calling it a 'social evil of a very serious character'. The Latter-day Saint gospel, the newspaper continued, 'has to remove the causes of every existing wrong, to heal up the wounds of society'. Indeed, the Mormons were 'looking for a day, that is not far distant, when the order of Enoch shall be established among the Saints'. Previous cooperative attempts in England and the United States were flawed because they were 'a combination of capital against capital, and of labour against capital'. Nevertheless, the paper stated with millennial fervour, 'The day is not far distant when the last vestige of class feeling will disappear, and injustice and equity govern every relation between labour and capital among all Latter-day Saints.'[44] While convinced that other cooperatives would fall short of what the Latter-day Saints could achieve, the *Deseret News* continued to report on cooperatives in Britain and elsewhere in Europe, suggesting that the Saints could learn much from these efforts.[45] In March 1869, an article declared,

> Co-operation as now conducted in the world, may not achieve all that is required to bring about this happy condition of affairs; but it is one means that can be used very effectively for the present, and it will, if properly

[43] 'Freighting, Co-operation and Money Saving', *Deseret News*, 30 November 1865.
[44] 'Capital and Labor—Employers and Employed', *Deseret News*, 27 May 1868.
[45] See, for example, 'Co-operative Societies in Switzerland', *Deseret News*, 17 April 1867; 'Co-operation and Its Benefits', *Deseret News*, 17 June 1868; and 'Results of Co-operation', *Deseret News*, 28 October 1868.

conducted, work out great results and prepare the people for the inaugura-
tion of higher principles and more advanced rules of life.[46]

The Latter-day Saints clearly felt a kinship with the cooperative institutions of Europe.

A series of articles in October 1868 in the *Salt Lake City Daily
Telegraph*, a Mormon newspaper, focused on the Rochdale Society of
Equitable Pioneers, which it distinguished from other communal efforts
such as Owenism and Communism. The *Telegraph* believed that its history of the Rochdale cooperative would demonstrate

> that when the working classes cease to quarrel with capital, and endeavor by
> prudent and skillful co-operation to become capitalists themselves, they help
> to solve a very difficult social problem, and elevate themselves as individuals,
> while at the same time they help to elevate the class to which they belong.[47]

The newspaper lauded other English and Scottish cooperatives, though
it recognized that 'there must be a general spirit of thrift among the
population, a persevering courage, and an amount of self-control sufficient to keep the members from the gin-shop or the public-house, before
such a society can anywhere take root'. Failed cooperatives in 'Sheffield,
Birmingham, Glasgow, Edinburgh, Liverpool, and London' suggested
that such cities did not have the proper conditions.[48] The article implied
that surely Salt Lake City did.

The *Telegraph* pointed to the intense interest in European cooperatives
among Utah citizens and advocated the establishment of cooperatives
among them.[49] Cooperatives would connect the Latter-day Saints with
the broader trans-Atlantic world:

> Co-operation in all the various forms ... is one of the most salient character-
> istics of the present age. It is co-operation that covers Europe and America
> with railways, lays down the Atlantic Cable ... and it is by co-operation, and
> the union of small savings, that the poor are learning how to diminish the
> hardships of their poverty, and to procure for themselves many of the enjoy-
> ments of the rich.[50]

[46] 'Co-operation Abroad', *Deseret News*, 24 March 1869. See also, 'Editorial Summary',
Deseret News, 2 June 1869.
[47] 'Co-operative Societies', *Salt Lake Daily Telegraph*, 16 October 1868.
[48] 'Co-operative Societies [continued]', *Salt Lake Daily Telegraph*, 19 October 1868.
[49] 'Co-operation', *Salt Lake Daily Telegraph*, 13 October 1868.
[50] 'Co-operative Societies [continued]', *Salt Lake Daily Telegraph*, 20 October 1868.

Though key differences existed between the Rochdale cooperative and the Mormon cooperatives in Utah, the British example doubtless influenced the Latter-day Saints.[51] As Leonard Arrington observed in his classic economic history of the Latter-day Saints, *Great Basin Kingdom*, 'Mormon missionaries in Europe had a particularly excellent opportunity to observe the operation of co-operatives in England, Scotland, and Scandinavia. Many of them vowed to assist in the establishment of similar institutions in Zion.'[52] Latter-day Saints who had served missions in England, and British converts who had been familiar with the cooperatives, were both instrumental in cooperative enterprises in Utah. In 1864, apostle Lorenzo Snow led an effort to establish a cooperative system in Brigham City, in which English converts—some of whom were likely acquainted with the Rochdale cooperative system—played key roles.[53] A cooperative store in Lehi—one of Utah's earliest, founded in 1868—was apparently influenced by Israel Evans, who had spent much of the 1850s on a mission to England. According to a community history, Evans 'had studied the Rochdale co-operative system, and now believed the same plan of co-operation could be utilized beneficially in his own city'.[54]

Louis Bertrand long hoped that communalism would be reinstated among the Latter-day Saints in Utah Territory, and just a few years before his death in 1875, Church leaders announced that Latter-day Saints should begin to organize communally into United Orders. In the vision of Brigham Young and other leaders, United Orders would cultivate unity, free the Mormons from dependence on outside merchants and eliminate poverty. 'The time has come', said apostle George Q. Cannon at the October 1872 general conference, 'when we must obey that which has been revealed to us as the Order of Enoch, when there shall be no rich and no poor among the Latter-day Saints.'[55]

The following day, Young elaborated on the communal societies that he envisioned would arise patterned 'after the Order of Enoch': 'A society like this would never have to buy anything; they would make and raise all they would eat, drink, and wear, and always have something to sell and

[51] Arrington, Fox and May, *Building the City of God*, pp. 94–5, 100–1.

[52] Arrington, *Great Basin Kingdom*, p. 293.

[53] May, 'One Heart and Mind', 146.

[54] Hamilton Gardner, *History of Lehi, Including a Biographical Section* (Salt Lake City: Deseret News, 1913), p. 187; Arrington, Fox and May, *Building the City of God*, p. 89.

[55] George Q. Cannon, 8 October 1872, *Journal of Discourses*, 26 vols (London and Liverpool: LDS Booksellers Depot, 1854–86), 15:207.

bring money, to help increase their comfort and independence.'[56] In 1876, John Taylor, the former missionary to the Icarians and now president of the Quorum of the Twelve Apostles, wrote, 'The united order is from God & was practiced by Enoch & his associates' as well as the disciples of Christ in both the New Testament and the Book of Mormon. The United Order, Taylor wrote, 'is an Eternal principle' that 'is Identified with the building up of the church & Kingdom of God the establishment of Zion & the renovation & regeneration of the Earth'.[57]

Mormon leaders showed significant flexibility with the Orders, allowing the members of each society to decide how to manage their affairs. In an April 1874 general conference session, two months after the establishment of the first United Order, Apostle Orson Pratt stated that the new orders would depart in ways from the system Joseph Smith had envisioned: 'I do not know that the common stock operation which God commanded us to enter into in Jackson County, M[issouri], will be suitable in the year 1874.'[58] In addition to differing from early Mormon communalism, the United Orders varied among themselves. Impoverished, rural settlements often favoured more communal living, while the older, more established urban centres generally adopted cooperative arrangements.

In their study of Mormon communalism, *Building the City of God*, Leonard J. Arrington, Feramorz Y. Fox and Dean L. May categorized the United Orders into four classes. The first category was organized around communal ownership of property and industry with differential wages and dividends rewarded for labour and initial capital stock investment. The second category was based on the model of Brigham City that featured community ownership of manufacturing and agriculture alongside private ownership of property and open-market labour and wages. The third category, mostly organized within individual wards (congregations) in urban areas, established a single cooperative enterprise in which members contributed both capital investment and labour. The fourth model, employed mostly among rural settlements, was arguably the closest to achieving Brigham Young's vision. These orders emphasized communal property ownership, equal dividends and community self-sufficiency.

---

[56] Brigham Young, 9 October 1872, *Journal of Discourses*, 15:223.

[57] CHL, Taylor to Culbert King, 30 September 1876, Kingston United Order journals, folder 1, LR 4463 22.

[58] Orson Pratt, 6 April 1874, *Journal of Discourses*, 17:33.

Financial distress brought about by the national Panic of 1873 expedited the formation of United Order societies throughout territorial Utah. By the end of 1875, over two hundred United Orders had been established throughout the territory. The majority of the United Orders, however, were dissolved by 1877, with rare exceptions surviving into the 1880s. The United Orders were victims of internal disorder, environmental challenges, the expansion of mining and other industries, the lure of outside merchants and goods, and the disruption of federal polygamy prosecutions.

John Alexander Dowie's Twentieth-Century Utopia

As these United Orders demonstrated, Mormon communalism drew from its trans-Atlantic context, but it also helped shape other trans-Atlantic communal traditions—none perhaps more noteworthy than John Alexander Dowie's 'twentieth-century Utopia': Zion City, Illinois.[59] Born in Edinburgh, Scotland, in 1847, Dowie emigrated back and forth from Australia in his early years. By 1882 he had established an independent ministry in Melbourne that centred on divine healing; Dowie reportedly healed hundreds over the next few years as part of his International Divine Healing Association. In response to a revelatory vision, Dowie felt called to move to the United States. But before he left Australia he had his first encounter with Latter-day Saints. Dowie became aware that a Mormon missionary was 'being persecuted' by local Protestants and publicly decried his mistreatment. The missionary and his family apparently spent some time with Dowie and his family and familiarized them with Mormon theology.[60]

Dowie arrived in the United States in early 1888, spent the next two years evangelizing the Pacific coast and then travelled to a new base of

---

[59] Philip L. Cook, *Zion City, Illinois: Twentieth-Century Utopia* (Syracuse University Press, 1996). On Dowie, see Grant Wacker, 'Marching to Zion: Religion in a Modern Utopian Community', *Church History*, 54:4 (1985), 503; Alden R. Heath, 'Apostle in Zion', *Journal of the Illinois State Historical Society*, 70 (1977), 98–113; Timothy E.W. Gloege, 'Faith Healing, Medical Regulation, and Public Religion in Progressive Era Chicago', *Religion and American Culture*, 23:2 (2013), pp. 185–231.

[60] 'False Swearers', *Leaves of Healing*, 24 November 1900, 144; D. William Faupel, 'What Has Pentecostalism to Do with Mormonism? The Case of John Alexander Dowie', in Quincy D. Newell and Eric F. Mason (eds), *New Perspectives on Mormon Studies: Creating and Crossing Boundaries* (Norman: University of Oklahoma Press, 2013), p. 86.

operations in Evanston, Illinois. En route, he spent three days in Salt Lake City, made a careful study of the community and met with Mormon leaders.[61] The managing editor of Dowie's periodical, Arthur Newcomb, later wrote that the Mormon 'Zion' 'made a deep impression upon him'.[62] During the next few years in Evanston, Dowie gained notoriety by loudly condemning all denominations and denouncing all medical professionals. His sermons and healings, especially among the crowds at the 1893 Chicago World's Fair, drew thousands of followers. In February 1895, Dowie began ecstatically announcing the possibilities for a city also to be called 'Zion' and described in detail the economic and moral possibilities of a city dedicated to living the communal life of the primitive Christians.[63] Two months later he dissolved his International Divine Healing Association to establish a church. He envisioned that God would '"build up" in the little city of Zion' and 'rapidly extend throughout the world a CHRISTIAN CATHOLIC APOSTOLIC CHURCH'.[64]

From 1895 to 1899, Dowie's business enterprises, philanthropic concerns, healings, evangelism, mass-circulation periodicals and following boomed. On New Year's Eve 1899, Dowie announced that he had secured 6600 acres 42 m north of Chicago along the shores of Lake Michigan, where his vision for Zion City could take form. This, as Grant Wacker has noted, was the moment when the local Illinois clergy's bemusement turned to alarm.[65] *The Independent*, for example, wrote that it had no bones to pick with Dowie's pre-millennialist effusions, literalist exegeses or healing exhibitions, 'but what requires serious warning is the new development which proposes to erect this Zion of Dr. Dowie's into a financial, perhaps political, organization very much like that of the Mormon Church'.[66] Such fears were not unfounded. By 1900, Dowie's denomination had 25,000 to 50,000 adherents worldwide and by 1905, 7500 to 10,000 of them were permanent residents in Zion City.[67]

The economic arrangements of Zion City echoed many of the Mormons' communal practices: producer cooperatives, profit-sharing,

---

[61] Faupel, 'What Has Pentecostalism to Do with Mormonism?' p. 86.

[62] Arthur Newcomb, *Dowie: Anointed of the Lord* (New York: Century Co., 1930), pp. 37–8.

[63] 'Editorial Notes', *Leaves of Healing*, 15 February 1895, 345.

[64] 'Editorial Notes', *Leaves of Healing*, 26 April 1895, 479.

[65] Wacker, 'Marching to Zion', 500–1.

[66] 'Dr. Dowie's "Zion"', *The Independent*, 11 May 1899, 1323.

[67] Wacker, 'Marching to Zion', 496–7, 502.

a strong emphasis on individual stewardship instead of communal own-ership, an avoidance of commercial entanglements with non-Dowieites and a universal ten per cent tithe on personal earnings. These were com-bined with a literal and materialistic millennialism: for example, residents received 1100-year land leases (extending into the Millennium) instead of clear property titles. Grant Wacker has described the arrangements as 'an ingenious yet inherently precarious combination of biblical, utopian, and modern notions'. Zion City Bank and major industrial operations in candy and lace, among other businesses, all owned and largely run by Dowie, 'pumped the community's financial lifeblood'.[68] Dowie shared around 90% of profits with the labourers, guaranteed employment to Zion City residents and protected them from strikes and labour conflict. During the first few years of cooperative effort, Zion City boomed and its motto pre-vailed in theory and practice: 'Where God Rules, Man Prospers.'[69] Dowie declared himself the Messenger of the Covenant, the third and final mani-festation of Elijah, and the prophet of the last days through whom God ruled Zion City. 'I have been raised up by God to do a work such as has never been done in modern times, nor in ancient times, by any other prophet of God', he declared.[70]

Zion City's economic foundations were trans-Atlantic from the begin-ning. The largest employer of the community, Zion Lace Industries, was an English transplant in toto.[71] Dowie's vision for Zion City had a profoundly global orientation. Much like Joseph Smith, Dowie saw his Zion City as the literal Zion from which Christ would soon reign in the Millennium and as the centre of a system of satellite cities that would rise in Jerusalem, and near major metropolises like London and Calcutta. To gather the elect in every nation, Dowie organized the 'Seventies' as a mis-sionary arm of the church and sent them out, two by two, 'to all the ends of the earth'.[72]

Zion City's Seventies demonstrate Mormon influences on Dowie. The Latter-day Saints had long ordained men as 'Seventies', based on the New Testament, to help in proselytizing and church governance.[73] When

[68] Wacker, 'Marching to Zion', 501.

[69] 'Where God Rules, Man Prospers', *Leaves of Healing*, 26 April 1902, 23–31.

[70] *Leaves of Healings* 11:764 (complete citation).

[71] Cook, *Zion City*, p. 35.

[72] Cook, *Zion City*, pp. 34–5.

[73] Luke 10:1 relates Christ appointing 'seventy' and sending them out two by two 'into every city'. Dowie's organization of Seventies drew directly from Mormonism but also drew,

Dowie began doing the same, he stated, 'I studied the Mormon Church. I watched that Seventy Movement of theirs and saw that they were able to send out common, apparently illiterate men into the world, who were devoted to their church, and were willing to die for it.'[74] Dowie spoke similarly of the rest of the Latter-day Saints' ecclesiology, calling it 'the best organized and most clearly scripturally organized of all churches' and the closest one to 'the Apostolic model'. He recounted that when he 'visited Salt Lake City' he 'was enabled to learn a great many things concerning the [Mormons'] internal organization'. The structuring of his own church and community suggests that he took the lessons to heart.[75]

Like Joseph Smith, Dowie sought to restore 'the Apostolic model' but ultimately reached past it, pulling freely from Old and New Testament practices as he constructed the Kingdom of God. At times, he also pushed beyond biblical precedents entirely, based on his own authority as a prophet. Thus, like the Mormon prophets, Dowie deemed himself not only 'First Apostle' but also 'High Priest'. Like Salt Lake City, Zion City also had a temple and tabernacle at its liturgical and geographical centre.[76]

Ultimately, it was not primarily in the particular economic practices of Zion City that Mormonism made its mark. Rather, it was in the open-ended restorationism that undergirded those practices, the material millennialism that directed them, the peculiar prophet-hood that authorized them and the vocabulary with which Dowie voiced them. Though Dowie's vision of Zion City only experienced prosperity for a few years, its progeny and influence continue to reverberate on both sides of the Atlantic, and its borrowings from Mormonism's communalism and millennialism were often commented on by contemporary observers.[77]

of course, from this New Testament account *through* a Mormon-influenced restorationist hermeneutic.

[74] 'Opening of Zion's Hall of Seventies', *Leaves of Healing*, 28 January 1899, 255.

[75] 'Opening of Zion's Hall of Seventies', *Leaves of Healing*, 28 January 1899, 255.

[76] Dowie's simultaneous insistence on a restoration of the New Testament church and literal identification with ancient Israel—two of the central conceptual foundations of his communal society—was distinctively Mormon and almost certainly drawn from the Latter-day Saints in Salt Lake City. See Joseph Williams, 'The Pentecostalization of Christian Zionism', *Church History*, 84 (March 2015), 171.

[77] For the historical and trans-Atlantic reverberations of Dowie's movement, see Adam Mohr, 'Zionism and Aladura's Shared Genealogy in John Alexander Dowie', *Religion*, 45 (April 2015), 239–51; Brian Stanley, 'Edinburgh and World Christianity', *Studies in World Christianity*, 17:1 (2011), 72–91; Adam Mohr, 'Out of Zion into Philadelphia and West Africa: Faith Tabernacle Congregation, 1897–1925', *Pneuma*, 32:1 (2010), 56–79. For more contemporary comparisons of Dowie and Mormonism, see 'False Swearers', *Leaves of Healing*, 24 November 1900, 144; Ernest Hamlin Abbot, 'Religious Life in America: New

Conclusion: Mormon Self-conceptions of Trans-Atlantic Communalism

Mormon leaders recognized the trans-Atlantic context of their efforts at communal life and economics. They were familiar with the communal societies that surrounded them in America and Europe, they noted converts like Louis Bertrand who traded trans-Atlantic socialism for the fellowship of the Saints and they watched the visions of other trans-Atlantic communalists flounder. Mormon leaders' awareness of influences on, engagements with and emulations of Mormon communalism within the Atlantic world ultimately led them to conceive of their own communal efforts in both trans-Atlantic and transcendent terms: trans-Atlantic because Mormonism had or would succeed where other communal groups on both sides of the Atlantic had failed; transcendent because the source of their success was their covenant relationship to God as the community that would prepare the earth for Christ's second coming. Mormon self-identity rested, in part, on contrasting themselves with other communal groups from throughout the Atlantic world.

In an address given at Temple Square in Salt Lake City in 1857, John Taylor detailed 'various social and politics movements, aided by philosophy, established among men in various ages of the world'. 'Almost, if not all of these', Taylor stated, 'have signally failed', pointing to the communities established by Robert Owen and Charles Fourier. In addition, establishing a theme that other Mormon leaders echoed throughout the century, Taylor juxtaposed the Icarian community that had collapsed in post-Mormon Nauvoo with the Mormons who had settled Utah despite more difficult circumstances.[78] He concluded that 'many societies of a similar nature, commenced in different parts of the world and at various times' had likewise 'commenced in the wisdom of man, and ended as speculative bubbles', proving that there was 'something associated with this people and with "Mormonism" that there is not with them'. For Taylor, the difference was that 'the [Mormon] society ... comes with the fear of God'.[79]

Sects and Old', *Outlook*, 13 September 1902, 125; 'Dowie and the "Mormons"', *Deseret Evening News*, 13 April 1906; Gilbert Seldes, *The Stammering Century* (New York: J. Day Co., 1928), 389.

[78] Other examples of the Icarian comparison include Brigham Young, 16 June 1867, *Journal of Discourses*, 12:61; George Q. Cannon, 6 April 1869, *Journal of Discourses*, 13:98.

[79] John Taylor, 13 September 1857, *Journal of Discourses*, 5:237–8. See also, Lorenzo Snow, 21 April 1878, *Journal of Discourses*, 19:349.

Leaders like Taylor saw a peoplehood forged by the authority of divine priesthood reflected in Mormon communalism. For them, Mormon priesthood and peoplehood fulfilled the frustrated ambitions of a trans-Atlantic communal quest. 'Fourierism, Communism ... and many other principles of the same kind have been introduced to try and cement the human family together', Taylor observed. 'But all these things have failed, ... because however philanthropic, humanitarian, benevolent, or cosmopolitan our ideas, it is impossible to produce a true and correct union without the Spirit of the living God, and that Spirit can only be imparted through the [priesthood] ordinances of the Gospel.'[80]

In this, Mormons were strikingly similar to many nineteenth-century Roman Catholics who used Fourier, Owen, George Ripley (the leading thinker behind the Brook Farm community) and others as object lessons. Each illustrated, in Catholic minds, that true community was established though papal authority in Christ's kingdom, that trans-Atlantic communalists tried to compensate for the absence of true community outside the Roman Church and that their attempts would never succeed.[81] Mormons, likewise, positioned themselves at the centre of the trans-Atlantic communal world, casting failed sectarian and secular utopias as peripheral proofs that the only true communalism was in God's institutional church and people.

Mormons knew that their own efforts at communal economics had failed at least as often as they had succeeded. Nevertheless, for them, the ultimate meaning of Mormon peoplehood and communal living was millennial: imperfect Mormon communalism in the present was always pressing towards full realization in the future. In an 1894 discourse delivered at the Tabernacle, George Q. Cannon, now a member of the Church's First Presidency, stated that God had 'revealed through Joseph Smith a plan by which union could be effected of such character as would remedy the evils that exist now in society'. The plan would 'stop the necessity for capital being arrayed against labor' and vice versa. The Saints, Cannon continued, had not yet been fully successful in implementing the plan, but would 'continue at work at this as long as we live', because they were 'the

---

[80] John Taylor, 10 October 1875, *Journal of Discourses*, 18:137.

[81] For examples, see J.W.G., 'Fourierism, and the Three Socialisms', *Catholic Telegraph*, 13 January 1844, 10–11; John B. Byrne, 'Protestantism—Its Tendencies and Results', *United States Catholic Magazine and Monthly Review*, April 1844, 239–41; Anna M. Mitchell, 'The Brook Farm Movement Viewed through the Perspective of a Half Century', *Catholic World*, 1 April 1901, 17–31.

people that can do it, and no other people'. Cannon situated this Mormon mission at the centre of a trans-Atlantic world where peripheral utopian prophets felt—as deeply as Mormons—that something was missing 'in the organization of society', yet lacked the priesthood and peoplehood to provide what was missing.

> These anarchists feel it; these societies of various kinds feel it; but their methods of reaching the desired end are not from God; therefore they fail. Fourier tried it; so did St. Simon. Owen tried in England, and afterwards in America. Many other reformers have tried ... but up to the present they have failed ... How shall these things be corrected? If they are not corrected by God raising up a people they never will be corrected.

Cannon envisioned a millennial timetable for the fulfilment of the Mormon people's communal mission and urged Mormons to prepare themselves to 'put in operation ... this perfect order'. 'We can divest ourselves of our selfishness ... And we shall live, if not in the flesh, to behold it and take part in that great millennial glory, towards which the eyes of all inspired men have been directed from the beginning.'[82]

These Mormon self-conceptions continued into the mid- and late twentieth century and, at times, merged seamlessly with condemnations of twentieth-century communisms. Although a full exploration is beyond the scope of this chapter, these echoes of nineteenth-century communalism in the twentieth century suggest the continuing power of trans-Atlantic communalism for Latter-day Saints. A trio of talks given in 1930, 1951 and 1962 by David O. McKay, a prominent apostle and eventually Church president, provides a salient illustration.[83] Each had a similar outline. First, McKay traced the Latter-day Saints' communal context, declaring 'a social Utopia has been the quest of the ages'. In the nineteenth century, 'observant people became dissatisfied with social and economic conditions, and thinking men sought for remedial changes'. Thus, Charles Fourier in France, Robert Owen in England and George Ripley in America all tried their hands at communal societies, McKay said, but each failed. Certainly, Mormonism emerged in this trans-Atlantic context, McKay acknowledged, noting one 'cynical writer' who argued that 'the Mormon Church was but one more excrescence of the fermenting body

---

[82] George Q. Cannon, 'Secret Combinations', *Deseret Weekly*, 7 April 1894, 479.

[83] David O. McKay, *Conference Report*, April 1930, 78–83; David O. McKay, *Conference Report*, April 1954, 22–6; David O. McKay, *Conference Report*, October 1962, 5–8.

politic of this religious-social reaction'. But, in McKay's mind, Latter-day Saints transcended their trans-Atlantic communal context. Although it shared the same social goals as other 'worthy' communal societies, the Church's communal efforts were organized by 'divine direction', had outlasted a century of social upheavals and were still supplying society's 'highest needs'.

McKay then drew a straight line from the nineteenth-century social ills that communal societies sought to ameliorate and the twentieth-century political problems which communist governments—like the 'dictatorship of the proletariat ... in Soviet Russia'—claimed to solve. As with the social, so with the political: McKay declared that the Church of Jesus Christ of Latter-day Saints had, by divine direction, 'that form of government which the nations today are seeking'.[84] Thus the formative trans-Atlantic context of nineteenth-century Mormon communal self-conceptions could still echo more than a century later in connection with mid-twentieth-century Mormon pronouncements on global politics. Such self-conceptions have been a lasting legacy of the trans-Atlantic world in which Mormonism was born—a world whose traces and trails led sporadically in and out of the Church's nineteenth-century communal efforts and millennial expectations.

[84] McKay, *Conference Report*, April 1930, 79–81.

CHAPTER 8

Trans-Atlantic Reputations: Protestant Communalism and Early Socialism

Philip Lockley

The trans-Atlantic history of Protestant communalism before 1850 was not restricted to the migrations, letter networks, recruitment missions or other internal initiatives of traditions and communities themselves. The interest and imitation provoked by communal groups outside their memberships and immediate settings also spanned the Atlantic. Their reputations were traceably trans-Atlantic, and in several cases their international influence grew some time after their last migrating believers had left Europe for America.

European notice of the Ephrata community, for instance, began in the late 1750s, some three decades after Conrad Beissel formed his first Pennsylvania community. By this date, a fashion for travel narratives encouraged colonial visitors to publish accounts of the sights and oddities of the North American interior. Israel Acrelius, the leading Swedish Lutheran whose observations of Ephrata were noted in Chap. 3, published his

P. Lockley
University of Oxford, Oxford, UK

© The Editor(s) (if applicable) and The Author(s) 2016   189
P. Lockley (ed.), *Protestant Communalism in the Trans-Atlantic World, 1650–1850*, DOI 10.1057/978-1-137-48487-1_8

account in Stockholm as *A History of New Sweden* in 1759.[1] Within a year, both the London *Royal Magazine* and the *Annual Register* also printed a description of the 'society called Dunkards, in Pennsylvania', this time by a 'gentleman of America'.[2] Ephrata's renown in Europe remained limited nonetheless, and subject to confusion: Voltaire's *Philosophical Dictionary* of 1764 misnamed the community as 'Euphrates', when describing this 'sort of religious hospitallers ... [g]one astray in a corner of the new world, far from the great flock of the Catholic Church'.[3]

In due course the Shakers and the Harmony Society featured in travellers' accounts that gained a trans-Atlantic readership.[4] One of the first descriptions of the Shakers to reach a European audience was by the Duke of Rochefoucauld-Liancourt, exiled from France after the Revolution, who published multiple editions of his *Travels through the United States of North America* in both London and Paris from 1799.[5] In 1806, the English Quaker Priscilla Bell Wakefield's *Excursions in North America* included an eyewitness account of a Shaker religious service and a report of the New Lebanon community.[6] Shakers also featured alongside the Ephrata 'Dunkers' in John Evans's popular London reference work, *Sketch of the Denominations of the Christian World* after 1807.[7] In 1812, Shakers received further passing mention in John Melish's *Travels in the United*

---

[1] Israel Acrelius, *A History of New Sweden, or the Settlements on the Delaware River*, trans. William M. Reynolds, reprinted in Felix Reichmann and Eugene E. Doll, *Ephrata as Seen by Contemporaries*, Proceedings of the Pennsylvania German Folklore Society, vol. 17 (Allentown, PA: Schechters, 1953), pp. 50–77. An English translation of this work was published in 1874. See pp. 48–50.

[2] *Royal Magazine; or, Gentleman's Monthly Companion*, 1:2 (1759), 61–3; *The Annual Register or a View of the History, Politicks, and Literature of the Year 1759* (London, 1760), pp. 341–3.

[3] Voltaire, *Dictionnaire philosophique* (1764), quoted in Reichmann and Doll, *Ephrata as Seen by Contemporaries*, p. 84.

[4] For a contemporary account of Moravian communities, see John Ogden, *An Excursion into Bethlehem and Nazareth in Pennsylvania in the Year 1799; with a Succinct History of the Society of United Brethren, Commonly Called Moravians* (Philadelphia, 1805).

[5] François-Alexandre-Frédéric, duc de Rochefoucauld-Liancourt, *Travels through the United States of North America: the country of the Iroquois, and Upper Canada, in the years 1795, 1796, and 1797*, transl. H. Neuman, 2 vols (London, 1799–1800), 2:92–100.

[6] Priscilla Bell Wakefield, *Excursions in North America. Described in Letters from a Gentleman and his Young Companion to their Friends in England* (London, 1806), pp. 201–3.

[7] John Evans, *Sketch of the Denominations of the Christian World* (London, 1807). See also John Evans, *Sequel to the Sketch of the Denominations of the Christian World ... and an account of the church government of the Shakers, who neither marry nor are given in marriage* (London, 1811).

States of America.[8] As Hermann Ehmer has noted in Chap. 5, Melish's more extensive account of his visit to Harmony, Pennsylvania, was among the earliest descriptions of the first Harmonist community.[9]

Melish's book was initially only published in Philadelphia. Trans-Atlantic Quaker connections brought the work to the attention of a leading London Quaker, William Allen, who extracted Melish's account of George Rapp's community to reprint in his monthly journal, *The Philanthropist*, in 1815.[10] It was this latter publication which was read by Allen's business partner, Robert Owen, the Welsh-born cotton master, philanthropist and secular social theorist. Owen's interest in the Harmony Society set in train a series of exchanges and events that would eventually lead him to purchase their second American community, New Harmony, Indiana, at the close of 1824.

Owen was behind the importing and republishing in London of a *Brief Sketch of the Religious Society of People Called Shakers* by W.S. Warder of Philadelphia in 1818.[11] Melish's account of Harmony was then reproduced or cited extensively in several publications linked to Owen in Britain by the early 1820s.[12] An article in the *New Monthly Magazine* in 1818 quoted Melish's book, Owen's view of the Shakers and a work on Moravian communities in Germany.[13] Accounts of the second Harmony settlement in Indiana, as well as more western Shaker sites, then reached Britain after 1819. An émigré scheme known as English Prairie settled the Illinois region west of Rapp's new community, and settlers, visitors and 'boosters' with a promotional interest in English Prairie frequently referred to nearby New Harmony in letters and publications, as they often passed

[8] John Melish, *Travels in the United States of America, in the years 1806 & 1807, and 1809, 1810, & 1811*, 2 vols (Philadelphia, 1812), 2:303.

[9] Melish, *Travels in the United States*, 2:64–82.

[10] *The Philanthropist: or, Repository for hints and suggestions calculated to promote the comfort and happiness of man*, no. 20 (1815).

[11] Robert Owen, *New View of Society: Tracts Relative to this Subject* (London, 1818), 69. Printed in pamphlet form as W.S. Warder, *A Brief Sketch of the Religious Society of People Called Shakers* (London, [1818]).

[12] 'Philanthropos' [John Minter Morgan], *Remarks on the Practicability of Mr Robert Owen's Plan to Improve the Condition of the Lower Classes* (London, 1818), pp. 68–72; 'Spencean Philanthropist', *Christian Policy in Full Practice among the People of Harmony* (London, 1818); Anon., *Mr. Owen's proposed arrangements for the distressed working classes shown to be consistent with sound principles of political economy* (London, 1819), pp. 96–102.

[13] *New Monthly Magazine*, 9 (1818), 116–18.

the community.[14] George Courtauld, a visitor to English Prairie, returned to Edinburgh in 1819 and published an open letter to Robert Owen in the *Glasgow Journal*, describing the 'remarkable establishments' of both the Shakers and Harmonists, which he considered to offer evidence for 'the superior advantages of a direct union of capital and labour'.[15]

As Arthur Bestor has recorded, the 1820s witnessed a marked rise in the number of accounts of Protestant communities printed for both an American and European readership, which persisted into the 1840s.[16] Travel narratives featuring descriptions of Shaker communities in New England, New York or western regions proliferated for some time.[17] The Harmonists' third settlement at Economy, Pennsylvania, drew reports by European visitors soon after its foundation, while the Pietist Separatists of Zoar, Ohio, attracted their own tourists and descriptions from the late 1830s.[18] This increased attention was the result of several factors, including improved transport links within the United States and across the Atlantic making touring easier, expanding book markets in both Europe and America, and a growing interest in America as a potential destination for emigration.

Yet, from the time of Robert Owen's first notice of the Harmonists and Shakers until well into the 1840s, a further ideological factor lay behind much of the interest in Protestant communal settlements, in Britain especially, but also parts of the United States: the emergence of the first forms of socialism. For much of the first half of the nineteenth century,

---

[14] Richard Flower, *Letters from Lexington and the Illinois* (London, 1819), pp. 98–100; George Flower, *History of the English Settlement in Edwards County, Illinois*, ed. E.B. Washburne (Chicago, 1882), pp. 56–8, 278. Morris Birkbeck's *Notes on a Journey in America* (1817) and *Letters from Illinois* (1818) featured descriptions of the Indiana *Harmonie* and were especially popular, going through numerous editions in Britain by 1820.

[15] *Glasgow Journal*, 3 November 1819. See also, *Mr. Owen's Proposed Arrangements*, p. 96.

[16] Arthur Bestor, *Backwoods Utopias*, second edn (Philadelphia: University of Pennsylvania Press, 1970), pp. 44–5.

[17] See, for example, Isaac Holmes, *An Account of the United States of America Derived from Actual Observation during a Residence of Four Years* (London, [1823]), p. 392; Isaac Candler, *A Summary View of America* (London, 1824), p. 217; Adam Hodgson, *Letters from North America, Written during a Tour in the United States and Canada*, 2 vols (London, 1824), 1:399–400.

[18] Karl Bernhard, Duke of Saxe-Weimar-Eisenach, *Travels through North America, during the years 1825 and 1826*, 2 vols (Philadelphia, 1828), 2:106–23; Basil Hall, *Travels in North America, in the years 1827 and 1828*, 3 vols (Edinburgh, 1830), 1:111–12. Sándor Farkas, Útazás Észak Amérikában [*Travel in North America*] (Klausenburg, 1834), pp. 231–44.

the earliest recognizable adherents of socialism in Britain, America and parts of Germany tended to believe that their vision of a more harmonious social future would be realized by establishing experimental rural colonies of shared property.[19] As they planned such communities, socialists were notably encouraged and emboldened by the examples and legacies of trans-Atlantic Protestant communal societies. Over time, many travelled purposely to observe these religious communities, and consciously compared the workings of communal property with the nascent free-market and individualist economies developing elsewhere in North America as well as back in Europe. By the 1840s, Protestant communal traditions born out of the early modern era had unwittingly secured a trans-Atlantic reputation linked to movements in radical social thought that would shape the modern world.

Robert Owen was a leading figure in the development of such ideas, and his decision to cross the Atlantic to found his own experiment in Indiana was an outworking of early socialist beliefs. Yet, the trans-Atlantic reputation of Protestant communalism generated links with a wider socialist culture in Owen's time: numerous other socialists and sympathizers also studied Shaker and Harmonist communities, as well as the Separatists of Zoar. Some socialists even converted to Shakerism for shorter or longer periods. A common perspective from Europe, articulated for a time even by Friedrich Engels, joint author with Karl Marx of the 1848 *Communist Manifesto*, was that communal Protestantism offered proof that socialism was a viable future reality.

This concluding chapter narrates the distinctive relationship which may be traced between the kinds of Protestant communal groups studied in this volume and early socialism. It re-examines the interactions between these secular and religious movements, exploring the personal links and convictions which brought reports of communal Protestantism in America back to, in particular, Britain to stir what may be identified as the early socialist imagination. The chapter underlines the trans-Atlantic reach of traditions of Protestant communalism in reputation as well as history.

[19] R.G. Garnett, *Co-operation and the Owenite Socialist Communities in Britain, 1825–45* (Manchester: Manchester University Press, 1972); Carl Guarneri, *The Utopian Alternative* (Ithaca: Cornell University Press, 1991); Carl Wittke, *The Utopian Communist: A Biography of Wilhelm Weitling, Nineteenth-Century Reformer* (Baton Rouge: Louisiana State University Press, 1950).

ROBERT OWEN'S EARLY INTERESTS

When Robert Owen first began to read about trans-Atlantic Protestant communities of shared property in 1815, he was among the most famous capitalists in Europe.[20] The lead partner and manager of one of the largest and most lucrative factories in the world—New Lanark cotton mills in southern Scotland—Owen was feted for combining philanthropic concern for his workers with high profits for his shareholders. Rising rapidly in the expansive Manchester textile economy of the 1790s, Owen had acquired both a boundless belief in his own ability to succeed and a scepticism towards revealed religion. Under the influence of Enlightenment philosophies, Owen dismissed all beliefs contrary to reason and looked to the progressive improvement of human nature by the conscious reform of institutions and conditions.

Since 1800, when New Lanark was acquired from his devout Presbyterian father-in-law, David Dale, Owen had assumed control of a factory village not unlike a sequestered frontier community. New Lanark was built in a steep-sided valley where almost 2000 employees lived and worked entirely under Owen's supervision. In this setting, Owen carried out a series of celebrated experiments in improving workers' conditions by excluding physical punishments, promoting temperance and order in the community, ensuring the quality and value of goods in the company store, and providing infant education. All such reforms were premised on a theory of environmental determinism—Owen's doctrine that 'the character of man is formed for him, and not by him'. As crime, ill-health and absenteeism fell, and profits rose, Owen's reputation spread, bringing thousands of visitors to his factory site. From 1813, Owen employed artful self-publicity to project lessons from New Lanark as a wider solution to social distress in a work entitled 'A New View of Society'.[21]

---

[20] Robert Owen was not the first British social radical to be interested in the trans-Atlantic tradition of Protestant communalism: the obscure figure of John Stewart, who may or may not have known Owen, learned of the Ephrata 'Dunkards', Moravians and Shakers while visiting the United States in the 1790s, though he did not publish his descriptions of their communities in Britain for some decades. Stewart strikingly anticipated elements of Owen's thought in his later advocating community of goods to be the 'highest state of social organization'. Stewart' s influence on socialism is, however, unproven, and his idiosyncratic publications little read. Gregory Claeys, '"The Only Man of Nature That Ever Appeared in the World": "Walking" John Stewart and the Trajectories of Social Radicalism, 1790–1822', *Journal of British Studies*, 53:3 (2014), 636–59.

[21] Robert Owen, *A New View of Society, or, Essays on the Principle of the Formation of the Human Character* (London, 1813).

As Owen read John Melish's description of the Harmony Society, he appreciated the industry, efficiency, working conditions and education of the Harmony Society more than the religion underpinning it. He took a similar view of the Shakers when he acquired W.S. Warder's account of their communities soon after.[22] Despite the 'degrading superstition … exhibited in the religious notions' of such communities, Owen wrote, he found in both the Harmonists and the Shakers 'the most triumphant and abundant proofs of the truths developed in … New View of Society'.[23] For Owen, the self-sufficient nature of these groups, living apart from existing societies, not only demonstrated how moral, industrious characters could be shaped by their environments, but also provided 'a simple but convincing proof of the effects of the principle of combined labour and expenditure'.[24] It was this latter principle that Owen, despite his background in factory-ownership, was increasingly convinced should be reintroduced to Britain, to combat the growing inequality between the rich with capital and the poor with only their labour to sell.

In 1817 Owen unveiled plans for 'villages of unity and mutual co-operation'—purpose-built communities of up to 1500 individuals combining agriculture and manufacturing. In the following few years, several more accounts of Shaker and Harmony Society communities in America appeared in Britain, invariably in literature dedicated to proving the 'Practicability of Mr Robert Owen's Plan'.[25] By 1821, the Owenite *Economist* journal was insisting 'it would be easy to form other societies, under all the regulations and principles of the Shakers which are really valuable—and rejecting, of course, their idle peculiarities—foolish prejudices—and disgusting prohibitions'.[26] By this date, Owen had further developed his views on how humanity might be freed from what he called 'the profit motive' and the social evils of competition. His projected cooperative communities began to incorporate proposals for shared property—the basis for what would soon be termed Owen's 'social system', and eventually 'socialism'.[27]

[22] Bestor, *Backwoods Utopias*, p. 96; E.D. Andrews, *The People Called Shakers* (New York: Dover, 1963), p. 106.

[23] Owen, *Tracts*, p. 69.

[24] Owen, *Tracts*, p. 69.

[25] *New Monthly Magazine*, 8 (1817), 164–5; 9 (1818), 116–18; [Morgan], *Remarks*, pp. 68–72.

[26] *The Economist*, 19, (2 June 1821), 289–91, 295.

[27] Robert Owen, *A New View of Society and Other Writings*, ed. Gregory Claeys (London, 1991), pp. xv–xvi, 250–308.

Significantly, it was in 1820 that Owen first wrote to George Rapp. His letter reveals how Owen consciously viewed the Harmony Society as an exemplar for a forthcoming society, as he explicitly acknowledged the value that he had so far placed on Melish's account of Harmony for its 'many details which to me appeared to promise many important future advantages'.[28] Claiming to have 'already placed under new circumstances' his own 'colony ... of about 2400 persons' (New Lanark), Owen described himself as 'now in the midst of preparing a further development of the system', and so approached Rapp for 'the full benefit of the experience' accrued from creating two 'colonies'. '[T]he particulars of the result of these two experiments would be of real value to me', Owen wrote, 'in order to ascertain the practical inconveniences which arise from changes to society from a state of private to public property'.[29]

No known reply from Rapp survives. However, this letter and the wider notice of the Harmonists among British Owenites laid the groundwork for events in 1824, when Rapp and his leading committee instructed a returning member of the English Prairie settlement in Illinois, Richard Flower, to advertise the entire estate of the Indiana New Harmony for sale in Britain, openly seeking to interest 'capitalists'.[30] Flower travelled more or less directly to New Lanark upon arriving in Britain, secured an audience with Owen, and was then reportedly amazed at how quickly Owen was convinced to buy.[31] Owen, as biographers commonly acknowledge, was a man prone to impulsive decisions and novel departures, despite his reputation for calculating business. Even so, the appeal of New Harmony was undoubtedly the affordable opportunity it offered for realizing a full-scale model community, the prototype for his imagined future society, which he had so far waited vainly to build in Britain. By October 1824, Owen was crossing the Atlantic.

---

[28] Robert Owen to George Rapp, 4 August 1820, George Flower family papers, 1812–1974, Chicago Historical Society, reprinted in K.J.R. Arndt (ed.), *A Documentary History of the Indiana Decade of the Harmony Society 1814–1824; Volume II 1820–24* (Indianapolis: Indiana Historical Society, 1978), p. 89.

[29] Arndt (ed.), *Indiana Decade*, pp. 89–90.

[30] 'Particulars of the Settlement and Town of Harmony, State of Indiana', quoted in Karl Arndt, *George Rapp's Harmony Society, 1785–1847*, second edn (Cranbury, NJ: Associated University Presses, 1972), pp. 291–2.

[31] Robert Dale Owen, *Threading my Way: Twenty-Seven Years of Autobiography* (London, 1874), pp. 209–11.

Upon arrival in the United States, Owen did not travel directly to Indiana, but, tellingly, took his earliest opportunity to visit a site of Protestant communalism: the Shaker community of Watervliet (originally named Niskeyuna) up the Hudson River. Owen was accompanied by his son, William Owen, and a Scottish friend and follower, Donald Macdonald. Each recorded in their diaries the positive impression created by the 'remarkably neatly and well contrived' Shaker living arrangements, and Owen's 'extremely agreeable' conversation with leading members on his own 'plans for communities'.[32] The Shakers 'seemed quite pleased, particularly as [Owen] ... explained many things he meant to do on their plans'.[33] The only note of discord sounded was in response to Owen's policy of free religious opinion: they 'shook their heads when they found it was for all sects'.[34]

After several weeks in New York and Philadelphia promoting his ideas, Owen further arranged to meet George Rapp in Pittsburgh, then accompanied him to nearby Economy—Rapp's already commenced third community.[35] According to Macdonald, 'Mr Rapp conversed with Mr Owen on the subject of forming human character, and seemed to have in many respects entertained similar opinions'; when Owen 'shewed his plans, the party were much pleased with them'.[36] William Owen likewise observed, 'Mr Rapp appeared to agree to all of it ... He seemed much pleased to find an individual with whom he had so many ideas in common.'[37]

In mid-December 1824, Owen finally reached Indiana and agreed terms with Rapp's representatives there.[38] In the early months of 1825, while the Pietists packed up their remaining goods and sailed back up the Ohio River to Pennsylvania, Owen himself returned to Philadelphia and Washington. Here he lectured to prominent audiences, including current and past American presidents, on the limitless prospects for New Harmony and the 'New System of Society', citing in his favour the wealth already

[32] Donald Macdonald, *The Diaries of Donald Macdonald, 1824–1826* (Indianapolis: Indiana Historical Society, 1942), pp. 186–91.

[33] William Owen, *Diary ... from November 10, 1824, to April 20 1825*, ed. Joel W. Hiatt (Indianapolis: Indiana Historical Society, 1906), pp. 7–26.

[34] Owen, *Diary*, p. 14.

[35] Macdonald, *Diaries*, pp. 227–33; Owen, *Diary*, pp. 51–6.

[36] Macdonald, *Diaries*, p. 230.

[37] Owen, *Diary*, p. 53.

[38] Arndt, *George Rapp's Harmony Society*, p. 298.

created by Shakers and Harmonists.[39] As newspapers debated his plans and audiences received him rapturously, Owen confidently assured William Allen back in Britain that 'the States west of the Allegheny Mountains have been prepared in the most remarkable manner for the New System ... the whole country is ready to commence a new empire upon the principle of public property and to discard private property'.[40]

AFTER NEW HARMONY

Events proved otherwise. Within two years New Harmony, and a host of other Owen-inspired communities established across New York, Pennsylvania, Ohio and Indiana, had failed.[41] Owen's publicity campaign attracted hundreds of families to New Harmony itself even before he had arrived back there in April 1825. Most were poor, unskilled and temperamentally unsuited to communal life, having previously eked out an existence on isolated family farmsteads.[42] Owen did not anticipate needing to resume his New Lanark role of overseer, assuming deputies could implement his 'new system'. He travelled back and forth from Indiana repeatedly, concentrating on securing eastern investors and intellectuals drawn to the romantic prospect of creating a new and enlightened society in the West. In Owen's absence, little was done to resume the organized industries and farming of Rapp's regime. When in residence, Owen concentrated on constitutional committee structures, principles of property and freedoms of religious opinion.[43] The New Harmony community soon disintegrated, with Owen selling off tracts of land for individual ownership to keep the core experiment afloat, and then finally signing over the remainder to his sons in perpetuity.

In Pennsylvania, the Harmonists were kept informed of the fate of their former home. Not long after Owen had begun his disorderly, wasteful experiment, George Rapp had reportedly denounced him as 'a tool of the Devil'.[44] Despite Donald Macdonald and William Owen's impressions of

---

[39] Anne Taylor, *Visions of Harmony* (Oxford: Oxford University Press, 1987), pp. 95–6.

[40] National Co-operative Archive, Manchester, GB 1499 ROC/1/18/1, Robert Owen to William Allen, 21 April 1825.

[41] Bestor, *Backwoods Utopias*, p. 279.

[42] Taylor, *Visions of Harmony*, pp. 104–5.

[43] Taylor, *Visions of Harmony*, pp. 150–4.

[44] Taylor, *Visions of Harmony*, p. 111.

significant shared ground between Owen and the communalists, substantial differences in view became clearer as Owen's American experiment came to fruition and fall. Owen's leadership at New Harmony offered a sufficiently alternative prospect to disrupt at least one Shaker community. Yet, this difference was ultimately not great enough to prevent the experience of failure in Owen-inspired communities, or the disillusionment of their demise, to lead a notable number of former Owenites—including British migrants to America—to consider new lives as Shakers.

The Shaker community at Pleasant Hill in Kentucky was the most affected by events at New Harmony in the mid-1820s. Situated close to one of the common routes west, several young men in the community learned of Owen during the course of 1825. The leader of the group, John Whitby, pressed for Pleasant Hill's communal structures to be reformed, to introduce a democratic element to the selection of Shaker leaders and a rearrangement of the Shaker community's assets along lines closer to Owen's theories. When forced out of the community, Whitby and his brother Richardson made their way to New Harmony, where John published an anti-Shaker tract in 1826.[45] The Whitbys joined at least one other former Shaker already at New Harmony: William Ludlow, once a resident of New Lebanon in New York.[46]

New Lebanon would, in time, become the Shaker community of choice for ex-Owenites, beginning with a substantial group from the Valley Forge community, west of Philadelphia. Valley Forge was one of the numerous communities established on Owen's principles independently from New Harmony. It formed and disbanded within the course of 1826 under the leadership of Abel Knight, a Quaker whose Philadelphia home was remembered as a headquarters for Owen's early disciples in the city.[47]

---

[45] Thomas D. Clark and F. Gerald Ham, *Pleasant Hill and Its Shaker Community* (Pleasant Hill, KY: Shakertown Press, 1968), pp. 39–40; John Whitbey (*sic*), *Beauties of Priestcraft; or, A Short Account of Shakerism* (New Harmony, 1826); Harlow Lindley (ed.), 'Letters of William Pelham', in *Indiana as Seen by Early Travelers* (Indianapolis: Indiana Historical Society, 1916), pp. 397, 411. Richardson Whitby went on to be involved in the Nashoba Owenite community: J.F.C. Harrison, *Robert Owen and the Owenites in Britain and America: The Quest for the New Moral World* (London: Routledge & Kegan Paul, 1969), pp. 167–8.

[46] William Ludlow, *Belief of the Rational Brethren of the West* (Cincinnati, OH, 1819).

[47] Frederick Evans, *Autobiography of a Shaker*, enlarged edn (Glasgow and New York, 1888), p. 17.

In May 1827, 'a party of seven' from Valley Forge made their way to New Lebanon 'desiring to see the Shakers and learn from them the secret of successful communism'.[48] The visitors stayed for a period 'to observe the workings of the community', then returned to Philadelphia. Shaker missionaries were then sent south to follow up the interest, and by 1828 about fifty former members of Valley Forge had joined, and returned with them to the Hudson Valley.[49] Among them were Abel Knight and his daughters Jane and Sarah, and George Wickersham—who alleged to have first 'heard the name Shaker mentioned' in a lecture given by Robert Owen in Philadelphia.[50]

After 1830, two further British-born Owenites joined New Lebanon: Frederick Evans and Daniel Fraser. Evans was originally from Worcestershire, and migrated to America aged 12 with his father and brother George Henry in 1820.[51] By 1825, both Evans brothers 'were radicals in civil government, and in religion ... materialists', and in the late 1820s were closely involved in the Owen-inspired freethought movement in New York City, including its journal the *Working Man's Advocate*.[52] In 1829, Frederick Evans walked to Ohio to join the Kendal Community, one of the longer-lasting Owenite experiments, though he witnessed its disintegration soon after his arrival.[53] Returning to New York, Evans joined another group planning a community, and was 'deputed to travel for information, and to find a suitable location'.[54] In the course of his researches, Evans called at New Lebanon 'interested ... in the community system and its operation as it existed there', but during his stay underwent a dramatic spiritual experience

[48] Anna White and Leila Sarah Taylor, *Shakerism: Its Meaning and Message* (Columbus, OH, 1905), p. 158.

[49] White and Taylor, *Shakerism*, p. 159.

[50] Western Reserve Historical Society, Cleveland, Ohio, MS VI:B-28, Calvin Green, 'Biographic Memoir' (1861); Jane Knight, *Brief Narrative of Events Touching Various Reforms* (Albany, NY, 1880); George M. Wickersham, *How I came to be a Shaker* (Mount Lebanon, NY, 1891).

[51] Evans, *Autobiography*, pp. 1–6.

[52] Sean Wilentz, *Chants Democratic: New York City and the Rise of the American Working Class, 1788–1850* (New York: Oxford University Press, 1984), pp. 197–207. G.H. Evans was subsequently a leading land-reform campaigner. See J.L. Bronstein, *Land Reform and Working-class Experience in Britain and the United States, 1800–1862* (Stanford: Stanford University Press, 1999).

[53] Evans, *Autobiography*, p. 14.

[54] Evans, *Autobiography*, pp. 15–16.

which led him to convert to Shakerism.[55] Evans went on to become the most prominent Shaker of his generation.

In contrast to Evans, Daniel Fraser's Owenite sympathies were bred first in Britain—in Yorkshire and London, though he was originally from Paisley, west of Glasgow.[56] Living near Huddersfield from the late 1820s, Fraser was drawn into various radical causes, including reform of factory conditions. On a visit to London, Fraser met Robert Owen, now returned from America, and became 'imbued with the sentiments of his communal ideas'. In 1834, Fraser 'left England for America, resolved ... to be instrumental in forming a community', being 'fully satisfied that our civilization needed a higher form of economic, and ... social life'.[57] Fraser's plans for an Owenite community crumbled on arrival, but he visited New Lebanon, where he met Frederick Evans and 'an organization already fulfilling his ideal', and never left.[58]

TRANS-ATLANTIC ATTENTION IN THE 1830s

During the 1830s, popular movements in Britain inspired by Robert Owen's 'social system' developed significant new interests and institutions. Model communities of shared property remained an aspiration for many, yet small-scale cooperative enterprises, trades unions, journals, lectures and weekly local meetings became the more immediate activities of those now calling themselves 'socialists'.[59] References to American religious communalism were rarer in socialist literature in this period, as the successful practice of shared property was less relevant to these other concerns.[60] However, interest in communal traditions re-emerged in the final years of the decade and in the early 1840s, when socialists revived their plans for community building. This notably coincided with the availability

---

[55] Evans, *Autobiography*, pp. 195–6.

[56] Daniel Fraser, 'Witness of Daniel Fraser' (1901), in *Shaker Autobiographies, Biographies and Testimonies, 1806–1907; Vol. 3*, ed. Christian Goodwillie (London: Pickering and Chatto, 2014), pp. 353–6. Autobiographical letters written by Daniel Fraser also appear in Evans, *Autobiography*, pp. 123–5, 253–7.

[57] Evans, *Autobiography*, p. 124; Fraser, 'Witness', p. 353.

[58] Evans, *Autobiography* (1888), p. 124; Andrews, *People Called Shakers*, p. 234.

[59] Garnett, *Co-operation and the Owenite Socialist Communities*, pp. 130–65.

[60] Exceptions included Thomas Wayland, *National Advancement and Happiness Considered in Reference to the Equalization of Property and the Formation of Communities* (London, 1832), p. 6.

of new accounts of American communal groups written by trans-Atlantic visitors consciously comparing their Protestant practices with socialist and cooperative theories circulating in Britain.

The most influential new description of the Shaker and Harmonist communities circulating in socialist circles was by Harriet Martineau—a prominent British Unitarian and feminist writer, who was not herself a socialist.[61] Martineau had achieved fame with her popular *Illustrations of Political Economy* (1832), an accessible introduction to liberal free-market economics largely at odds with Owen's discontent with competition.[62] Between 1834 and 1836, Martineau toured the United States with a female companion, returning to Britain to publish an extensive social analysis based on her observations: *Society in America* (1837). Martineau visited two Shaker communities, Hancock and New Lebanon either side of the Massachusetts–New York border, and the Harmonists at Economy.[63] Her descriptions revealed a strong prejudice against the celibacy and religious views of each community. Yet Martineau was impressed by the 'moral and economical principles of these societies', and adjusted her existing theories when she saw 'the produce of co-operative labour being so much greater than in a state of division into families'. Celibacy, Martineau insisted, could not be the cause of their wealth, as the Shakers recruited so many new members from outside who were as much a drain on the community as children would be. For Martineau, 'whatever they have peculiarly good among them is owing to the soundness of their economical principles; whatever they have that excites compassion, is owing to the badness of their moral arrangements'.[64]

Martineau echoed the earlier assumptions of Robert Owen when she admired the 'co-operation and community of property' of the Shakers and Harmonists, regretted their religion, then wondered how much more might be achieved 'among a more intelligent set of people, stimulated by education, and exhilarated by the enjoyment of all the blessings which Providence has placed within the reach of man?'[65] A decade of Owenite failures since *The Economist* first assumed it 'would be easy' to form such

[61] Barbara Taylor, *Eve and the New Jerusalem: Socialism and Feminism in the Nineteenth Century* (London: Virago, 1983), p. 62.

[62] R.K. Webb, *Harriet Martineau: A Radical Victorian* (London: Heinemann, 1960).

[63] Harriet Martineau, *Society in America*, 3 vols, second edn (London, 1837), 1:215–20, 2:54–65.

[64] Martineau, *Society in America*, 2:54–8.

[65] Martineau, *Society in America*, 2:57.

societies probably influenced Martineau to acknowledge that 'the problem is to find the principle by which all shall be induced to labour their share'. 'They smile superciliously upon Mr. Owen's plan', she noted of the Harmonists, as Owen followed 'a wrong principle'. To Martineau, however, 'it seems only reasonable' that 'the co-operative methods of the Shakers and Rappites might be tried without any adoption of their spiritual pride and cruel superstition'. Some section of the 'more complicated', divided and agitated societies on the European side of the Atlantic should therefore 'make a trial of the peaceful principles which are working successfully elsewhere', Martineau concluded; 'it will never now rest till it has been made [a] matter of experiment'.[66]

This conclusion, together with Martineau's authoritative endorsement of cooperative and communal economics, stirred Owenite interest. Extracts from Martineau's description of the Harmonists and Shakers quickly appeared in Samuel Bower's *Competition in Peril* (1837), in the series *Social Tracts* (1837–1838) and in William Hawkes Smith's *Letters on the State and Prospects of Society* (1838).[67] Martineau's work continued to feature in Owenite literature into the early 1840s, from which time it was supplemented by extracts from the earliest British notice of the Separatist community of Zoar, Ohio, begun in 1817, and a yet more recent travel account of the 'Shaker villages' and the 'the co-operative community of the Rappites' by James Silk Buckingham.[68] Buckingham was a former Member of Parliament with radical sympathies who toured the United States before 1840. His view of these communities corroborated Martineau's in seeing the Shakers and the Harmonists as 'an irresistible proof' that cooperation was more productive than competition. Buckingham more willingly

---

[66] Martineau, *Society in America*, 2:58–9, 64.

[67] Samuel Bower, *Competition in Peril: or the Present Position of the Owenites, or Rationalism considered: Together with Miss Martineau's Account of Communities in America* (Leeds, 1837; London, 1839); Samuel Cornish (ed.), *Social Tracts: Observations upon Political and Social Reform with a Sketch of the Various and Conflicting Theories of Modern Political Economists* (1837–38), reprinted in Gregory Claeys (ed.), *Owenite Socialism: Pamphlets and Correspondence, Volume 5* (London: Routledge, 2005), pp. 54–60. William Hawkes Smith, *Letters on the State and Prospects of Society* (Birmingham, 1838), reprinted in Claeys (ed.), *Owenite Socialism*, pp. 244–56.

[68] The account of the Zoar community first appeared in *The Penny Magazine*, no. 26, (October 1837), 411–12. Extracts appeared in Robert Owen, *A Development of the Principles and Plans on which to Establish Self-Supporting Home Colonies* (London, 1841), appendix II, pp. 11–15. See also, Charles Bray, *The Philosophy of Necessity*, 2 vols (London, 1841), 2:519–29.

acknowledged the Shaker 'religious peculiarities' to be important to their group cohesion, but not their economic success: 'when divested of this hindrance', Buckingham confidently concluded, the principle of cooperation 'will someday or other make a great change in the social arrangements of mankind'.[69]

Samuel Bower, the Bradford author of *Competition in Peril*, was one of many younger socialists in Britain in the late 1830s unfamiliar with the notice given to Protestant communalism in the early Owenite movement.[70] Used to having his own communal aspirations dismissed as 'utopian' and unrealistic, Bower wrote of experiencing a 'feeling of delight ... at the realisation of some dream of happiness' when he first read Martineau's 'facts and observations on Communities in America'.[71] In her account, Bower found 'the great, inappreciable fact of the complete success of Communities in America ... triumphantly recorded'.[72] For Bower and other British socialists, the Shakers and the Harmonists once again became a vindication of hope, evidence that their 'principles of Associated Labour and Community of Property' were viable. In *Competition in Peril*, Bower enthusiastically answered Martineau's concluding thought, by announcing Owenite plans 'for submitting their principles ... to the stern test of experiment in England!'[73] By 1838, the Owenite national congress had reaffirmed its commitment to establishing a model community, and in 1839 secured a site for an official experiment in Hampshire, known as Queenwood or 'Harmony Hall'.[74] Bower was one of its earliest members.[75]

Before arriving at Queenwood, Bower already had a reputation for combining his socialist commitment to reforming external circumstances with an interest in personal, inward reformation through self-denial and

---

[69] James Silk Buckingham, *America, Historical, Statistic, and Descriptive*, 2 vols (New York and London, 1841), 2:56–87, 285; idem, *The Eastern and Western United States of America*, 3 vols (London, 1842), 2:205–36, 292–93, 421–30. Buckingham used the examples of Moravian, Shaker and Harmonist communities in support of a scheme for non-Owenite 'home colonies' in Britain in the 1840s, and later influenced the Garden City movement.

[70] Bower also wrote *The Peopling of Utopia* (Bradford, 1838) and *A Sequel to the Peopling of Utopia* (Bradford, 1838).

[71] Bower, *Competition in Peril*, p. 6.

[72] Bower, *Competition in Peril*, p. 7.

[73] Bower, *Competition in Peril*, p. 3.

[74] Garnett, *Co-operation and the Owenite Socialist Communities*, pp. 151–9.

[75] Edward Royle, *Robert Owen and the Commencement of the Millennium* (Manchester: Manchester University Press, 1998), pp. 85, 135.

a plain, vegetarian diet. George Jacob Holyoake remembered Bower living 'chiefly upon grey peas, of which he carried a supply about, and strenuously insisted that that peculiar diet should be universally adopted'.[76] Behind such views lay a reservoir of contemporary ideas about bodily humours and stimulants, the relation of ingestion to behaviour and ultimately a concept of moral purification concerning the physical as well as the spiritual self.[77] For a section of socialist opinion, ideas of avoiding the 'stimulating' effect of meat, caffeine or alcohol on the body connected with principles of imaginative education and the shaping of surroundings to offer the hope of creating not just a 'new moral world' but a newly moral humanity, less subject to 'temptation' in all its forms. In due course, up to half the inhabitants of the Queenwood community were vegetarian, with formal debates organized on the practice.[78] Yet for some, including Bower, ascetic individual denial came to dominate their vision of communal living.

ASCETIC SOCIALISTS AND SHAKERS

Leaving Queenwood in August 1840, Bower became associated with the Ham Common 'Concordium' in Surrey, a small community on the borders of the British socialist movement, instituting a regime of uncooked vegetarian food, cold baths and celibacy.[79] Founded by the 'Sacred Socialist' James Pierrepont Greaves, the Concordium offered a distinctly 'mystical' alternative to the materialism of mainstream Owenism, aiming to produce conditions for the 'divine progress in humanity' and a return to the sinless circumstances of Eden.[80] Related ideas and ambitions circulated within the contemporary Transcendentalism movement in New England. The two groups shared intellectual roots in the Romantic idealism of Samuel Taylor Coleridge, yet were also closely aligned through

[76] G.J. Holyoake, *The History of Co-operation*, rev. ed., 2 vols (London: T.F. Unwin, 1908), 1:220.

[77] This would produce a variety of dietary 'fads', such as 'Grahamism'. James Gregory, *Of Victorians and Vegetarians* (London: I.B. Tauris, 2007).

[78] Royle, *Robert Owen*, pp. 142, 168.

[79] *New Moral World*, 6 (1845), 432. Greaves's biography is Jackie Latham, *Search for the New Eden: James Pierrepont Greaves (1777–1842), the Sacred Socialist and His Followers* (Cranbury, NJ: Associated University Presses, 1999).

[80] *A Prospectus for the Establishment of a Concordium* (London, 1841).

friendships, correspondence and print networks.[81] The school attached to Ham Common was named 'Alcott House', after the Transcendentalist educationalist A. Bronson Alcott. And it was Alcott who effected the most significant trans-Atlantic connection between the two movements by visiting the Concordium in 1842, then convincing several leading members, including Bower and a journalist, Charles Lane, to follow him back to Massachusetts. There they founded a further ascetic community, Fruitlands, close to a Shaker community near the town of Harvard.

Among Transcendentalists in the region, the Protestant communal traditions in general and this Harvard Shaker community in particular had already provoked much interest. Rising distress and inequality in the emerging industrial economy of New England motivated the circle of Boston intellectuals to reflect on social reform and the ideal community.[82] Ralph Waldo Emerson repeatedly visited the Harvard Shakers, initially finding the drabness and melancholy of their 'Protestant monastery' unappealing, yet altering his views as he became acquainted with several elders and their communal principles.[83] In 1840, Emerson wrote of the need for wider society to 'sift' the Shaker 'experiments' for what was 'false and adopt and embody in a new form the advantage'—a view akin to that of Martineau, Owen and others. Yet Emerson's reflection was notably without the prejudgement that the 'false' was necessarily their religion.[84] George Ripley drew up plans to found a more 'complete' ideal community, explicitly seeking to overcome the negative aspects that Transcendentalists saw in Shaker life—the sacrifice of 'family' and 'individuality', and the making of 'enormous wealth ... at the expense of all manly pursuits and

---

[81] The most recent works to reconstruct these networks are, Latham, *Search for the New Eden*, and Richard Francis, *Fruitlands* (New Haven: Yale University Press, 2010).

[82] Anne Rose, *Transcendentalism as a Social Movement, 1830–1850* (New Haven: Yale University Press, 1981).

[83] P.J. Brewer, 'Emerson, Lane and the Shakers: A Case of Converging Ideologies', *New England Quarterly*, 55:2 (1982), 254–75.

[84] R.W. Emerson, *The Journals and Miscellaneous Notebooks of Ralph Waldo Emerson*, ed. William Gilman et al., 16 vols (Cambridge, MA: Harvard University Press, 1960–82), 7:394–5. Elizabeth Palmer Peabody, writing in the Transcendentalist periodical *The Dial*, notably acknowledged the 'religious communities ... the Moravians, the Shakers, even the Rappites' as having 'partially entered into ... Christ's Idea of Society', despite having 'narrowed' this idea 'by creeds and tests'. Peabody, 'A Glimpse of Christ's Idea of Society', *The Dial*, 2, (October 1841), 214–15.

attainments'.[85] Ripley founded Brook Farm community near Boston in 1841, which was soon drawn into a new American communal movement, this time influenced not by Owen but by the alternative 'socialism' of the French theorist Charles Fourier.[86] Many 'Associationists', as Fourier's American followers called themselves, purposely visited Shaker communities to 'seek a lesson from them'.[87] Shaker celibacy was commonly criticized as a 'reduced pattern of humanity', yet Shakers were still heralded as an 'exceptional manifestation of the social instincts ... an invincible argument for Association'.[88]

For the trans-Atlantic 'sacred socialists' migrating to form the Fruitlands community with Bronson Alcott in 1843, the Shaker neighbours in Harvard were intriguing. Coming themselves from the celibate Concordium, and in significant contrast to other visitors who flatly denied that Shaker economic success could have anything to do with celibacy, the Fruitlands members considered it 'worthy of enquiry' just how far 'the great secular success of the Shakers; their order, their cleanliness, intelligence ... are attribual [sic] to their peculiar doctrine'.[89] Samuel Bower visited the Shakers in June 1843, accompanied by two members of Brook Farm, and was 'much attracted by them'.[90] Charles Lane also visited the Harvard community with Alcott, and reportedly pressed for the adoption of celibacy at Fruitlands as a means of 'conquering self'. By August 1843, Emerson was writing 'Mr. Lane is very much engaged with the Shakers ... & perhaps may join them.'[91] Lane published an article, 'A Day with the

[85] Peabody, 'A Glimpse', 214–15; George Ripley to Charles Dana, 18 March 1842, in J.H. Wilson, *The Life of Charles A. Dana* (New York, 1907), p. 40. Ripley and his wife Sophia were further influenced by visiting the Separatists of Zoar, Ohio: Sophia Ripley, 'Letter from Zoar', *Dial*, 2 (July 1841), 125.

[86] Guarneri, *Utopian Alternative*, pp. 51–9.

[87] Horace Greeley, 'A Sabbath with the Shakers', *Knickerbocker*, 11:6 (June 1838), 532; J.S. Dwight, 'The Shakers at New Lebanon', *Harbinger*, 21 August 1847, 176.

[88] Dwight, 'Shakers', 176.

[89] 'The Consociate Family Life', *New York Evening Tribune*, 1 September 1843.

[90] Francis, *Fruitlands*, p. 174; Charles Lane to William Oldham, 28 June 1843 quoted in Joel Myerson, 'William Henry Harland's "Bronson Alcott's English Friends"', *Resources for American Literary Studies*, 8:1 (1978), 46–8.

[91] Emerson to Margaret Fuller, 7 August 1843, quoted in Brewer, 'Emerson, Lane and the Shakers', 267.

Shakers', in Emerson's influential journal *The Dial* in October, by which time Lane had also sent back a description to Surrey for the *Concordium Gazette*.[92]

The Fruitlands community lasted barely a year, collapsing at the close of 1843, though Samuel Bower had left in August, finding the communal rubric restrictive and 'Mr Alcott ... arbitrary or despotic'.[93] Bower was reportedly offered some land where he could indulge his bean diet and burgeoning fondness for the further asceticism of nudity, though little came of this scheme.[94] In December, Bower was present at a Fourierist convention in Boston, but in the new year he resolved to join the Shakers back at Harvard.[95] Charles Lane also became a Harvard Shaker in January 1844, along with his young son William, who had accompanied him to America.[96]

From the Shaker community, Lane composed another article for *The Dial*, lamenting the 'considerable prejudice ... harboured against the Millennial Church' on the grounds of its teachings against marriage.[97] Lane now encouraged celibacy among socialists by explicating the Shaker view of sexual practice. This was a compliance not with the 'order of nature' but with the 'order of grace'—the Shaker hope for 'God's law of grace ruling in the soul'. For Lane, the Christian prayer for the Kingdom to come, and the doing on earth as in heaven, was ultimately a prayer for socialism; yet, the scriptural teaching that 'in heaven they are neither married nor given in marriage' should direct such Christians to adopt celibacy as a way towards 'heavenly love'. This was an argument closely aligned with the mystical theology of the Ham Concordium.

Despite this confidence of the recent convert, Lane did not remain a Shaker for long. Within two years he declared the community a 'system of spiritual despotism which does not allow a man to think for himself, to

---

[92] Charles Lane, 'A Day with the Shakers', *Dial*, 4 (Oct. 1843), 167; *New Age, Concordium Gazette, and Temperance Advocate*, 1 (1 Aug. 1843), 75–6.

[93] Francis, *Fruitlands*, p. 205.

[94] Francis, *Fruitlands*, p. 205. Louisa May Alcott described Bower in her satirical memoir of the Fruitlands experiment, *Transcendental Wild Oats* (1883), as 'a bland, bearded Englishman, who expected to be saved by eating uncooked food and going without clothes'. She gave Bower the witty pseudonym 'John Pease'.

[95] David Edgell, 'Bronson Alcott's "Autobiographical Index"', *New England Quarterly*, 14:4 (Dec. 1941), 713.

[96] Brewer, 'Emerson, Lane and the Shakers', 270–2.

[97] Charles Lane, 'Millennial Church', 4 (Apr. 1844), 537.

feel that his soul is his own or ... God's'.[98] Lane returned to Surrey and the Concordium in 1846—though it was not until 1848 before his son could be legally extricated from a Shaker apprenticeship. Bower also eventually found the Shakers too restrictive for his idiosyncrasies, and by 1849 was resident elsewhere in Massachusetts, declaring 'the true question' now to be 'a proper Individualism ... nothing that is good and desirable in Socialism can come but after this'.[99]

TRANS-ATLANTIC TRAVELLERS OF THE 1840S

Since joining the Shakers in New York State in 1834, Daniel Fraser, the Huddersfield radical, had occasionally written home to friends in Britain, describing his new life. In the summer of 1842, this trans-Atlantic correspondence brought Fraser a visit from an old ally, Lawrence Pitkethly, a leading Yorkshire political radical also originally from Scotland, who stayed several days at New Lebanon during his own extensive tour of North America.[100] Pitkethly was a Chartist rather than a socialist: he campaigned principally for political rights, believing full democracy would overturn the social and economic injustices suffered by British working people sooner than model communities. Pitkethly undertook his American tour on behalf of Chartism—to research conditions among American artisans and the viability of a Chartist emigration scheme. His journal was serialized in the Chartist newspaper *Northern Star*.[101] Pitkethly's account, which included a detailed description of his Shaker stay, was nevertheless appreciated by socialists back in Britain—many of whom read the Chartist press. Pitkethly was well known among Owenites in Yorkshire, and acknowledged during his tour that he was 'acquainted with Mr. Owen ... I was with him some time before I left England ... but I was not one of his disciples.'[102]

[98] Letter to the Editor, *New York Tribune*, 17 July 1846.

[99] Samuel Bower to Joseph Palmer, 6 November 1849, in C.E. Sears (ed.), *Bronson Alcott's Fruitlands* (Boston, 1915), pp. 141–2.

[100] On Pitkethly, see Harrison, *Robert Owen*, p. 227; Michael Brook, 'Lawrence Pitkethly, Dr Smyles and Canadian Revolutionaries in the United States, 1842', *Ontario History*, 57:2 (June 1965), 79–84.

[101] *Northern Star*, 1 April 1843–1 July 1843. Ray Boston, *British Chartists in America, 1839–1900* (Manchester: Manchester University Press, 1971), pp. 39–40.

[102] *Northern Star*, 24 June 1843, 3; Edward Royle, 'Owenism and the Secularist Tradition: The Huddersfield Secular Society and Sunday School', in Malcolm Chase and Ian Dyck (eds), *Living and Learning* (Aldershot: Ashgate, 1996), pp. 199–217.

Pitkethly used his time with the Shakers to examine their skilled manufacturing, living conditions and structured lifestyles, in addition to attending Shaker worship. Despite having a reputation back in Huddersfield as a sceptic, Pitkethly offered an open-minded description of Shaker worship, and during his stay 'read a portion of the Memoirs of Ann Lee'.[103] Pitkethly appreciated the neatness, efficiency and quality of Shaker goods and labour, and found the community 'happy and cheerful with each other. No strife; but, on the contrary, love and affection, reign throughout their abode; and unequalled order and regularity are witnessed in every department.' 'They are like bees in a hive', Pitkethly further reflected, 'with a constantly increasing mass of wealth, I consider they ought to relax a little'. Such a state of affairs notably contrasted with the wretched conditions Pitkethly had previously noted among Boston and New York artisans. Yet Pitkethly made little of this juxtaposition. His journal drew few conclusions beyond admiration and gratitude for generous hospitality. Readers of the *Northern Star* were left to believe that Pitkethly had crossed the Atlantic and discovered, as he put it, 'a very paradise'.[104]

When Pitkethly returned to Britain from New York in October 1842 he carried a letter for John Finch, a leading Owenite socialist and first and current governor of the Queenwood community.[105] It is unclear when Pitkethly and Finch met, but the following April, Finch himself set out on his own tour of North America, also keeping a journal intended for publication, this time in the socialist *New Moral World*. Finch's mission was a more deliberate investigation of American communal experiments—socialist and religious. He visited first Brook Farm and other Fourier-influenced communities in New England, then the Harmonists in Pennsylvania, the Separatists in Ohio, the Mormons in Nauvoo, Illinois, the remains of New Harmony, Indiana, and finally the Shaker Pleasant Hill community in Kentucky, before making the journey back to Britain by December 1843. Finch's subsequent series of 'Letters' in the *New Moral World* early in 1844 offered not only descriptions of these communities,

---

[103] *Northern Star*, 6 May 1843, 7.

[104] *Northern Star*, 6 May 1843, 7.

[105] *Northern Star*, 24 June 1843, 3. Finch was governor of Queenwood from October 1839 to May 1840, then again from August 1842. John Saville, 'Finch, John (1784–1857)', in J.O. Baylen and N.J. Gossman (eds), *Biographical Dictionary of Modern British Radicals*, 2 vols (Hassocks: Harvester, 1984), 2:118–20.

but also his measured assessment of their strengths, weaknesses and lessons for British socialists, for Queenwood, and any future experiments.[106] Finch preceded his analysis by listing the common objections voiced 'whenever we have advocated the formation of Communities of United Interests in England': 'we have been met ... with this scornful reply— "Utopian, visionary, impracticable! Contrary to human nature and human experience ... the desire for private property is inherent in our race. All attempts that have hitherto been made, by yourselves and others ... were all miserable failures."'[107] Finch now assured his socialist readers: 'I therefore feel peculiarly happy that my travels in America have enabled me to answer all these objections by facts—by what I have seen, heard, and experienced.' He then cited the size, scope, persistence and wealth of the Shakers, 'Rapp's community' and the Zoar community as his principal evidence:

> Instead of these societies having been failures, they have far more than realized all the objects for which they were formed. The desire for private property is thus proved not to be *natural*, for there it does not exist. ... [T]hey never have any poor ... they do not know what trouble is: they have *many* continuing cities [i.e. settlements]...[108]

In subsequent articles, Finch offered 'an impartial portraiture' of most of the communities he had visited, though he wrote little on the Mormon community at Nauvoo, to whom he lectured on socialism.[109] At points Finch deliberately corrected, as he thought necessary, assessments of the American groups already known to British socialists. 'It has been erroneously asserted, by Mr Buckingham and others', Finch declared, 'that their religion is the binding principle that holds the Shakers and Rappites together'.[110]

[106] *New Moral World*, 13 January 1844–6 July 1844.

[107] *New Moral World*, 3 February 1844, 249.

[108] *New Moral World*, 3 February 1844, 249.

[109] The Mormon founder, Joseph Smith, Jr, recorded: 'I attended a lecture at the Grove, by Mr. John Finch, a Socialist, from England, and said a few words in reply ... I attended a second lecture ... and after he got through, I made a few remarks, ... I said I did not believe the doctrine ... Elder John Taylor replied to the lecture at some length.' Joseph Smith, *History of the Church of Jesus Christ of Latter-day Saints*, ed. B.H. Roberts, 7 vols (Salt Lake City, 1902), 6:33.

[110] *New Moral World*, 10 February 1844, 257.

> No greater mistake could be made; their religion, on the contrary, has pre-
> vented thousands of the most valuable characters from joining them ... the
> real binding principles of the Shakers are,—their obedience to their leaders,
> their great order, complete organization, and the many temporal comforts
> they enjoy. ... [U]nion, co-operation, and order ensured them a better sub-
> sistence than they could obtain in competitive society.[111]

Finch's central argument echoed once again the assumptions of Owen,
the *Economist* and Martineau before him: 'if, under such unfavourable circumstances, communities of united interests can secure so much wealth,
peace, and happiness, how much more may we expect under our superior arrangements, if we are equally diligent and economical'?[112] The
Protestant communities across the Atlantic were not only living evidence
that cooperative principles and community of property worked, but their
achievements had manifested themselves *despite* their religion and other
'unfavourable' aspects of their practice.

For Finch, the Separatists at Zoar offered the highest ideal of community, above the Shakers and Harmonists, because their religion appeared
to him 'more rational', and a less central concern: 'they have no creed',
he claimed, 'and do not interfere with the private opinions of their members'.[113] He consequently presented the constitution of the Zoar community as an exemplar for socialists to follow, even as he repeatedly assured
his readers in Britain that their own experiment in Hampshire would prove
itself a greater achievement:

> ... these communities, excellent as they are, are far inferior to what our
> own may be made at Harmony [Hall] ... These accounts should stir up all
> our Branches, officers, and members, to renewed and untiring exertions to
> complete ... the experiment at Harmony, ... [which] I believe, may soon be
> made the most perfect model the world has ever yet seen.[114]

Finch and Pitkethly were comparatively unusual among early socialists and Chartists for crossing the Atlantic then returning the same year,

---

[111] *New Moral World*, 10 February 1844, 257.

[112] *New Moral World*, 10 February 1844, 258.

[113] *New Moral World*, 23 March 1844, 305.

[114] *New Moral World*, 23 March 1844, 306; *New Moral World*, 30 March 1844, 313.
Unlike many Owenites, Finch was not opposed to a Christian case for socialism, and had,
controversially, introduced religious services while governor of Queenwood. Royle, *Robert
Owen*, p. 132.

as many others emigrated and settled.[115] Among those who left permanently, some retained an ongoing interest in the viability of socialism in their new home, as well as back in Europe, and conducted their own research into both Protestant communal traditions and American socialism. A.J. Macdonald, a Scottish Owenite printer, moved to the United States in about 1842 and worked in New York. For more than a decade he compiled material for a book on 'all the social and co-operative experiments' in America, to be called *The Communities of the United States*, but died in 1854, before his manuscript could be published.[116] Macdonald's surviving notes in the Beinecke Library at Yale University reveal he paid particular attention to Owenite and Fourierist communities, visiting and composing eyewitness accounts of their sites and their ongoing existence. This material was utilized by another author, John Humphrey Noyes of the Oneida community, in a later work, *History of American Socialisms* (1870).[117] Yet Macdonald also compiled notes never published on the varieties of Protestant communalism, past and present, on his newly adopted continent. He drew up short chapters on the Moravians, the Shakers and Zoar, among others, though the Harmonist communities did not feature beyond a discussion of Owen's New Harmony.[118]

Macdonald visited in person the Zoar Separatists and two Shaker communities—Watervliet, New York, and Union Village, Ohio. 'Zoar', Macdonald wrote, 'was a place I had read about long ago—Robert Owen, Miss Martineau [*sic*] and many other social reformers have spoken of it and to me the very name seemed blended with something almost holy'.[119] Macdonald's imagination had been so stirred by the knowledge such a community could exist; 'the idea of being so near [this] place … put me in a state of the most pleasurable anticipation … I left the canal boat when within three miles of Zoar … I ran all the way.'[120] His subsequent

[115] Royle, *Robert Owen*, p. 103. Wilentz, *Chants Democratic*, pp. 339–40.

[116] These materials remain in manuscript form in the Beinecke Rare Book and Manuscript Library, Yale University, A.J. Macdonald Collection of Utopian Materials, *c.*1840–65 (hereafter Macdonald Collection).

[117] J.H. Noyes, *History of American Socialisms* (Philadelphia, 1870).

[118] Macdonald Collection, ff. 432–6, 437–45, 485–92, 493–6, 578–615, 639–59.

[119] Zoar does not feature in Martineau's *Society in America*, so Macdonald probably misattributed to her the 1837 article on Zoar in the *Penny Magazine*.

[120] Macdonald Collection, ff. 486–7.

description indicates Macdonald found the community happy and healthy, though not 'a model of order' when contrasted with the Shakers.[121]

At the latter's Union Village, which Macdonald visited with a fellow socialist, he described 'three or four hours spent' discussing socialism with Elders, telling them 'some of our peculiar views and in what we had been engaged and how anxious we were to be good and to find out the truth'.[122] 'We have known many like you', came an Elder's reply; '[w]e know all about these Community movements and we know that they are all in vain and can never succeed, you will have to do like us or you will never succeed', Macdonald was told.

The conversation ranged over arguments for 'celibacy especially ... and the subject of Divine Revelation'. This led Macdonald to confess, 'I could say no more, but express how impossible it was for me to believe in such things and how unreasonable they appeared to be.' Macdonald's handwritten notes ended with a sense of poignancy, suggestive of the tension felt within himself—and perhaps shared by other socialist visitors—of being strongly drawn to such an effective, working communal life, but repelled by the religious and relational requirements:

> ...we left the place in a strange state of mind and wended our way in the Sunset, from the Shaker village—We saw with pleasure as we passed, their clean houses their fine orchards and their beautiful fields and woods we also gazed upon their horses and cows and concluded they were the finest we had ever seen, but we could not live happy, if we had to adopt the (to us) gross Superstitions and absurdities of the Shakers.[123]

'COMMUNIST COLONIES' AND IMAGINED FUTURES

Friedrich Engels, the influential German communist, was not in a position to tour the United States in the 1840s, but early in the decade he set out to acquire as many published descriptions of trans-Atlantic Protestant communities as he could. By late 1844, Engels had read the journal accounts of both John Finch and Lawrence Pitkethly, and consulted 'the works of Miss Martineau, Messrs Melish and Buckingham and many

---

[121] Macdonald Collection, ff. 487–90.
[122] Macdonald Collection, f. 680.
[123] Macdonald Collection, ff. 680–1.

others'.[124] In October 1844, Engels published an article quoting these works and enthusiastically endorsing the apparent outcomes of Protestant communalism: abundant food and material produce, no crime and no poverty.[125] Engels pointedly identified the 'colonies' of the Shakers, the Harmony Society and the Separatist Society of Zoar in the United States as practical examples of 'communism'. Defining 'communism' at this time as 'social existence and activity based on community of goods', Engels sought to answer the objections that he claimed to hear often in Europe, namely that it was 'impossible ever to put such things into practice in real life'. 'Communism', he retorted, 'is not only possible but has actually already been realised in many communities in America ... with the greatest success.'[126]

Engels wrote his article at home in Barmen, western Germany, shortly after spending two years working in Manchester, in northwest England. Here, Engels had been involved in 'Owenite' socialism—the continuing movement of Robert Owen's followers.[127] Absorbing early socialist ideas through friendships and radical newspapers, Engels was influenced especially by Owen's public antagonism to Christianity and conviction that socialism would come about by building model communities of shared property. Both these influences were apparent in the article, as Engels declared 'irrational religion ... an obstacle in the way of communal living', then acknowledged, 'if communal living is successful in real life despite this, how much more feasible must it be with others who are free of such inanities'.[128] In common with these assertions, almost all the opinions expressed in Engels's article on 'communist colonies' had been articulated in the foregoing lineage of British Owenite and radical interest in

[124] Friedrich Engels, 'Description of Recently Founded Communist Colonies Still in Existence', in *Marx and Engels Collected Works* (hereafter *MECW*) (London: Lawrence & Wishart, 1975–2005), 4:222.

[125] *MECW*, 4:214–28. This article was published anonymously, though Engels confirmed his authorship in subsequent writings (*MECW*, 4:240).

[126] *MECW*, 4:214–22.

[127] Gregory Claeys, 'The Political Ideas of the Young Engels, 1842–45', *History of Political Thought*, 6:3 (1985), 456–9. Scholarly notice of Engels's 1844 article is comparatively rare. See also, Lewis Feuer, 'The Influence of the American Communist Colonies on Engels and Marx', *Western Political Quarterly*, 19:3 (Sep. 1966), 456–74; David Leopold, '"Socialist Turnips": The Young Friedrich Engels and the Feasibility of Communism', *Political Theory*, 40:3 (2012), 347–78.

[128] *MECW*, 4:215. Engels also described the Owenite community of Harmony Hall in Hampshire in the latter part of the article.

American Protestant communalism: that Shakers, Harmonists and the Zoar community 'proved' community of property to be both possible and successful; that their cooperative labour was superior to the competitive system; and that their religious disciplines, including celibacy, were irrelevant to the viability of their whole enterprise. Along with the Owenite *Economist* journal, Harriet Martineau, John Finch and others, Engels expressed his confidence that a secular community, founded without such disciplines and beliefs, would prove itself just as prosperous and persistent.

Scholarly analyses of communal societies have long since contradicted these radical and early socialist assumptions, especially concerning the role of religious practices in a community's success.[129] This was, of course, the view of the groups themselves at the time, including those Shakers who 'shook their heads' at Robert Owen, and later informed A.J. Macdonald he would 'have to do like us or you will never succeed'. The longevity, discipline and cohesion of the Harmony Society, the Zoarites and the Shakers are now commonly attributed to shared religious principles, the endorsement of authority in religious terms and the individual commitment to the whole encouraged by collective religious rituals and experiences.

When Engels turned to write another, longer and better-known text derived from his Manchester experience—*The Condition of the Working Class in England* (1845)—his view of how socialism could be made a reality changed dramatically.[130] The stark divisions and resentments between social 'classes' that Engels witnessed in the north of England became the new muse for his imagination, and no longer far-off communal America. Projecting the future from this ruptured industrial present, Engels contemplated a new prospect of inevitable class-conflict and violent upheaval before socialism could be achieved. This attention to class-consciousness and belief in the threat of revolution would be Engels's most significant contribution to the theories of historical progress and revolutionary change he worked out with Karl Marx by 1848.[131] The *Communist*

---

[129] Example studies include: Rosabeth Moss Kanter, 'Commitment and Social Organization', *American Sociological Review*, 33:4 (Aug. 1968), 499–517; K.H. Stephan and G.E. Stephan, 'Religion and the Survival of Utopian Communities', *Journal for the Scientific Study of Religion*, 12:1 (March 1973), 89–100; Richard Sosis et al., 'Religion and Intragroup Cooperation', *Cross-Cultural Research*, 34:1 (2000), 70–87; see also Noyes, *History of American Socialisms*, pp. 646–57.

[130] Friedrich Engels, 'The Condition of the Working-class in England from Personal Observation and Authentic Sources', *MECW*, 4:295–596.

[131] Claeys, 'Young Engels', pp. 468–71.

Manifesto of that year contained no thought of Shakers proving socialism feasible or practical. Shakers were instead just another 'utopian' expression of a temporary present which could only distract from the disruptive demise of capitalism that Engels and Marx imagined taking place around them in Europe.[132]

As Engels's evolving interests illustrate, early socialism was a movement forged in the individual imagination and the dream of a better future in this world. Within the various socialisms which emerged by the 1840s—whether Owenite, Fourierist or other theories—material to inspire an imagined future was crucial, and the living reality of Protestant communalism in the early nineteenth century proved among the most influential such material. For a time, the early socialist imagination was trans-Atlantic in scope: from Europe and within America it was willing to look to the rural communal landscape of the United States for current precedents and prototypes for its hoped-for future. Individual journeys to visit working communities of shared property, and the individual consumption of literary descriptions of such distant communities, each contributed to this trans-Atlantic imagining.

The rise of Marxist socialism after 1848 might appear to have severed this link between socialism and Protestant communalism in the trans-Atlantic world. The Marxist vision of how a better future could be proven to be possible allowed only for a prediction forwards from revolutionary conditions in a contemporary, localized context. An envisaged future could never be a projection sideways, as it were, from circumstances known or believed to be already a reality elsewhere in the world. Despite this, socialists continued to visit Protestant communal settlements, including the Inspirationist Eben-Ezer colony, into the 1850s.[133] Later studies of communalism, including the work of Charles Nordhoff, were also born out of personal quests for alternatives to free-market capitalism.[134]

The external reputations of some communal traditions in the later nineteenth century were alternatively shaped by their own efforts at self-promotion. The most striking example of this was the Shakers, who undertook a series of trans-Atlantic missions back to Britain in the 1870s, led

---

[132] Karl Marx and Friedrich Engels, *The Communist Manifesto* (London: Allen Lane, 2002), pp. 254–6; Feuer, 'Influence', 473.

[133] Wittke, *Utopian Communist*, pp. 170–1. Parke Godwin, whose 1848 description of Eben-Ezer was quoted in Chap. 6, was a Fourierist Socialist at the time.

[134] See especially, Charles Nordhoff, *The Communistic Societies of the United States* (London: J. Murray, 1875), pp. 11–22.

by Frederick Evans, the former Owenite.[135] Yet Evans continued to draw explicit links between socialism in Europe and the religious practice of communalism in America. Commenting on the progress of the Paris revolutionary commune in 1871, Evans declared: 'Communism is the greatest good that thousands can see in the future; and the fact that the Shakers make it a practical thing, a success, is a constant source of congratulation, and of hope.'[136]

Evans's own evoking of views of the future and the pertinence of existing Shaker practices demonstrates that the connection drawn between Protestant communalism and socialism was not, after all, an exclusively external perception: communal traditions themselves capitalized on the comparison.

CONCLUSION

Tracing the trans-Atlantic reputation of Protestant communalism within early socialism reveals a striking similarity in attitudes to anticipating the future. The early socialist concern to identify and inaugurate in the present their own blueprints of the future shared much in common with strands of Protestant 'future-thinking' identified elsewhere in this study. As my first chapter in this volume made clear, and the subsequent chapters on respective traditions have reiterated, eschatological thinking, prophetic inspiration and the vision of an imminent millennium were frequently implicated in the practice of communal property in the trans-Atlantic world. Attempts to live in the here-and-now as believers imagined life was or would be like in some future Kingdom or heavenly society lay at the heart of what many Protestant communalists thought they were doing. Shakers and Harmonists in particular were either 'foreshadowing' or 'actualizing' a future expected imminently across the whole earth or deemed in the process of realization in the present.

For early socialists, the model or prototype community which proved the possibility of the socialist vision amounted, in pragmatic terms, to evidence that socialism worked. But it also constituted a realizing of some kind of secular eschatology, as the imagined future of socialism was

---

[135] Stephen Stein, *The Shaker Experience in America* (New Haven: Yale University Press, 1992), pp. 223–8.

[136] New York Public Library, Manuscripts and Archives Division, Shaker Manuscript Collection, Frederick Evans to the Elders, 2 August 1871.

brought closer, as if almost within reach, by the knowledge that 'communist colonies' existed, and could be visited and experienced.

It is this which ultimately makes sense of the eagerness and emotion
apparent in socialist responses to Protestant communalism—from Robert
Owen's readiness to make personal contact with distant Shakers and
Harmonists, to Samuel Bower's later 'feeling of delight' when learning
of 'the great, inappreciable fact' of such American communities, as well as
A.J. Macdonald's 'most pleasurable anticipation' of reaching Zoar, running the final miles. It was the appeal of personally living in a manner that
transcended the contemporary state of nineteenth-century society, coming closer to the kind of alternative future anticipated for all humanity,
which further explains the allure to certain socialists of a Shaker conversion. In the case of those individuals who considered conversion, from the
50 members of Valley Forge community to Macdonald again, each faced a
moment of decision whether or not their own imagined future remained
with socialism's projected society, or instead lay in the alternative understanding of forthcoming life offered within Christian community.

The recognition of this allure and the points of decision it provoked
arguably allow an aspect of life on the inside of Protestant communal
groups to be better acknowledged: the degree of individual consent and
imaginative commitment required for the full functioning of the collective body. For generations of Protestant Christians practising community
of property, communal life and work were paradoxically nearly always
bounded and defined by individual decisions. Believers shared their property and effort, and in celibate communities curtailed inclinations to family
life, as individual agents. While the persuasive power of group majorities,
charismatic prophets, or the simple fear of insecurity in a foreign land
should not be underestimated as factors contributing to communal commitment, those who remained in communities for any length of time were
most often drawn into association by personal choice and the assent of
faith. Alternative Protestant cultures promoting independence and private
property were, after all, readily at hand to console any who withdrew or
doubted in most surrounding settings.

Taking account of their whole histories, each migration of communal
traditions, across oceans or continents, further involved appeals to individual imaginations to garner assent. Believers within the gathered group—
be they Rapp's Harmony Society, Metz's Inspirationists or in some cases
communal Mormons—had each to be captured in themselves by the
hope offered by movement, and a future lived in a subsequent collective

settlement, whether it anticipated the Kingdom of God, prepared them for a new divine dispensation or actualized a prophetic ideal of Christian community. In common with the missionary efforts of Ephrata and the Shakers, every trans-Atlantic tradition offered a theological vision drawing the individual into communal activity as part of a people believing themselves intimate with the Christian God. Instances of dissent, departure and dissolution in every community history testify to the persisting potential for members to imagine a future for themselves outside the communal endeavour. And yet for many individuals, over an expansive period, communalism proved an especially dynamic, committed and hopeful way of being Protestant in the early modern trans-Atlantic world.[137]

[137] Research for this chapter was supported by the award of a British Academy Postdoctoral Fellowship, and by funding for archive research in the United States from the Central New York Humanities Corridor (for research in Hamilton College Library and Syracuse University Library), from the Houghton Library at Harvard University and from the Beinecke Library at Yale University. I acknowledge my sincere gratitude to each of these remarkable institutions for their generosity and support.

INDEX

© The Editor(s) (if applicable) and The Author(s) 2016
P. Lockley (ed.), *Protestant Communalism in the Trans-Atlantic World, 1650–1850*, DOI 10.1057/978-1-137-48487-1